A CENSUS OF SHAKESPEARE'S PLAYS IN QUARTO

1594-1709

AMS PRESS
NEW YORK

PUBLISHED UNDER THE AUSPICES
OF THE
ELIZABETHAN CLUB
YALE UNIVERSITY

A CENSUS OF SHAKESPEARE'S PLAYS IN QUARTO

1594-1709

By
HENRIETTA C. BARTLETT
AND
ALFRED W. POLLARD

NEW HAVEN: YALE UNIVERSITY PRESS
LONDON: HUMPHREY MILFORD
OXFORD UNIVERSITY PRESS
MDCCCCXVI

Reprinted from the edition of 1916, New Haven

First AMS edition published 1971

Manufactured in the United States of America

International Standard Book Number: 0-404-00669-8

Library of Congress Catalogue Card Number: 70-135724

AMS PRESS INC.
NEW YORK, N.Y. 10003

DEDICATED
TO THE MEMORY OF
THOMAS RAYNESFORD LOUNSBURY
PROFESSOR OF ENGLISH IN YALE UNIVERSITY

BY THE ELIZABETHAN CLUB
AND THE EDITORS

INTRODUCTION.

Few literary prophecies have been so strikingly fulfilled as that of "A neuer writer" who in the preface which follows the revised title of the first edition of *Troilus and Cressida* (1609) predicted of Shakespeare "when hee is gone and his Commedies out of sale you will scramble for them, and set up a new English Inquisition." It used to be thought much to say of a book that it was worth its weight in gold, but copies of the earliest Shakespeare quartos are worth their weight in banknotes and those notes by no means for the smallest sums. Nor is this money value unreasonable. It is based, as all money values will be found to be in the case of books, on intrinsic interest, the intrinsic interest, in this case, of the plays in themselves and secondly of these early editions as such. It is enhanced, moreover, as money values must always be, if they are to exceed the ordinary, by an exceptional degree of rarity.

We may take the question of rarity first, as the more quickly dealt with. How great it is this Census itself abundantly reveals. Of the earliest quarto with which Shakespeare's name has been connected, the 1594 edition of *Titus Andronicus* (we may both hope and believe that Shakespeare's share in it, if any, was of the very smallest) only one copy is known. Of the second, the first edition of *Richard II*, three copies are recorded, two of them in solid public ownership and so presumably beyond any chance of changing hands. Of the third, the first edition of *Richard III*, there are four copies and a fragment, of which two and the fragment are unpurchasable. Of the pirated *Romeo and Juliet* of 1597 only four copies are registered, three of them publicly owned; of the better text of 1599 as many as eleven, of which no fewer than seven are in private hands. In the case of the First Part of *Henry IV* there is a fragment of four leaves, which may be the scanty remains of an entire edition published early in 1598, and three copies (two in public ownership) of the edition of that year which usually passes as the first. Of *Love's Labors Lost* reasons have been given in *Shakespeare Folios and Quartos** (pp. 70 sq.) for believing that a pirated first edition has entirely perished. Of the good text of 1598, which passes as the first, there are as many as ten copies, no fewer than six being in private hands. The fact that nearly as large a number of copies exist of this quarto as of Burby's edition of *Romeo and Juliet* reinforces the argument for a pirated edition of the one play as of the other having helped, by taking off the edge of the demand, to save Burby's from being thumbed to pieces. On the other hand it can only be reckoned a coincidence, though a very curious one, that the present ownership of the ten copies of the one play, and of the eleven of the other is with one exception exactly the

* *Shakespeare Folios and Quartos: a study in the bibliography of Shakespeare's plays, 1594-1685.* By Alfred W. Pollard. With 37 illustrations. Methuen and Co. 1909.

INTRODUCTION

same.[1] Three other cases need special mention, the first of these being the Second Part of *Henry IV*, of which Sheet E in the first edition exists in two states, four copies of the first and four of the second issue being in public ownership, and three of the first and six of the second in private. In the case of *Hamlet* we have a double complication, an earlier text and a later, and for the later text two states of the title-page. Of the earlier edition only two copies are known (one public, one private); of the later text three copies with the title-page dated 1604 (one public, two private), and two (both public) with the last figure of the date altered to a 5. Lastly of *Troilus and Cressida* there are two issues of 1609, one with a mention on the title of its having been acted (two copies in public ownership, one in private), the other (five public, two private) withdrawing this statement and adding the preface, from which we have already quoted, which takes credit for the play "not being sullied with the smoky breath of the multitude." Adding the editions which need no comment to those already mentioned we can present the whole series of First Editions in a list, variant issues being counted together, but editions with different texts kept apart.*

First Editions.

	Public Ownership.	Private Ownership.	Total.
Titus Andronicus, 1594		1	1
Richard II, 1597	2	1	3
Richard III, 1597	2 + frag.	2	4 + frag.
Romeo and Juliet, First Text, 1597	3	1	4
Romeo and Juliet, Second Text, 1599	4	7	11
Henry IV, Part I, 1598	2	1 + frag.*	3 + frag.*
Love's Labors Lost, 1598	4	6	10
Merchant of Venice, 1600	9	8	17
Henry V, 1600	4	2	6
Much Ado about Nothing, 1600	8	7	15
Henry IV, Part II, 1600	8	9	17
Midsummer Night's Dream, 1600	5	3	8
Merry Wives of Windsor, 1602	3	2	5
Hamlet, First text, 1603	1	1	2
Hamlet, Second text, 1604-05	3	2	5
King Lear, 1608	6	4	10
Troilus and Cressida, 1609	7	3	10
Othello, 1622	9	4	13
	80 + 1 frag.	64 + 1 frag.	144 + 2 frag.

* The fragment of *Henry IV*, Part I, from the Perry Collection is reckoned with the 1598 edition, as if the same text. Logically, either the fragment or the 3 copies of the 1598 edition should be excluded.

[1] The Elizabethan Club owns a copy of *Romeo and Juliet* and none of *Love's Labors Lost*. Trinity College, Cambridge, owns a copy of *Love's Labors Lost* and none of *Romeo and Juliet*. The other owners are the Bodleian Library, the Earl of Ellesmere (each copy having been catalogued by the Second Earl of Bridgewater in 1649), the British Museum, Edinburgh University (each copy presented by William Drummond of Hawthornden), Mr. Folger (two copies of *Love's Labors Lost* and three of *Romeo and Juliet*), Mr. Huntington (two of each) and Mr. W. A. White.

INTRODUCTION

Thus of these eighteen editions which, as we shall see, have great, if varying, importance for the construction of a text, the average number of copies extant is just eight apiece, and less than half of these are in private hands, though probably enough remain unregistered to bring the two classes to an equality and make the average number of copies still extant nine instead of eight.

The hypothetical pirated First Edition of *Love's Labors Lost,* if it ever existed, has left no trace behind except a possible allusion on the title-page of Burby's edition. The First Edition of *Henry IV,* Part I, is represented by a fragment of four leaves, *Titus Andronicus* by one copy, the first *Hamlet* by two, *Richard II* by three, the first *Romeo and Juliet* by four, *Richard III* by four and a bit, the *Merry Wives* and second *Hamlet* by five, *Henry V* by six. There is no seven, nor nine, nor twelve, nor fourteen, nor sixteen; otherwise from zero to seventeen all the numbers are filled. Is there any basis for a guess, or guesses, why so many more copies of some plays should have been preserved than of others? Mr. Falconer Madan, in commenting on the story of the original Bodleian copy of the First Folio, which disappeared from the library in the Seventeenth Century (it was probably sold as a duplicate when the third edition appeared in 1663) and was bought back in 1906 for £3000, found evidence of the degrees of popularity of different plays in the comparative amount of wear and tear shown by the leaves on which they were printed. We may safely invert the deduction and connect the disappearance of copies with the popularity of the plays, or (which is not quite the same thing) their vogue with the play-reading public at the moment of issue. It is noteworthy that the four quartos which everyone admits to have been pirated, the first *Romeo and Juliet, Henry V,* the *Merry Wives* and the first *Hamlet,* only muster seventeen copies between them, or just half the average of the First Quartos as a whole. We are not to attribute this fewness of copies to any high minded objection of book buyers to piracy, leading them to purchase copies in order to burn them, or even to burn them after they had been read, as scrupulous people might burn foreign editions of copyright novels which they had brought home to finish. We should rather remember that the pirate *ex hypothesi* always got out his edition at least a little before the time when the players would have printed the play of their own accord. If he could not effect his piracy when the vogue of a play was at its height, he must needs come in as soon as possible after this, or he would have had no temptation to take the risk of getting himself into trouble. What concerns us is that the nearer to the psychological moment his edition appeared the more likely would it be to be thumbed to pieces.

Turning to the quartos which we believe to have been printed with the players' consent we find that *Richard II, Richard III* and *Henry IV,* Part I, represented respectively by three, four and three copies of the first edition, went through five or six editions apiece before 1623, whereas *Henry IV,* Part II, of which nineteen copies survive, was never reprinted in quarto. It is disconcerting to find that, on the theory this suggests, so fine a play as

INTRODUCTION

the *Merchant of Venice,* of the Heyes edition of which seventeen copies survive, comes next to *Henry IV,* Part II, at the wrong end of the list. We are forbidden, however, to regard the survival of so many copies as accidental by the fact that the play was not reprinted until 1619. In the same way in the case of *Much Ado about Nothing,* of which fifteen copies are extant, we may take the absence of any quarto reprint as confirming the suggested deduction that the First Quarto was not very successful. Possibly the fact that all these three plays were published in the same year (1600) had something to do with their apparently very moderate degree of success; but the *Midsummer Night's Dream,* though it also was first printed in 1600, by which time it must have been quite an old play, was much more severely bethumbed, only eight copies surviving.

While the fact of a play being permanently popular, or the vogue of the moment, seems to have been the main cause of copies of the first edition disappearing, something must be allowed for contributory causes. A time certainly came when editions without Shakespeare's name on their titles would stand less chance of preservation than those which bore it. Again, it is only natural that *Titus Andronicus,* which was first published nineteen years before the First Folio, should have been more hardly used than *Othello,* which came out when the First Folio was already being printed. After all, moreover, "habent sua fata libelli," and into the mysteries of fate we must not pry too closely.

There is one explanation of the variation in the number of the copies surviving in the case of different plays which may be decisively rejected; that, namely, which would have us believe that fewer copies of any given play have come down to us because fewer were printed. It would be more reasonable to argue inversely and find in the scantiness of the remnant an indication that the edition which has left so few survivors was probably a large one. The bibliographers' maxim that the number of copies extant is likely to vary inversely with the number printed is indeed only a generalization from the points about popularity already noted. Large editions, low prices, popularity and careless handling all go together, and where we find one, in the case of works which have in them the possibility of success, we may look out for the others. Our information about the cost of paper and print at the end of the Sixteenth Century is not sufficiently precise to justify any positive statement, but it is probable that even if only quite a small sum, say forty shillings, were spent on obtaining the text of a play, either by bribery or purchase, unless something like a thousand copies could be sold at the customary price of sixpence apiece, the temptation to a publisher to print a full-length play of Shakespeare's would have been very slight. It is more likely, indeed, that the full maximum of 1200 copies, to which the Stationers' Company, in the interest of compositors and good workmanship, restricted an edition, was the number printed, and even if 1200 copies were sold the publisher's profit was probably well under ten pounds. From the sale of an edition of only five hundred copies he would have done little more than clear his expenses.

We pass from these money matters to the intrinsic value of the texts of

INTRODUCTION

the First Quartos, which has seldom or never been frankly admitted, even by editors who have seen the necessity of relying on them rather than on that of the First Folio as the basis of their own. If a document has once been interpreted in a particular sense and that interpretation has survived unchallenged sufficiently long for men to be educated in it, it is no small task to win acceptance for any other view. From an imperfect knowledge of the facts the reference to "stolne and surreptitious copies" in the preface to the First Folio* was taken to refer to all the quarto editions of Shakespeare's plays, though such an interpretation can only be maintained on the supposition that the publishers of the Folio were bent on damaging their own credit and property, and that Shakespeare and his fellow sharers in the Globe were more conspicuously helpless in defending their rights than any other set of Englishmen since the world began. The address "To the great Variety of Readers" in the First Folio gives no hint as to the number of the "stolne" copies to which it refers. It merely says that whereas, or wherever ("where" may have either meaning) readers had been abused by pirated editions with bad texts, even in these plays they would now find the texts sound and perfect. As the reference is to "copies" in the plural, it must relate to at least two plays, but if only two plays could be found in which the Folio editors had replaced the text of the First Quarto by a conspicuously better one, only two plays could on any reasonable interpretation be brought under the accusation of piracy. Two such plays exist in *Henry V* and the *Merry Wives of Windsor,* for neither of which was any good text in quarto ever printed. In the case of *Romeo and Juliet* and *Hamlet,* possibly also in that of *Love's Labors Lost,* an original bad text in quarto was replaced by a better one in the same form. In other plays there are divergences between the Folio and the Quartos which may be susceptible of different interpretations, but which did not prevent Malone from declaring roundly, in the Introduction to his Shakespeare of 1790, as regards the text of the plays, that "the editors of the folio, to save labour, or from some other motive, printed the greater part of them from the very copies which [according to the stereotyped interpretation accepted, alas, even by Malone himself] they represented as maimed and imperfect." Common sense would suggest that if a passage is susceptible of two interpretations, in one of which it is accurate and helpful, and in the other inaccurate and confusing, and raises difficulties of many kinds, the accurate and helpful should be preferred. But in the present case this interpretation does not seem even to have occurred to any of the bold gentlemen who have undertaken to expound so difficult a text as that of Shakespeare and yet, from an idle indulgence in the humour which delights to make out that everything is as bad as possible, have thus mischievously misrendered a simple passage in the "Address to the Readers." Malone knew from his collations what use the Folio editors had made of the Quartos, but the

* "We pray you do not envie his Friends, the office of their care, and paine, to have collected & publish'd them; and so to have publish'd them, as where (before) you were abus'd with diverse stolne and surreptitious copies, maimed and deformed by the frauds and stealthes of iniurious impostors, that expos'd them: even those are now offer'd to your view cur'd, and perfect of their limbes; and all the rest absolute in their numbers as he conceived them," &c.

INTRODUCTION

old blunder was by his time part of the Eighteenth Century Shakespearian creed. Thus he could not get away from it, but says sweepingly of the Quartos, in the very sentence in which he is confessing their merits, "undoubtedly they were all surreptitious, that is stolen from the playhouse, and printed without the consent of the author or the proprietors."

Can Malone, or anyone else who has upheld this extraordinary theory, ever have thought out what it involved? If all the plays of Shakespeare published before 1623 were "stolen from the playhouse and printed without the consent of the author or the proprietors," are we to suppose that his works were the sole objects of attack, or were the couple of dozen other plays acted by his company which found their way into print while he was still in London, i.e., between 1594 and 1608, also pirated? And if all or most of the quartos of plays acted by Shakespeare's company were pirated, what about the rest, produced at other theatres? If the theory in its full implications is to be maintained there must, in some years, have been a piracy once a fortnight. If it be said that in the case of Shakespeare's plays we have a positive statement, which does not apply to the others, about which we may therefore adopt a hopeful agnosticism, we must recur to our point that the positive statement as to Shakespeare's plays need apply to no more than two of them. But let us accept the position, absurd as it is, that only the plays performed by Shakespeare's company, and among these only those in which he himself had a hand were singled out for attack. This would still oblige us to believe that in the thirteen years 1597 to 1609 there were some fourteen successive piracies. Now to pirate a single play of some two thousand five hundred or three thousand lines would be no easy matter, unless, indeed, as Mr. Fleay once suggested in the case of *Romeo and Juliet*,* a prompter were kind enough to "throw aside" a superfluous copy, where it could be picked up by a dishonest servant. Piracy from the wastepaper basket, piracy by stenography, piracy by the treachery of a "hired man,"—we can imagine all these feats to have been performed once; but unless the players were pleased to have their plays stolen, surely some steps must have been taken to prevent the recurrence of these thefts, and the steps cannot have been so ineffective as to allow nearly all Shakespeare's early plays and several of his later ones to be appropriated. Many of these quarto editions appeared some years after the first production of the play. Was it impossible to keep both the prompt-copy and the actors' parts securely locked up, even when a play was not being performed? In 1597 and again in 1600 several plays by Shakespeare were published one after the other. Were these outbursts of piracy the result of a burglary at the theatre? The topical character of Elizabethan plays is often emphasized, even over-emphasized; is it not remarkable that we hear little or

* "Q_2 is, according to this theory, a revised version made on a complete copy of an early version of the play, while Q_1 is printed from the prompter's copy of the same early version. When the revision took place this copy would be thrown aside as worthless; and any dishonest *employé* of the theatre could sell it to an equally dishonest publisher, who would publish it as the play now acted." (A Chronicle History of the Life and Work of William Shakespeare. By F. G. Fleay, 1886, p. 193.) If piracies were frequent, is carelessness of the kind here supposed easily conceivable?

INTRODUCTION

nothing about thefts of this kind in play, prologue or preface of Shakespeare's day (contemporary complaints of piracy are mainly concerned with poems or essays passed round in manuscript by men of fashion), and have to seek it in the much later prefaces of Heywood.* Surely if piracy were thus frequent some honest apprentice must have brought down his cudgel on a cheating stenographer's hand, and himself not have passed unsung.

In opposition to the theory that Shakespeare (that excellent man of business, as we have been taught to consider him) and his fellows submitted to being defrauded of their property fourteen successive times within thirteen years, it has elsewhere been contended, and will be contended as often as a hearing can be obtained, that while the pirates were able not only to get out editions of *Henry V* and the *Merry Wives,* but to convey copyright in them to their confederates, and had the profits of single editions of *Romeo and Juliet* and *Hamlet,* and possibly also of *Love's Labors Lost,* the players after each of these attacks, as also after that on *Pericles* in 1609, can be seen protecting other plays by staying notices, sometimes openly of that character, more often in the form of entries on the Stationers' Register, which while seeming to pave the way for publication were really meant to delay it. Here and now as much has been said as to this fight with the Pirates as there is space for. We must pass on from this negative and defensive support of the Quartos to claim for them positive qualities not easily compatible with piracy, and which give to them a much higher character than they have hitherto been allowed.

In the passage already cited from Malone's Introduction to his Shakespeare of 1790 that great critic wrote, with a truth only marred by his acceptance of the current application of the words "stolne and surreptitious":

"Fifteen of Shakespeare's plays were printed in quarto antecedent to the first complete collection of his works, which was published by his fellow comedians in 1623.... The players when they mention these copies represent them all as mutilated and imperfect; but this was merely thrown out to give an additional value to their own edition and is not strictly true of any but two of the whole number; The Merry Wives of Windsor and King Henry V. With respect to the other thirteen copies, though undoubtedly they were all surreptitious, that is, stolen from the playhouse, and printed without the consent of the author or the proprietors, they *in general* are preferable to the exhibition of the same plays in the Folio; for this plain reason, because, instead of printing these plays from a manuscript, the editors of the folio, to save labour or from some other motive, printed the greater part of them from the very copies which they represented as maimed and imperfect, and frequently from a late instead of the earliest edition; in some instances with additions and alterations of their own. Thus, therefore, the first folio, as far as respects the plays above enumerated, labours under the disadvantage of being at least

---

* The passages in question occur in the preface to the 1630 edition of *The Rape of Lucrece* and in "a prologue to the Play of Queene Elisabeth as it was last revived at the Cock-Pit" printed in Heywood's *Pleasant Dialogues and Drammas,* 1637.

INTRODUCTION

a second, and in some cases a third, edition of these quartos. I do not, however, mean to say that many valuable corrections of passages undoubtedly corrupt in the quartos are not found in the folio copy; or that a single line of these plays should be printed by a careful editor without a minute examination and collation of both copies, but those copies were in general the basis on which the folio editors built, and are entitled to our particular attention and examination as *first editions."*

It is a thousand pities that Malone should not only have misunderstood the attack on previous editions in the First Folio to "represent them *all* as mutilated and imperfect," but while having the courage to deny that any but two of the Quartos* were "mutilated and imperfect" should have abstained from denying that any but these specified exceptions were "stolne and surreptitious." As a vindication, however, of the text of the First Quartos nothing could be better. As he says, these editions must be reckoned in general as good texts, and the main argument on this topic advanced in *Shakespeare Folios and Quartos* in 1909 was that since the good texts, with easily explainable exceptions, were regularly entered on the Stationers' Register, and the bad texts were either not entered at all or entered irregularly, by the logical method of Agreement and Difference we are entitled to assume a causal connection between good texts and regular entries and between bad texts and irregular entries or no entries at all. This causal connection we find in the fact that an honest publisher who printed a play with the Players' consent would naturally get as good a text as they could give him and have no reason to avoid taking it to Stationers' Hall, whereas a dishonest publisher would naturally get hold of an obsolete or vamped up text and would fear to take it to be registered lest the Wardens of the Stationers Company should "stay" it till he was able to produce authority for printing it. In the introduction to the facsimile of the unique third quarto of *Richard II*, recently identified in the library of Mr. W. A. White of New York, this argument has been carried further and it has been shown by an analysis of the readings of the successive editions that while nothing in the text forbids us to believe that the First Quarto (1597) was set up from Shakespeare's autograph there is at least some slight ground for believing that this was really its origin.

The two negative arguments for this contention are: (a) that the number of readings in the First Quarto rejected as erroneous by the editors of the Cambridge text (our nearest approach to a *textus receptus* of Shakespeare) being far fewer than the number of new errors introduced by the same printers in reprinting the play the next year for a second edition, the proved carelessness of the printers suffices to account for the errors of the First Quarto and it is thus superfluous, and therefore illegitimate, to assume that before it reached the printer the text had already been corrupted by being copied by scriveners; (b) that no evidence can be found either in the later Quartos or in the First Folio that the original manuscript had been used for the correction of the play as a whole, but that the good readings in

---

* The *Hamlet* of 1603 had not been discovered when Malone wrote. As regards the bad quarto of *Romeo and Juliet* printed in 1597, he made the necessary exception in another passage.

INTRODUCTION

the Folio are best explained as reaching it in the form of casual corrections on a prompt-copy. The positive arguments advanced on the same side are: (a) that some of the errors of the First Quarto suggest that it was set up not from a clean copy such as a scrivener would have made, but from a manuscript which, though generally clear, presented some difficulties, so that now and again the master-printer was driven to read it out to the compositor; (b) that the punctuation of the set speeches is a dramatic punctuation with peculiarities which, despite much carelessness, incline us to believe that it was derived from the author himself; (c) that this is true also of the method of using Emphasis Capitals. The punctuation, it is shown, is generally much lighter and the use of emphasis capitals more moderate than in the First Folio, and this fits in prettily with Shakespeare's views as set forth in Hamlet's exhortation to the players: "Speak the speech I pray you as I pronounc'd it to you, trippingly on the tongue, but if you mouth it as many of our Players do, I had as lieve the town-cryer spoke my lines."

When we consider the question with reference to other plays we find that it can be readily proved that the source of the text of most of the good quartos was a prompt-copy and that such scanty evidence as survives shows that it was not unusual for a prompt-copy to be made by the prompter writing his notes on the author's autograph manuscript. There is thus a high probability that at least some of the good Shakespeare quartos were set up from his autograph, a printed copy subsequently taking the place at the theatre of the manuscript thus destroyed and, after it had received casual correction and alterations, becoming in turn the ultimate source of the "corrected" Folio text. If this theory wins acceptance it is hoped that "probably printed from Shakespeare's autograph" may prove an adequate counter-cry to the "probably stolen and surreptitious" of so many prefaces, and the estimation of the First Quartos be correspondingly enhanced. But if we advance no further than Malone's position their importance remains very great. Malone believed that all the Quartos were in some unexplained manner "stolen from the playhouse," but that the texts thus clandestinely obtained, so far from being maimed and imperfect, were the best versions we possess of what Shakespeare wrote. This is the essential point, and to anyone who admits it, the value of these First Quartos may well seem inestimable.

When we pass from the First Quartos to the reprints of them the most ardent collector must be sensible of a notable fall in temperature. In this Census all quarto editions are included down to the publication of Rowe's Shakespeare in 1709, the first edition to which an editor put his name. All of them are of interest for the evidence which they offer of the popularity of Shakespeare in the Seventeenth Century as compared with the other playwrights of his day, and of the popularity of some of his plays as compared with others. Textually in themselves not one of them has any direct importance, with the apparent rather than real exception of the *Richard II* of 1608 in which 166 lines of the "Parliament Scene" appeared for the first time, but in a form so mutilated (almost certainly

INTRODUCTION

put together by stenographers) that they have only the very smallest value. There is no evidence in the case of any of these later quartos pointing to the original manuscript having been collated afresh in order to improve the text, or of access having been had for this purpose to any new one. The theory that all the quartos were stolen and surreptitious has had this one good effect, that it has prevented editors from formally maintaining that recourse was had to any such authoritative source, old or new, when the later quartos were printed. Unfortunately it has not prevented them from adopting some of the readings of these later quartos into their own texts. Of course if these readings had been clearly marked off as "early conjectures" the editors adopting them would have been well within their rights. A printer's reader of Shakespeare's day was at least as likely to make a good guess at a missing word as Rowe, Theobald or Hanmer. But these emendations from the early reprints have been treated as "variants," invested with an authority of their own by the dates at which they appeared. A reprint, however, even if it appeared within a few months of the First Edition, derives its authority exclusively from that and cannot be set up against its source. Textually, therefore, the later quartos in and by themselves are negligible and should be neglected, the extent to which they have influenced the text of Shakespeare being distinctly matter for regret. Indirectly on the other hand they are of importance as the source of a vast number of readings in the First Folio which could never have been rightly appraised if the intermediate quartos had disappeared. Each time the text of a play was reprinted new errors were introduced and the majority of these errors were carried over from one quarto to the next. At the threshold of the First Folio, which usually followed the latest quarto, many of them were stopped, but many others got through, and in some cases there is clear proof that the new reading of the Folio is a mere botching of an error which first appears in an intermediate Quarto. By the help of the quartos all these errors can be eliminated from the Folio text, and the modern editor has nothing to consider save the original readings of the First Quarto and the original readings, right or wrong, introduced by the Folio. This genealogical value of the intermediate quartos, though subsidiary in character, is very great.

As a basis for further discussion we may now present the results of this Census as it affects the quartos which appeared between the First Editions in this form and the First Folio in the following table.

INTRODUCTION

INTERMEDIATE EDITIONS BEFORE 1623.

	Public Ownership.	Private Ownership.	Totals.
Titus Andronicus, 1600	1	1	2
Titus Andronicus, 1611	6 (7)	8 (9)	14 (16)
Richard II, 1598a	4	4	8
Richard II, 1598b	0	1	1
Richard II, 1608	3	5	8
Richard II, 1615	6 (13)	7 (17)	13 (30)
Richard III, 1598	4	3	7
Richard III, 1602	2	1	3
Richard III, 1605	2	2	4
Richard III, 1612	6	4	10
Richard III, 1622	5 (19)	1 (11)	6 (30)
Romeo and Juliet, 1609	3	3	6
Romeo and Juliet, n. d.*	6 (9)	4 (7)	10 (16)
Henry IV, Part I, 1599	6	5	11
Henry IV, Part I, 1604	2	0	2
Henry IV, Part I, 1608	2	5	7
Henry IV, Part I, 1613	6	4	10
Henry IV, Part I, 1622	6 (21)	6 (21)	12 (42)
Merchant of Venice, 1600 [1619]	11	12	23
Henry V, 1602	1	1	2
Henry V, 1608 [1619]	12 (13)	18 (19)	30 (32)
Midsummer Night's Dream, 1600 [1619]	11	14†	25
Merry Wives of Windsor, 1619	12	16	28
Hamlet, 1611	9	7	16
Hamlet, n. d.*	7 (16)	8 (15)	15 (31)
King Lear, 1608 [1619]	11	17‡	28
	144	157	301

The number of editions registered in this table is twenty-six, giving an average of five and one half copies in public, and six in private ownership, or a total of eleven and one half copies extant per edition, a result, however, which, as will be shown, is affected by a special circumstance, and hardly entitles us to say that these intermediate quartos as a class are less rare than the First Editions, which yielded an average of eight. The lowest figures in our new list are one for the single copy of the newly differentiated third quarto (the second of 1598) of *Richard II*, two apiece for *Titus Andronicus* (1600), *Henry IV*, Part I (1604) and *Henry V* (1602), three for *Richard III* (1602) and four for *Richard III* (1605). As to the rarity of *Titus Andronicus* we may recall the fact that of the original edition of 1594 only one copy survives without attempting any further explanation. The other five editions are all of popular chronicle plays and the figures are not in themselves very surprising. It may be just worth noting, however, as the dates lie so close together, that in 1599 Sir

* Perhaps after 1623.
† No. 557 assumed to be of this edition.
‡ No. 358 assumed to be of this edition.

INTRODUCTION

John Hayward was imprisoned for his prose history of *Henry IV,* which he had too effusively dedicated to the Earl of Essex, and that in 1602 an "old play" of *Richard II* (opinions differ as to whether it was Shakespeare's) was acted before the Essex conspirators. It is just possible that between 1598 and 1605 these happenings and the accession of a new dynasty may have created a special interest in historical plays, especially in those connected with changes of the crown, and thus account for these five editions being exceptionally hardly used.

At the opposite end of our list we have thirty copies extant of the *Henry V* of "1608," twenty-eight apiece of the *Merry Wives* of 1619 and *King Lear* of "1608," twenty-five of the *Midsummer Night's Dream* of "1600" and twenty-three of the *Merchant of Venice* of "1600," a total of 134 copies (or 132 if the two doubtful copies, Nos. 358 and 557, which have been reckoned with the majority, are excluded) giving an average of nearly twenty-seven copies of each edition. The corresponding figures for the First Editions are six, five, nine, eight and (for the *Merchant of Venice*) seventeen, a total of forty-five for the five plays, or an average of nine copies extant apiece, just a third as many as in the case of the reprints.

In Chapter IV of *Shakespeare Folios and Quartos* (1909) an elaborate argument was submitted to prove that these five plays, despite their varying dates, had all been printed and published in one volume (copies may also have been sold separately) in the same year, 1619, together with four others, viz., the *Whole Contention between the two famous houses, Lancaster and York* (n. d.), *Pericles* (1619), *A Yorkshire Tragedy* (1619) and *Sir John Oldcastle* (1600), and the fact that they had been thus preserved in exceptional numbers was an important link in the chain of evidence.* The only volume now known in which all the nine plays are still found together is that in the library of Mr. Marsden Perry of Providence, R. I., bearing the stamp of the Seventeenth Century collector EDWARD GWYNN. But a similar volume belonging to Mr. Hussey was only broken up in 1906 and others must have belonged to Capell, Garrick and other early collectors.

The arguments put forward in *Shakespeare Folios and Quartos* to prove that all the nine plays were printed in 1619 were numerous and elaborate. They started with Mr. W. W. Greg's demonstrations from the watermarks, devices and large numerals on the title-pages, and followed up with others based on the short imprints on the titles, on the types, on the spelling, on the number of copies extant, on an entry as to the *Merchant of Venice* in the Stationers' Register in 1619, and on the hitherto unexplained continuity of the signatures of the undated *Whole Contention* and *Pericles* of 1619. The chapter was well received by reviewers, but Mr. Alfred Huth preferred an earlier theory of the same writer's, which accepted the dates on the title-pages as truthful and supposed that new and

---

*The number of copies of the five plays at that time known to Mr. G. W. Cole, the Cataloguer of the Church collection, who had made a special study of the question, was 105, or an average of 21 apiece.

INTRODUCTION

old copies had been bound up for sale in 1619 by way of clearing off "remainders," and the arguments which he advanced in the *Library* for January, 1910, though they were not left unanswered, were quite impressive. In October, however, of the same year, Mr. William J. Neidig, an instructor in English in the University of Wisconsin, in articles in *Modern Philology* and the *Century Magazine*, by a composite photograph in which the *Merchant of Venice* of "1600" was superimposed on the *Pericles* of "1619" proved that the words "Written by W. Shakespeare," the "Heb Ddieu heb Ddim" device and the word "Printed" came in exactly the same positions in each title-page, and pointed out also identical flaws of one kind in the W of "Written" and of another kind in the W of Shakespeare's initial in each case. It was thus made certain that portions of the title-page of *Pericles* had been used over again in the title-page of the *Merchant of Venice,* without having been shifted in the form, and the impossibility of the two editions being separated by nineteen years was demonstrated in a manner appreciable even by readers with no bibliographical training. In this Census the falsity of the dates 1600 on the *Merchant of Venice* and *Midsummer Night's Dream* and 1608 on *King Lear* and *Henry V* has thus been regarded as definitely proved, the correct date, 1619, being added in each case in brackets.

It is obvious that editions printed for inclusion in a stout quarto volume are in a much better position for resisting wear and tear than those issued separately in paper wrappers. These five editions thus stand in a class by themselves. If we deduct them and the number of copies of them still extant from the totals of these Intermediate Quartos given above, we get 169 extant copies to be divided among twenty-one editions, or the same average of eight apiece as in the case of the First Quartos. These 169 copies, it is interesting to note, are divided between public and private collections, giving totals of a little over eighty and an average of four to each.

We now give our final table of editions.

INTRODUCTION

Later Editions, 1624-1709.

	Public Ownership.	Private Ownership.	Totals.
Richard II, 1634	9	8	17
Richard III, 1629	7	6	13
Richard III, 1634	11 (18)	6 (12)	17 (30)
Romeo and Juliet, 1637	10	12	22
Henry IV, Part I, 1632	5	5	10
Henry IV, Part I, 1639	8	11	19
Henry IV, Part I, 1700	10 (23)	6 (22)	16 (45)
Love's Labors Lost, 1631	9	12	21
Merchant of Venice, 1637	9	8	17
Merchant of Venice, 1652	7 (16)	7 (15)	14 (31)
Merry Wives of Windsor, 1630	6	4	10
Hamlet, 1637	11	13	24
Hamlet, 1676 (2 editions)	9	10	19
Hamlet, 1683	3	9	12
Hamlet, 1695 (2 editions)	4	7	11
Hamlet, 1703 (2 editions)	7 (34)	10 (49)	17 (83)
King Lear, 1655	7	7	14
Othello, 1630	10	14	24
Othello, 1655	10	8	18
Othello, 1681	4	7	11
Othello, 1687	5	2	7
Othello, 1695	7	7	14
Othello, 1705	7 (43)	6 (44)	13 (87)
Taming of the Shrew, 1631	12	9	21
Macbeth, 1673	4	3	7
Julius Caesar, 1684	3	6	9
Julius Caesar, Undated (4 editions)	9	20	29
Julius Caesar, 1691	6 (18)	11 (37)	17 (55)
	209	234	443

In this final period we have a total of thirty-four editions, with an average of thirteen copies apiece still extant, six of them in public ownership and seven in private. The distribution as between public and private libraries would probably have been still nearer equality if public librarians had earlier become aware of the three variant editions of the *Hamlets* of 1676, 1695 and 1703 and the four undated editions of *Julius Caesar*. In this case, however, that they left more copies to fall into private hands is no great matter. It is the business of large libraries to lighten the task of the bibliographers of great writers by enabling as many editions as possible to be confronted and compared under the same roof. But when bibliography has done its work, the final cause of the editions is often achieved and they become of little importance. These later Shakespeare quartos have no shred of authority for the formation of Shakespeare's text, though many of those published before 1660 have been laboriously collated for variants. They do not, like our intermediate class, the editions other than the first printed before 1623, enable us to eliminate errors from the Folios,

INTRODUCTION

as these have their distinct line of descent and owe nothing to the late quartos. Their only, yet quite dignified, justification for existing is the testimony they bear to the extent of Shakespeare's popularity with the class of bookbuyers who preferred "books of the play" to complete editions. From this point of view it would be pleasing if more of them, or (as would serve as well) indisputable traces of more of them, even though lost, could be discovered. The unsold copies of the 1637 edition of the *Merchant of Venice* were reissued with a new title-page in 1652; an edition of *Henry IV*, Part I, was printed as late as 1700; otherwise, not only all the comedies which had never had large sales as separate quartos, but all the histories, which had been so popular right up to 1623, were in the eyes of the owners of the copyright no longer worth producing separately after 1639. What may be called Shakespeare's permanent, as distinct from his contemporary, popularity begins with the revival of his tragedies in the last quarter of the Seventeenth Century. In the long interval there had been some haphazard editions, an *Othello* in 1630 and another in 1655 and a *Hamlet* in 1637. *Macbeth* was separately printed for the first and only time in the Seventeenth Century in 1673. But between 1676 and 1705 there were seven editions of *Hamlet,* six of *Julius Caesar* and four of *Othello,* and this betokens a notable, if limited, revival. Other plays, as we know, were more or less popular, in more or less irreverent adaptations.

Meanwhile the four large Folio editions were being absorbed, one after the other, by the literary readers of Shakespeare, and here and there we find anticipations of the respectful treatment of the quartos which in our own day has ripened till they occupy an inner shrine in the book-collector's temple. In 1627 William Drummond presented copies of the 1598 *Love's Labors Lost,* 1599 *Romeo and Juliet* and some other plays to Edinburgh University. In 1649 the Second Earl of Bridgewater entered in the catalogue of his library copies of these same three editions and of the *Richard II* (second edition) and *Richard III* of 1598, *Henry IV,* Part I, of 1599, and *Henry IV,* Part II, *Merchant of Venice, Midsummer Night's Dream* and *Much Ado about Nothing* of 1600, a very pretty little nosegay to have been originally acquired for a crown, but which it is pleasing to find not thought unworthy of cataloguing on that account. Why, a little later on, Pepys did not add to the delight of his library by doing his best to collect a complete set of the quartos is hard to guess. A later benefactor made good the loss to Cambridge, but a picked set of Shakespeare quartos in Pepys' bindings would have been a very pleasant addition to the good things of the world.

Probably if Pepys had started on the quest of our quartos he would not have acquired more than a haphazard selection of them, for when books are still purchasable for pence there is little temptation to owners to ransack their libraries or lumber rooms to see if they have any to sell. It is only fair to the Eighteenth Century editors to remember that the Quartos have only come somewhat slowly and capriciously to light. When Pope was completing his edition of Shakespeare he very properly added

INTRODUCTION

at the end of the last volume a "Table of the several editions of Shakespear's [sic] Plays made use of and compared in this Impression." They comprise

    Hamlet, 1605, 1611.
    Henry IV, Part I, 1599, 1604, 1608.
    Henry IV, Part II, 1600.
    Henry V, 1600, "1608" [1619].
    King Lear, "1608" [1619].
    Love's Labors Lost, 1598.
    Merchant of Venice, 1600, 1600 [1619].
    Merry Wives, 1619.
    Midsummer Night's Dream, "1600" [1619]
    Othello, 1622.*
    Richard II, 1598, 1608, 1615.
    Richard III, 1598, 1602, 1612.
    Romeo and Juliet, 1597, 1599.
    Titus Andronicus, 1611.
    Troilus and Cressida, 1609 (both issues).

The list is quite a good one; nevertheless it omits the first version of *Hamlet* and the first editions of *Henry IV*, Part I, *King Lear*, *Merry Wives of Windsor*, *Midsummer Night's Dream*, *Much Ado about Nothing*, *Richard II*, *Richard III* and *Titus Andronicus*, i.e., Pope had the right editions of less than half the quartos. It is at least possible that if all the good quartos had been available for editorial use from the outset, we should have heard less about their being "stolne and surreptitious."

Theobald and Capell both printed lists similar to that of Pope's, and these enable us to follow the gradual discovery of the quartos. Of first editions Theobald added to those known to Pope the *Merry Wives of Windsor*, *Midsummer Night's Dream*, *Much Ado* and *Richard III*, while Capell supplied those of *Henry IV*, Part I, *King Lear* and *Richard II*. After this there were no more finds of First Editions until 1823 when the first version of *Hamlet* (1603) was discovered by Sir H. E. Bunbury in a volume of old plays. Of *Titus Andronicus* a copy of the first edition was written of by Langbaine in a way that made Malone think he had it before him, but if so it disappeared without having been seen by any editor, and it was not until 1905 that a copy was discovered in Sweden which is now, apparently, reposing in one of Mr. Folger's inaccessible boxes. Even of the second edition, that of 1600, no copy had been heard of until, in 1800, one that had been peacefully reposing in the Bridgewater Library for a century and a half was brought to light. At what dates the various other intermediate and the later editions were first localized and registered it would be tedious to ascertain and hardly less tedious to recite. But that the possibilities of discovery are not yet exhausted is made credible by the recent identification as a new edition of a 1598 *Richard II* in the

* Apparently, as Malone notes, with the title mutilated, as Pope speaks of it as issued soon after Shakespeare's death, instead of by its date.

INTRODUCTION

library of Mr. W. A. White of New York, which with sportsmanlike promptitude he has caused to be reproduced in facsimile.

Early editors of Shakespeare expected their book-collecting friends to lend them their quartos, but Pope possessed some of his own and these according to Malone (see his note quoted under No. 573) were sold in David Mallet's sale on 10 March, 1766. The printed catalogue offers no corroboration of this statement, but in the auctioneer's copy, preserved in the British Museum, at the end of a section of "Plays in quarto" there is a manuscript entry: "Shakespeare. 2 vol. 3.3.0." No doubt these were Pope's copies, and the two volumes, according to the practice of Eighteenth Century binders, may have contained a dozen or more pieces. The three guineas realized must be considered a fair price, since other volumes of early plays fetched only a few shilling apiece, though the 1575 edition of *Gammer Gurton's Needle,* with the help of a separate entry and italics, had a few minutes before been worked up to as much as 7s. 6d. Lewis Theobald, Pope's critic and successor in editing Shakespeare, must have had a good many of the later quartos among the 195 old plays* which he left behind him, as there were at least three with his collations in the Dodd sale of 1797-1798, one of which, the 1637 *Hamlet,* is now in the Dyce Collection with a quaint reference to Theobald by a subsequent owner. His copy of the *Merchant of Venice* of "1600" [1619], moreover, was No. 1279 in the Steevens sale. But the plays not being "set out" in the catalogue of his sale in October, 1744, what others he owned cannot here be stated. As for Warburton it was he who put Pope's quartos into Mallet's sale in 1766, so probably these were all he possessed. Thus Edward Capell seems to have been the first editor-collector of Shakespeare quartos on a large scale, and certainly made a very diligent use of them. In his edition of "Mr. William Shakespeare his Comedies, Histories and Tragedies, set out by himself in quarto, or by the Players his Fellows in folio, and now faithfully republish'd from those editions" he speaks of having been at work on it for over twenty years. He may have begun collecting at a still earlier date, perhaps in 1737, when he was appointed deputy inspector of plays. In June, 1779, nineteen months before his death, he handed over his Shakespeare collection to Trinity College, Cambridge. As recorded in Mr. Greg's catalogue of this, the quarto editions of the plays number just fifty, of which as many as fourteen, according to our classification, rank as first editions, making up a complete set save for the *Hamlet* of 1603, the 1597 and 1599 editions of *Romeo and Juliet,* the *Titus Andronicus* of 1594 and the later variant of the *Henry IV,* Part II, and earlier of *Troilus.* It must be said also that the collection is not only the fourth in order of importance, but one of the pleasantest to handle, the plays being bound together in convenient volumes in Eighteenth Century brown calf and in size averaging about seven and one fourth by five and one eighth inches. The nine plays of the volume of 1619 all appear in this collection, divided between two volumes, but with the uniform size,

* Not 295, as stated in the article "Theobald" in the Dictionary of National Biography. A copy of Theobald's Catalogue is in the Bodleian Library.

[xxv]

INTRODUCTION

seven and one half by five and five eighths, and standing together as Q 11 and Q 12.

The credit of being the first to collect plays and present them to an important library does not belong to Capell, and though he only missed it by a few months, it is probable that he was an imitator rather than an initiator. The Capell collection was accepted by the Masters and Seniors of Trinity College on 11 June, 1779. On the twentieth of the preceding January David Garrick had died, bequeathing, by a will made 24 September, 1778, all his "collection of old English plays to the Trustees of the British Museum for the time being for the use of the public." Garrick and Capell were old friends and though they were estranged towards the end of their lives, it seems likely that Capell's presentation was inspired by Garrick's bequest. The Shakespearian portion of this is markedly inferior to Capell's, comprising a total of thirty quartos as against fifty, and only five first editions as against fourteen. Moreover, save for the plays of the volume of 1619, which measure over seven and one half by five and three quarter inches, the copies as a rule are not as good as Capell's either as to size or as to condition. None the less the collection was a very valuable one, or rather a very valuable part of a bequest to the total importance of which only Charles Lamb, who made such fine use of it, could do full justice.

Perhaps we may anticipate a little and having described the nucleus of the British Museum collection of Shakespeare quartos complete our account of its formation. The first addition to Garrick's bequest was that of twenty-two quartos, comprising six first editions, which formed part of the library of King George III and came to the Museum in virtue of an arrangement between his successor and the British Government. These also were for the most part rather poor copies, the King's librarian having apparently considered it much more important to secure spotless copies of books printed in the Fifteenth Century than of the first editions of Shakespeare. Up to this time, indeed, and beyond it, the great libraries and most of the great collectors thought it beneath their dignity to concern themselves with anything of Shakespeare except the Folios, neither Mr. Cracherode nor Mr. Grenville ever buying a play of his in quarto, though the latter admitted some of his poems. It may even be doubted whether, except more or less accidentally, any of the quartos entered any great library by purchase until Antonio Panizzi bought the Jolley copy of the *Richard II* of 1608 (first issue) in 1845. His successor, Mr. John Winter Jones bettered this instruction by spending a thousand pounds in November, 1858, to such good advantage that leave has been obtained to quote the invoice in full. Here it is:

INTRODUCTION

The Trustees of the British Museum
Drs. to J. O. Halliwell, Esq.

1. The first edition of Hamlet, 1603.
2. The famous victories, 1617.
3. Richard the third, 1598.
4. Sheet E of Henry IV, 1600.
5. Pericles, 1611.
6. Richard the third, 1605.
7. Pericles, the novel, 1608.
8. The first edition of Lear, 1608.
9. Another copy with textual variations.
10. Henry IV, 1608.
11. Romeo and Juliet, 1609.
12. Henry IV, 1613.
13. Another copy with textual variations.
14. Pericles, 1630. The imprint unique.
15. The first edition of Sir J. Oldcastle, 1600.
16. The first* edition of Troilus and Cressida, 1609.
17. Richard the third, 1634.
18. Richard III, 1622.

£1000 0 0

———
£1000 0 0

For various reasons the name of Halliwell-Phillipps is not held in great esteem by librarians, but there can be no doubt that in this instance he did, and meant to do, the British Museum a great service, and the transaction was equally creditable to him and to Winter Jones, who furthermore carried off one of the most expensive first quartos, that of *Love's Labors Lost,* from the Daniel sale in 1864. After this there seemed but little chance, as prices continued to rise, that the Museum set would ever be made more complete, but in 1910 Mr. Alfred Huth's bequest added the three important editions which were lacking, the *Richard II* and *Richard III* of 1597 and *Merry Wives* of 1602 (all Daniel copies). By the addition of these the Museum has now, with the exception of the doubtfully Shakespearian *Titus Andronicus,* the text of all the plays issued in quarto in the first editions, though it lacks the variant title-pages of the *Hamlet* of 1604 and the *Richard II* of 1608, if the inclusion for the first time of the Deposition scene justifies the reckoning of this last among first editions.

Returning to the Eighteenth Century we find ourselves still mainly concerned with the professed students of Shakespeare and his dramatic exponents, though other collectors begin to appear. Few of the sales are interesting to us, as most of the entries of Shakespeare quartos are either of plays from the volume of 1619, or late editions published after the First Folio. Thus the Rev. Thomas Crofts (sale in 1783) had six of the plays of the volume, a *Titus Andronicus* of 1611 and *Richard II* of 1615. Major Thomas Pearson (sale in 1788) had a *Richard III* of 1612, un-

---
* The second issue, with the preface, which Halliwell mistook for the first.

INTRODUCTION

dated *Hamlet, Merry Wives* of 1619 and five later quartos. James William Dodd, of the Theatre Royal, Drury Lane (sale in 1797-1798) had all the plays of the volume except *Henry V*, and about a dozen late quartos (some with Theobald's collations), but also *Henry IV*, Part II, of 1600, the Heyes *Merchant of Venice* of 1600, *Romeo and Juliet* of 1599, *Titus Andronicus* of 1611, *Richard II* of 1615, *Richard III* of 1621 and *Henry IV* of 1622. Dr. Farmer (sale in 1798) had all the plays of the volume entered in an order which suggests that it may have been intact while in his possession and only broken up for the sale, also a dozen late quartos, a collection hardly worthy of his reputation; Samuel Ireland (sale in 1801) had six or seven plays of the volume (some of the descriptions are imperfect) and a few later quartos (one of them Theobald's); Samuel Tyssen (sale in 1801) had the first edition of *Henry IV*, Part II, *Richard III* of 1602, *Richard II* and *Henry IV* of 1608, and all the plays of the volume except *Lear* and the *Yorkshire Tragedy*. Richer than any of these, though again hardly equal in this category to its reputation, was the famous Roxburghe sale in 1812 at which were sold at least five first editions (good text of *Romeo and Juliet*, 1599; *Much Ado about Nothing*, *Merchant of Venice* and *Henry IV*, Part II, all of 1600, and *Troilus*, 1609) also *Richard II* of 1598 and 1615, *Henry IV* of 1599, 1608 and 1613, *Richard III* of 1612, *Titus Andronicus* of 1611, *Romeo and Juliet*, 1609 and *Hamlet* of 1611 and n. d., also a probably complete set of the plays of the volume and a few later quartos. The one really important sale of this period, however, was that of George Steevens (May, 1800) the entries of which are here epitomized with prices and purchasers' names.

			£	s	d
1263	Hamlet, 1611. No title. MS. Notes by Mr. Steevens.	Nicol.	2	2	0
1264	Hamlet, 1637.	Stevenson.		7	0
1265	Henry IV, Part I, 1599.	Nicol.	3	10	0
1266	Henry IV, Part I, 1608.	Nicol.	1	7	0
1267	Henry IV, Part I, 1613. MS. Notes by Mr. Steevens.	Combes.	1	2	0
1268	Henry IV, Part I, 1632.	Stevenson.		10	0
1269	Henry IV, Part II, 1600. First edit. "printed by V. S."	Nicol.	3	13	6
1270	Henry IV, Part II, 1600. First edit. "printed by Val. Simmes."	Barker.	2	15	0
1271	Henry V, 1600. First edit. Inlaid on large paper.	Hill.	27	6	0
1272	Henry V, 1608.	Forster.	1	1	0
[1273]	True Tragedie of Richarde Duke of Yorke, 1600.	Nicol.	1	16	0
[1274]	Whole Contention, n. d.	Barker.	1	5	0
[1275]	John, King of England, 1611.	Nicol.	1	18	0
[1276]	John, King of England, 1622.	Fillingham.	1	0	0
1277	King Lear, 1608. First edit.	Hill.	28	0	0
1278	King Lear, 1608. Another edition differing in title-page and signature of first leaf.	Fillingham.	2	2	0
1279	Merchant of Venice. Printed by J. Roberts, 1600. First edit. (!). Inlaid on large paper. With Theobald's Collations.	Baker.	2	0	0

INTRODUCTION

			£	s	d
1280	Merchant of Venice. Printed by J. Roberts, 1600. Inlaid on large paper.	Nicol.	2	2	0
1281	Merry Wives of Windsor, 1602. First edit.	Malone.	28	0	0
1282	Merry Wives of Windsor, 1619.	Stephenson.	1	4	0
1283	Merry Wives of Windsor, 1630.	Stace.		10	6
1284	Midsummer Night's Dream. For Tho. Fisher, 1600. First edit. Part of one leaf wanting.	Malone.	25	10	0
1285	Midsummer Night's Dream. Another copy, inlaid.	Barker.	1	15	0
1286	Much Ado about Nothing, 1600. First edit.	Nicol.	2	12	6
1287	Othello, 1622. MS. Notes, etc., by Mr. Steevens.	Hill.	29	8	0
1288	Othello, 1630.	Combes.		13	0
1289	Othello, 1655.	Combes.		4	0
1290	Richard II, 1598.	Nicol.	4	14	6
1291	Richard II, 1608.	Hill.	10	0	0
1292	Richard II, 1615. MS. Notes, etc., by Mr. Steevens.	Fillingham.	1	12	0
1293	Richard II, 1634.	Combes.		5	0
1294	Richard III, 1602. Defective at end.	Forster.		10	0
1295	Richard III, 1612. MS. Notes, etc., by Mr. Steevens.	Forster.	1	5	0
1296	Richard III, 1629.	Combes.		7	0
1297	Richard III, 1634.	Stace.		6	0
1298	Romeo and Juliet, 1599. A fragment.	Forster.		5	6
1299	Romeo and Juliet, 1599. Complete, inlaid on large paper.	Nicol.	6	0	0
1300	Romeo and Juliet, 1609. MS. Notes, etc., by Mr. Steevens.	Nicol.	2	2	0
1301	Romeo and Juliet, 1637.	Combes.		9	0
[1302]	Taming of the Shrew. "First edit." Inlaid on large paper.	Hill.	20	0	0
1303	Taming of a Shrew.	Fillingham.		11	0
1304	Titus Andronicus, 1600. Inlaid.	Nicol.	2	12	6
1305	Troilus and Cresseide. First edit.	Nicol.	5	10	0
[1306]	Locrine, 1595.	Nicol.	3	5	0
[1307]	London Prodigall, 1705 [! i.e. 1605].	Forster.	1	9	0
[1308]	Pericles, 1609.	Fillingham.	1	2	0
[1309]	Pericles, 1619.	Nicol.		15	0
[1310]	Sir John Oldcastle, 1600.	Fillingham.		10	0
[1311]	A Yorkshire Tragedy, 1619.	Combes.		9	0

It is quite clear from our Census that in addition to these quartos Steevens also bought others which he must have sold again after putting his name in them. Every owner of a "Steevens" copy, however, has naturally identified it with the copy sold at auction in 1800, and as it has often been impossible to decide between rival claims of this kind, all the information available is given here.

We may now pass on to the Malone collection, one of the finest brought together, and ennobled by its presentation to the Bodleian Library at Oxford, but cruelly marred like the Kemble-Devonshire collection, formed about the same time, by the outrageous mishandling of the copies, all of which have been trimmed close round the text and then inlaid in large paper. The object of this cruel treatment was apparently to enable every edition to be collated with every other edition. But not very much in this way has been done in either set, while to the booklover all the charm

INTRODUCTION

of the old volumes has been destroyed. On 1 January, 1801, however, the author of all this havoc surveyed his collection in a very complacent mood. He first wrote out "A List of the various Quarto editions of Shakespeare's Plays, hitherto discovered," adding a star to those of which he had copies and asserting roundly "the later editions of these quartos are of no value whatsoever," a verdict which he repeated successively with special reference to the 1631 *Love's Labors Lost;* 1630 *Merry Wives;* 1637 and 1652 *Merchant of Venice* and 1655 *Othello.* The *Hamlet* of 1603 was as yet undiscovered, also the *Othello* of 1630, while Malone seems to lump together the *Titus Andronicus* of 1594 and 1600, but leaves both of these out of his reckoning on the ground that the play is not by Shakespeare. He then proceeds complacently: "This collection of Shakespeare's Plays and Poems in seven Quarto volumes (with which several pieces on which he constructed dramas, bound up among my *Shakesperiana,* must be considered as connected) forms perhaps the most complete Assemblage of the early editions of his productions that has ever been made. It wants only the *Hamlet* of 1604, *King Richard II,* 1597, *King Henry IV,* Part I, 1598, and *Venus and Adonis,* 4to, 1593, to make it complete, and of those three plays it contains very early copies, carefully collated with those original editions, and of the fourth piece (the *Venus and Adonis* of 1593) no copy was ever seen by any of the collectors of these precious rarities, or is now known to exist, though I have no doubt that at some future time it will be discovered.

"Having now finished my collection, and amassed as many ancient editions of this great author's pieces as I shall probably* ever be able to procure, which I have bound up in such a manner that they shall be forever preserved, I have been led to compare it with other similar assemblages."

He then proceeds to compare it with the editions mentioned by Pope (this in a note), and with "1. Mr. Capell's, now preserved in the Library of Trinity College, Cambridge; 2. the late Mr. Steeven's, now dispersed; 3. that formed by the late Mr. Garrick, preserved in the Museum; 4. the collection of Mr. Kemble of Drury Lane theatre, and 5. that of the late Mr. Jennings of Gopsal in Leicestershire, now the property of Lord Curzon." From the standpoint here adopted he could claim no more than an equality with the Capell collection which, while it also lacked the *Hamlet* of 1604 (and 1603), possessed the 1597 *Richard II* and 1598 *Henry IV* as against his 1597 *Richard III* and 1599 *Romeo and Juliet.* Over the other collections his superiority was marked. That of Steevens contained nothing which Malone had not, and lacked three genuine plays which he had; the Garrick as against its inclusion of *Henry IV* lacked six other plays; the Kemble as against the 1604 *Hamlet* and 1597 *Richard II* lacked four genuine plays, and the Jennings as against the 1604 *Hamlet* wanted as many as nine others which Malone possessed.

* "Probably" is interlineated. The *Venus and Adonis* of 1593 Malone himself acquired in 1805. The following further additions have been made to the collection: *Henry IV,* 1608, 1622; *Merchant of Venice,* 1637; *Richard II,* 1634; *Richard III,* 1598, 1622, 1629, 1634; *Romeo and Juliet,* 1609 and *n. d.*

INTRODUCTION

Edmund Malone on his death in 1812 bequeathed all his collection, manuscript and printed, to his brother, Lord Sunderlin, with unfettered discretion as to the disposal of it. Ten years later it was presented by Lord Sunderlin to the Bodleian, of which it is one of the many glories.

In 1821, almost contemporaneously with the Malone collection being transferred to Oxford, John Philip Kemble, the famous actor, sold for £2000 to the Duke of Devonshire a great collection of plays, including an important set of Shakespeare quartos, which he had brought together in imitation of Garrick and cropped and mounted in imitation of Malone. It was this collection, which with some added quartos, including the better of the two known copies of the 1603 *Hamlet,* was sold by the present Duke to Mr. Henry E. Huntington in 1914, thereby raising the latter's collection to the very front rank where only that of the British Museum can challenge, and that doubtfully, its claim to pre-eminence.

After the transference of the Malone and Kemble collections the next important event for us was the second Heber sale in June, 1834, which included fourteen First Editions, but lacked both the *Hamlets* of 1603 and 1604, *Richard II* of 1597 and both issues of 1608, *Henry IV* of 1598, *Titus* of 1594 and one issue of *Troilus.* In Part 4 of the Sale, held at Evans's in December of the same year, duplicates were sold of the *Midsummer Night's Dream, Merchant of Venice, Henry IV*, Part II (4 leaves) and *Lear,* while there were altogether over a score of second and later editions ranging in date between 1598 and 1655, besides a good set of the spurious and doubtful plays. Altogether Heber's collection of Shakesperiana must be reckoned as fine a one as had yet been got together, and it is interesting to note that £41.9.6 for the *Richard III* of 1597 was the highest price paid for any of the plays.

Compared to Heber's the Shakesperiana in the Jolley sale of 1844 were unimportant and we may pass on to 5 May, 1847, to look over the shoulder of George Daniel at his house at Canonbury with a newly acquired copy of the 1597 *Richard II* before him into which he proceeds to write the following note, surely the prettiest piece of humour in the annals of bibliography:

> "King Richard 2: Valentine Simmes for Andrew Wise. 1597, of most excessive rarity. In no collection of which I am aware not even in that of Mr. Heber."
>
> Dr. Dibdin, who is so often incorrect touching the first quartos of Shakespeare; (he gave to Sir Francis Freeling the 4to King Lear printed by Nathaniel Butter and are to be sold at his shop in St. Paul's &c., viz. the *first,* when the worthy Baronet had only a very indifferent copy of the *second:* and to Mr. Heber the *first* edition of Romeo and Juliet instead of the *second:** to say nothing of his assertion that the second edition of Venus and Adonis bears the date 1596 instead of 1594; and of his calling

---

* According to his sale catalogue Heber had both, though the 1597 edition lacked the title and was otherwise undesirable.

INTRODUCTION

the edition of 1602 the 3d instead of the 4th &c &c)   Dr. Dibdin is in the above statement perfectly *right* . . . *This edition of Richard 2d is* UNIQUE.

George Daniel: 1847. Canonbury.

Surely no barrister can have first vilified a witness and then accepted his evidence with such delightful unexpectedness, and the jest is the prettier because the unhappy Dibdin was *not* "perfectly *right*" in his statement that this *Richard II* was unique, as copies existed, and exist, in two such well-known and accessible collections as the Capell at Trinity College, Cambridge, and the Malone at the Bodleian.*

This beginning of Daniel's note has been quoted for the mere joy of it. What follows is more to our purpose, for this is a list of eleven "first editions" (including *Pericles*), headed by four of the very rarest, those of *Richard II, Richard III, Love's Labors Lost* and the *Merry Wives,* which in turn are followed by the *Midsummer Night's Dream, Henry V, Much Ado, Merchant of Venice, Troilus,* and *Othello,* and among Second Editions by the 1599 *Romeo and Juliet* which textually must count among the Firsts. With these are other early editions of plays and poems, first editions of the spurious plays, "the finest and most genuine copy known" (no vain boast) of the First Folio, and "sound, large and most beautiful copies" of its three successors.   Finally comes the statement: "The above Volumes quite perfect and in fine, very many in most beautiful and all but uncut condition are in my possession," with the signature "George Daniel, Canonbury, May 5, 1847," and then we may imagine that Mr. Daniel put down his pen and felt very happy indeed.

At his sale in 1864 the four quartos to which he had given the pride of place fetched from 325 to 335 guineas apiece, prices which long remained records.   The *Love's Labors Lost* was carried off by the British Museum, the other three became the property of Mr. Henry Huth, and by the liberality of his son also found their way to the Museum in 1911, thereby giving to its collection a degree of completeness which had seemed past hoping for, and enabling its officials to rejoice, without any pang, at the prospect that one day some great American library may be equally fortunate.

The passage of a full half of the extant Shakespeare Quartos across the Atlantic which was beginning very quietly about this time is the only chapter in our story which still remains to be told.   In 1869 Alexander Dyce bequeathed to the South Kensington (now the Victoria and Albert) Museum, as part of his valuable library, a little collection of quartos, mostly late, but including three or four first editions.   In 1872 Halliwell-Phillips made an addition of some importance to the quartos presented by Drummond to Edinburgh University in 1627.   The gatherings of other English collectors since George Daniel have all, or nearly all been harvested

---

* A doubt seems to have crossed Daniel's mind for later on he added in a smaller hand the qualification "but (I believe) for a copy in ye library of ye Earl of Ellesmere," which did not make matters any better.

INTRODUCTION

in the United States, and it is with the story of the American collections that they may best be fitted in.

The honor of being the first American collector* of Shakesperiana belongs to Thomas Pennant Barton, who was born in Philadelphia in 1803 and began collecting about the time of the Heber sale in 1834, and continued adding to his stores until a year or two before his death in 1869. Fortunately his library, by the liberality of his widow, was sold, at a price much below its market value, to the City of Boston, and remains intact in the Boston Public Library, an excellent monument to his skill, the usefulness of which is much increased by an unusually good catalogue. Barton was a scholar and a student, and when he could not afford originals he supplied their places with the best reprints he could procure. But his originals included First Editions of the *Merchant of Venice, Midsummer Night's Dream, Much Ado about Nothing* and *Othello* (mostly Heber copies), a dozen of the second and later editions issued before the First Folio (including the earlier *Richard II* of 1598 and a set of the 1619 plays) and a considerable number of the later Seventeenth Century editions to which he seems to have paid special attention.

While Mr. Barton spread his purchases over many years, Mr. Lenox acquired all his Shakespeare Quartos by a single transaction of which we may quote the account given by the seller, Mr. Henry Stevens of Vermont in his "Recollections" of his celebrated customer:

> A large part of 1855-1856 Mr. Lenox spent in Europe and picked up rare books wherever he met with them. . . . He had set his heart on "the four folios," and by changing and chopping about, besides having secured the famous Baker copy, he had secured nearly all the variations known, including all the variations of the third folio of 1663. But I could never induce him to invest in the Shakespeare quartos until December, 1855. I then offered him while he was still in Paris in one lump about forty of the quartos, all in good condition and some of them very fine, for £500, or including a fair set of the four folios, for £600. This offer upset his previous resolutions, and he bought the whole, thus becoming at one step, the possessor of perhaps the finest Shakespearian collection then in private hands.
>
> An exact list of the quartos will enable an expert to judge of the prices compared with what such a collection would bring now. They were, *Merry Wives*, 2nd and 3rd editions, 1619 and 1630; *Midsummer Night*, 2nd, Roberts, 1600; *Loves Labor's Lost*, 2nd, 1631; *Merchant of Venice*, 1st, 2nd, 3rd and 4th editions, 1600, 1600 Roberts, 1637, 1652; *Taming of the Shrew*, 1st edition, 1631; *Richard II*, 4th and 5th editions, 1615, 1634; *Henry*

---

*Thomas Jefferson possessed the plays of the volume of 1619, which entered the library of the University of Virginia in 1853, by gift of his nephew, Thomas Mason Randolph, and were destroyed by fire in 1895. If he had bought the plays separately he might have qualified on them as an anticipator of Barton, but as he possessed only these he must be supposed to have picked them up as a volume, and one volume does not make a collector!

INTRODUCTION

IV, 2nd, 5th and 8th editions, 1599, 1613, 1639; *Henry V*, 3rd edition, 1608; *Richard III*, 4th, 7th and 8th editions, 1612, 1629, 1634; *Romeo and Juliet*, 5th edition, 1637; *Macbeth*, 1st edition, 1674; *Hamlet*, 4th and 7th editions [1607], 1637; *Lear*, 1st and 3rd editions, 1608, 1655; *Othello*, 1st, 2nd and 3rd editions, 1622, 1630, 1655; *Pericles*, 3rd and 5th editions, 1619, 1635; *Henry VI*, 2nd part, 4th edition [1619], and 3rd part, 3rd edition [1619]; *Sir John Oldcastle*, 1600; *Lord Cromwell*, 1602, unique; *Yorkshire Tragedy*, 1619; *Rape of Lucrece*, 16mo, 1616; *Birth of Merline*, 1662; *The Puretaine*, 1607; *The London Prodigal*, 1605; and two or three others, besides the four folios, all for £600! He was greatly pleased with his bargain, but I could never tempt him to go further in the Shakespeare quartos.*

The value of this haphazard collection had no doubt increased greatly at the time that Stevens wrote, and now that another thirty years have passed has increased greatly again, but to suggest that in 1855 it was "perhaps the finest Shakespearian collection then in private hands" suggests either a curious ignorance or still more curious bluff.

In May, 1856, Halliwell sold at Sotheby's a first edition of the *Merchant of Venice*, a *Richard II* of 1598, half a dozen plays from the volume of 1619, and a dozen later editions, and a twelvemonth later a smaller but rather nice lot of quartos which included first editions of *Much Ado* and *Henry IV*, Part II; in 1858, as we have seen, he sold a much more interesting collection, including a *Hamlet* of 1603, to the British Museum; gave another lot to Edinburgh University in 1873; and still had a few to sell in 1889; while a further collection of "Rarities" passed in 1897 to Mr. Marsden Perry of Providence, R. I. In 1864 came the sale of the Daniel collection already described from his own memorandum of 1847. At this Mr. Henry Huth was the chief purchaser. He was then mid-way in his career as a collector, and before his death in 1878 had brought together a fine set of Shakespeare Quartos, including the *Hamlet* of 1604, *Henry IV*, Part II (six leaves), *Henry V, Merchant of Venice, Midsummer Night's Dream* of 1600, *Othello*, 1622, *Richard II*, 1597 and 1608 (first issue), *Richard III*, 1597; *Romeo and Juliet*, 1599, and the second issue of *Troilus and Cressida*, besides a complete set of the plays of the volume of 1619, in the discussions as to which his son joined in an article in *The Library*. Most of his copies were in very fine condition, and the Elizabethan Club of Yale has abundant cause to be grateful for the munificence which secured them so fine a set intact, save for the three which passed to the British Museum.

In 1871 came the sale of the sixth part of the collection of the Rev. Thomas Corser, which was somewhat less strong in Shakespearian Quartos than might have been expected; in 1874 that of Sir William Tite, the well-known architect, and at this the chief buyer of Shakesperiana was

---

* Henry Stevens: Recollections of Mr. James Lenox, 1886, pp. 47 *sq.*

INTRODUCTION

Frederick Locker, a collector of exceptional taste and judgment, by the aid of which, though he never spent any very large sums on his hobby, he brought together a charmingly compact collection of early editions of English poems, essays, novels and plays, which rightly enjoyed a reputation far in excess of its pecuniary cost. Among his Shakesperiana were both the issues of the *Henry IV*, Part II, of 1600, besides the *Henry V, Much Ado,* and *Merchant of Venice* of that year, the *Romeo and Juliet* of 1599, the second issue of *Troilus and Cressida,* and a good many of the intermediate quartos, including all those of the volume of 1619. His eldest son Godfrey proved himself worthy of his father, in the first instance by the skill with which he added to the English treasures which he inherited a similar collection of foreign ones, and secondly by the pluck with which he parted with both sections of his library at a call to which Mr. Locker himself would certainly have responded in the same way. One of the issues of the *Henry IV*, Part II, was first sold at Sotheby's in 1904, and the following year the whole collection was bought by Dodd, Mead & Co. by arrangement with Mr. E. Dwight Church, who took from it all the books he wanted, leaving the rest in the hands of the firm. The *Midsummer Night's Dream* of 1600 thus found a home in Stratford-on-Avon, and a *Titus Andronicus* at Providence, R. I., but the bulk of the Shakesperiana was retained by Mr. Church and passed after his death to Mr. Henry E. Huntington, who also acquired in January, 1914, from the present Duke of Devonshire the famous Kemble collection of plays purchased by the Sixth Duke in 1822 for £2,000. Most of the other Shakesperiana which have been on the market during the last thirty years have drifted into the possession of Mr. Folger, whose appetite for them appears to be insatiable. It, perhaps, reached its maximum in the year 1907, in the course of which he acquired the so-called "Halliwell Rarities" sold in 1897 to Mr. Marsden Perry, the quartos belonging to Bishop Gott, and those of Lord Howe (bequeathed in 1773 to his ancestor W. P. A. Curzon by Charles Jennens). In or about 1907 Mr. Folger also acquired the "Jonas" quartos. Before this he already, it is believed, possessed quartos which had belonged to Messrs. Griswold and Kalbfleisch, and probably also a set from Warwick Castle, as to the original provenance of which information has not been obtained, though their dates suggest the modern auction-room rather than early possession. Most of these purchases *en bloc* yielded Mr. Folger one or more valuable editions, though all the Jonas quartos were of 1619 or later, and the best of the Kalbfleisch was a *Richard II* of 1598. Among the Griswold copies was a *Much Ado* of 1600; among the Warwick a *Romeo and Juliet* of 1599 and *Merchant of Venice* of 1600, nothing else being earlier than 1608; among the "Halliwell Rarities," a fragment of what may be the first edition of *Henry IV*, another *Merchant of Venice* and a *Love's Labors Lost* of 1598 and *Lear* of 1608; among the Gott quartos, a *Midsummer Night's Dream* of 1600, and other copies of *Love's Labors Lost* and of the second *Romeo and Juliet;* amongst the Howe books an *Othello* of 1622, *Richard III* of 1597 and *Hamlet* of 1604 (a great prize), besides a third *Romeo and*

INTRODUCTION

Juliet of 1599 and a second *Richard II* of 1598 and *Lear* of 1608. A few quartos seem to have been bought singly at various auctions or taken over from booksellers who so purchased them, and in 1905 Mr. Folger acquired through Messrs. Sotheran the only known copy of the *Titus Andronicus* of 1594, which had remained in Sweden since the death of its first recorded owner, Mr. Charles Robson at Stockholm in 1794. Next to Mr. Huntington, Mr. Folger and the Elizabethan Club, the best collection of Shakespeare Quartos in the United States is that of Mr. W. A. White of Brooklyn, who owns two copies of the E 6 issue of *Henry IV*; Part II, a *Lear, Love's Labors Lost, Merchant of Venice, Midsummer Night's Dream, Much Ado, Othello,* and *Troilus* (second issue) in first editions, besides the 1599 *Romeo and Juliet* and 1608 *Richard II*, and many intermediate and later editions, including an apparently unique one of *Richard II* dated 1598, and reprinted from the earlier quarto of that year. The foundation of Mr. White's collection appears to have been laid at the Perkins sale in 1889. The only other collection we have space here to mention is that of Mr. Marsden Perry which is chiefly notable for its containing the one unbroken copy of the volume of 1619 now known to exist.

The passage of so many Shakespeare Quartos across the Atlantic has been deplored by an English writer as "lamentable," and interpreted by an American bibliographer as a conclusive proof "that Englishmen value their sovereigns more than literary treasures." Neither comment seems quite reasonable. What matters is that serious students of Shakespeare on both sides of the water should have easy access to the original editions necessary for the construction of his text. In England there were, and are, fine sets of these editions at the British Museum, at the Bodleian Library, Oxford, and at Trinity College, Cambridge; also supplementary sets at Edinburgh University and elsewhere. Besides these there were, twenty years ago, as many or more important editions in private hands, of which very slight use was being made. Most of these privately owned English copies are now privately owned in the United States. If they continue to be privately owned in their new habitat, the English-speaking world is no worse off than before; if they pass into public ownership it is much better off. Professional librarians must own, with some shame but more gratitude, that the great treasures in the world's libraries are only to a very small extent of their buying. Shakespeare Quartos are too expensive for any public library to buy nowadays, and the curious thing is that they always have been too expensive for any public library to buy, even when they were obtainable for a few pence. It is to the imagination, the foresight, the pluck of the private collector that libraries in the British Isles owe 90 per cent of their finest treasures. As a rule the most that the professional librarian has done has been to fill up gaps. In the United States the movement is gaining strength, which in Great Britain Wm. Drummond anticipated when he gave his Shakespeare Quartos to Edinburgh University, which Garrick inaugurated, and Capell, Storer, Malone, Dyce, Halliwell and Huth continued. The United States is not

INTRODUCTION

going to remain forever with the Barton collection at Boston, and the Lenox collection at New York as the only Shakespeare Quartos (there is one at the Library of Congress) which a student can see without obtaining an introduction to a private owner.

The present Census is in a manner a celebration of a gift to a corporation which plays its part in a great university, and it needs no prophet to be sure that the movement will continue, nor can any wise Englishman wish that it should be stopped by any refusal of English private owners to sell in order that as many Shakespeare Quartos as possible may be kept in the British Isles. Now and again old books, as in the case of the Bridgewater quartos, may have stayed so long in the same family that, unless they are urgently needed elsewhere, it becomes an impiety to sever the connection. But as soon as the ardor of collecting wanes the possession of rare books becomes a burden, and if they are of the intrinsic interest and importance of the early Shakespeare quartos, a very heavy one. Here, indeed, is a kind of property which brings with it the maximum of duties and the minimum of rights. In the Sixteenth Century rich men were content to be public institutions, and thought that to maintain a great library and show patient hospitality to scholars desirous of using it was no ill way of acquiring merit. But the pleasure of being a public institution has long since palled, even upon dukes, and why should a man play dog-in-the-manger with Shakespeare Quartos when others are yearning to present them to public libraries where they are sorely needed?

The following two tables will show at a glance the present ownership: (1) of the early quartos which rank as First Editions, (2) of the intermediate quartos printed before 1623 and necessary for the understanding of the First Folio.

INTRODUCTION

I. First Editions.

		Bodleian	Boston	Bridgewater	British Museum	Crichton Stuart	Dyce	Edinburgh	Elizab. Club	Folger	Huntington	T.C.C.	White
Hamlet	1603				1						1		
Hamlet	1604 / 1605				1					1	1	1	
Henry IV.	1598				1					1	1+1	1	
Henry IV, Part II.	1600 a	1			1	1					1+1		1+1
	1600 b	1		1	1+1			1			1+1		
Henry V.	1600	1			1								
Lear	1608	1+1			1+1					1+1	1+1	1	1
L. L. L.	1598	1		1	1			1		1	1+1	1	1
M. o. V.	1600	1	1	1	1+2	1	1		1	1+2	1+1	1	
Merry Wives	1602	1			1						1+1	1	
M. N. D.	1600	1	1	1	1				1	1	1	1	
Much Ado	1600	1	1	1	1+1		1	1	1	1	1+1	1	1
Othello	1622	1	1		1+1		1	1		1+1	1	1	1
Richard II.	1597				1						1	1	
Richard II.	1608 a / b	1			1	1			1		1+1		1
Richard III.	1597	1			1				1	1	1		
R. & J.	1597	1			1						1	1	
R. & J.	1599	1		1	1		1	1		1+2	1+1		1
Titus	1594									1			
Troilus	1609 a / b	1			1	1	1				1	1	1
		23	15+1	4	6	20+6	4	4	4	11	11+7	20+9	14	9+1

Owners of three editions or fewer: Mr. Marsden Perry (*Henry IV*, Part II, a, *Much Ado, Richard II*, 1608 a); New York Public Library (*Lear, M. o. V., Othello*); Britwell (*Much Ado*); Eton College (*Troilus* b); Hunterian Museum (*Henry IV*, Part II, a).

INTRODUCTION

II. Intermediate Editions.

		Bodleian	Boston	Bridgewater	British Museum	Crichton Stuart	Edinburgh	Elizab. Club	Folger	Huntington	New York	Perry	T.C.C.	White
Hamlet	1611	1	1		1+1		1	1	1+1	1+2			1	1
	n. d.	1	1		1+1			1	1+2	1	1	1	1	1
Henry IV.	1599	1		1	1+1	1		1	1	1+1			1	
	1604	1											1	
	1608	1			1	1			1	1		1		1
	1613	1			1+1			1	1+1	1+1	1		1	
	1622	1	1		1	1	1		1+2	1		1	1	
Henry V.	1602									1			1	
	"1608"	1	1		1+1	1	1	1	1+4	1+1		1	1	1
Lear	"1608"	1	1		1+2	1	1	1	1+3	1+2	1	1	1	1
M. o. V.	"1600"	1	1		1+1		1	1	1+2	1+2	1	1	1	
M. W.	1619	1	1		1+1	1		1	1+4	1+1	1	1	1	1
M. N. D.	"1600"	1	1		1+1	1	1	1	1+3	1+2	1	1	1	1
Richard II.	1598	1	1	1	1				1+1	1			1	
	1598													1
	1605	1	1		1		1		1+1	1+1	1		1	1
Richard III.	1598	1		1	1+1					1+1			1	
	1602				1					1			1	
	1605	1								1		1		
	1612	1			1	1	1			1	1+1		1	1
	1622	1			1+2					1			1	
R. & J.	1609	1			1				1	1+1			1	
	n. d. (2)	1	1		1		1	1	1	2			1	1
Titus	1600			1			1							
	1611	1	1		1+1	1		1	1+1	1+1		1	1	1
		26	21	12	4	21+14	9	10	11	16+25	23+16	9+1	10	21	12

Owners of six editions or fewer: H. H. Furness (6+2); J. P. Morgan (5); Dyce Collection (4); Eton College (4); Shakespeare Birthplace (4+1); Dodd (3); John Murray (3); Britwell (2); Quaritch (2+1); Trowbridge (2); A. T. White (2); Balliol College (2); Clawson (2); Terry (2); Birmingham Public Library, Carrington, Earle, Hunterian Museum, John Carter Brown Library, Library of Congress, Pickering, Shakespeare Memorial, Valentine, Royal Library Windsor, one each. Of these Balliol owns *Hamlet*, 1611; Clawson, *Richard II*, 1615; Dyce, *Hamlet*, 1611, and *Henry IV*, 1622; Furness, *Hamlet*, 1611 and n. d., and *Richard III*, 1612; Hunterian Museum, *Henry IV*, 1599; Quaritch, *Titus*, 1611. All the other copies belong to the volume of 1619. The Bridgewater Library is included in the list itself because of the rarity of some of its four editions.

INTRODUCTION

In the first of these tables the 1608 *Richard II* has been included with some reluctance, as although it gives the first edition of part of the Deposition Scene this hardly entitles it to rank with first editions of whole plays, still less by virtue of its alternative titles to rank as two. In this case, however, as in those of the *Hamlet* of 1604-1605, the *Henry IV*, Part II, of 1600, and the *Troilus* of 1609, whether the two issues are counted twice or not, as it chances, makes no difference to the order of precedence of the chief collections. At the head of this come the British Museum and Mr. Huntington, each only lacking the doubtfully Shakespearian *Titus Andronicus* of 1594 and two variant titles. Mr. Huntington has nine duplicates against six owned by the Museum, and from a textual standpoint this gives him a slight advantage; on the other hand the cropping and mounting of the Kemble plays would probably make most collectors prefer the Museum set. The Bodleian and Capell collections follow some little way behind, and then come Mr. Folger, the Elizabethan Club, and Mr. White. The total number of copies here registered as on the English side of the Atlantic is seventy-seven and on the American seventy-eight.

As regards our second table the benefit of the doubt has been given to the undated *Hamlet* and *Romeo and Juliet*, though some bibliographers place them as late as 1630. As Mr. Huntington is the only possessor of copies of both the title-pages of the *Romeo and Juliet*, this is in his favor and gives him a total of twenty-three against twenty-one in the British Museum, while Mr. Huntington has sixteen duplicates and the Museum fourteen. The Bodleian and Capell collections each have twenty-one editions, Mr. Folger being fifth with sixteen editions and twenty-five duplicates, mostly of plays of the volume of 1619.

The total of the copies in American hands is again a little larger than those registered as in British collections, although as it is probable that there are more unregistered copies in Great Britain the difference either way is very slight. In the third section, of editions after 1623, in which English collectors have taken little interest, the American predominance is more marked.

A few notes and explanations remain to be added. The scope of our researches has been determined for us by the earlier work of Sir Sidney Lee, who has already dealt with the First Folio and with *Pericles* and the Poems. Our limit has been taken at 1709, the year of the publication of Rowes text, the first which bore an editor's name. This introduction and the details of the larger English collections down to 1660 are mainly the work of the English partner in this enterprise, while the later quartos in English hands, all those in the United States and the List of Unidentified Copies and Index are due to the American. But the partners have exchanged much information and are quite willing to share the burden of each other's responsibilities. American copies are allocated to their owners in the autumn of 1915, British ones to those who held them at the outbreak of the European War, which may also be mentioned as having precluded any attempt to trace the few quartos on the Continent of Europe, and

INTRODUCTION

interrupted a correspondence with the late Lord Ninian Crichton Stuart, who later on died very gallantly at the head of his battalion of the Welsh Regiment. The lack of information as to his copies and Mr. Folger's is greatly regretted. In other respects we could wish our work were better, but the difficulties of collaboration under the circumstances of the last eighteen months have been great.

Two small points to be noted are that the measurements of type-pages and of most copies have been taken from sig. Ci, and that the catchwords of the first page of each quire are given as a help to identifying imperfect copies. These catchwords have been found excellent tests in differentiating the undated editions of *Hamlet* and *Julius Caesar* which have hitherto been confused. The differentiation of Mr. W. A. White's 1598 edition of *Richard II* from the other examples bearing this date has already been mentioned incidentally, and may perhaps also be placed to the credit of this Census.

Our thanks are due to His Grace the Duke of Devonshire and his librarian, Mr. J. P. Maine; His Lordship the late Earl of Ellesmere and his librarian, Mr. Strachan Holme; Mr. S. R. Christie Miller, Britwell Court; Mr. John Murray, London; Mr. W. A. White, Brooklyn; Mr. H. E. Huntington, New York; Mr. H. H. Furness, Philadelphia; Mr. Marsden J. Perry, Providence, R. I.; to the librarians of the various public institutions in England and America which have Shakespeare Quartos; and lastly to all collectors in both countries who have kindly and generously opened their libraries to us and assisted us in every way with information in regard to their books.

HENRIETTA C. BARTLETT,
ALFRED W. POLLARD.

February, 1916.

A CENSUS OF SHAKESPEARE'S
PLAYS IN QUARTO
1594-1709

HAMLET.

HAMLET, 1603.

The | Tragicall Historie of | Hamlet | Prince of Denmarke | By William Shake-speare. | As it hath beene diuerse times acted by his Highnesse ser-|uants in the Cittie of London: as also in the two V-|niuersities of Cambridge and Oxford, and elsewhere. | [Ling's device] | At London printed for N.L. and Iohn Trundell. | 1603.

First edition. Title, 1 leaf; B-I^4; total, 33 leaves. Type-page, 6 x 3 $\frac{3}{8}$".
Catchwords: Bi, There-; Ci, *Ham.*; Di, For; Ei, *Ham.*; Fi, *Gil.*; Gi, I; Hi, *Leartes*; Ii, *Hor.*

COPIES.

BRITISH MUSEUM. 6 $\frac{15}{16}$ x 4 $\frac{11}{16}$". Title lacking; irregularly interleaved with text of modern edition of later version pasted on interleaves and also quotations from Theobald; a few variant readings on margins of text. "Bought 9 November 1858" stamped on I$_4$ verso; crown stamp on Bi recto. Pasted on wrapper is the note: "This is the rare & most precious Edition of the Hamlet of 1603, of which the only other known copy is in the collection of the Duke of Devonshire. I purchased this volume of Messrs Boone in Sept. 1856 for £120. J. O. Halliwell". Inside cover is pasted this printed entry from catalogue: "No perfect copy is known of this, the original sketch of Shakespeare's Hamlet. All the older commentators were ignorant of its existence and it was not until the year 1825 that a copy, wanting the last leaf, was discovered. That copy, long supposed to be unique, is now in the possession of the Duke of Devonshire. The present one has the last leaf but wants the title. It is otherwise perfect in firm sound genuine condition throughout, and most of the leaves remarkably fine." The Rooney of Trinity College, Dublin (sold, 1856), Boone (sold, September, 1856), Halliwell (sold, November 9, 1858) copy. Kept in grey wrappers pasted over brown paper as at time of purchase, within red morocco case. Pressmark, C. 34. k. 1. [1

HUNTINGTON. 6 $\frac{5}{8}$ x 4 $\frac{5}{16}$". I$_4$ lacking; some headlines cropped. Found by Sir H. E. Bunbury at Barton, 1823, in volume containing other quartos; probably belonged to his grandfather, Sir William Bunbury. The Bunbury (exchanged, 1823), Payne & Foss (sold, 1823), Devonshire (sold, January, 1914) copy. Inlaid and bound with Henry IV, 1600, and other plays in Vol. 542 of the Devonshire Collection. [2

A CENSUS OF SHAKESPEARE QUARTOS

HAMLET, 1604.

The | Tragicall Historie of | Hamlet, | Prince of Denmarke. | By William Shakespeare. | Newly imprinted and enlarged to almost as much | againe as it was, according to the true and perfect | Coppie. | [Ling's device] | At London, | Printed by I.R. for N.L. and are to be sold at his | shoppe vnder Saint Dunstons Church in | Fleetstreet. 1604.

Second edition, earlier title. Title, 1 leaf; B-N^4; O^2; total, 51 leaves. O2 is wrongly marked G2. Type-page, 6 $7/16$ x 4 $13/16$".

Catchwords: Bi, *Mar;* Ci, But; Di, Being; Ei, You; Fi, tifull; Gi, Of; Hi, *Enter;* Ii, May; Ki, The; Li, Let; Mi, Clambring; Ni, My; Oi, O.

COPIES.

ELIZABETHAN CLUB. 7 $1/4$ x 5 $1/4$". Some leaves stained in margins. Bookplates of Plummer and Huth; signature "Jacobus Cumming, P.H." on Bi. Discovered by H. Staunton in collection of Plummer of Selkirk and sold to Messrs. Hatchard who resold it to Mr. Huth. The Huth (November, 1911, No. 1202), Cochran (presented, December, 1911) copy. Bound in red straight-grained morocco. [3

FOLGER. 7 x 5". K$_3$ to O$_2$ injured on lower outer corners, some words supplied in manuscript; title stained; Ii-K$_2$ mended in outer lower margins; cropped at foot, injuring a few signatures and catchwords. With note in old handwriting on title following author's name: "who (with some errors not to be avoided in that age, had undoubtedly a larger Soule of Poesie then for any of our Nation) was the first who to shun ye pain of continuall rhymg invented that kinde of writing which we call blanch verse, but ye French more properly Prose Mesurée; into which the English tongue so naturally falls." The Jennens (collected c. 1740, bequeathed 1773 to W. P. A. Curzon, ancestor of Lord Howe), Howe (sold, December, 1907) copy. Bound in half blue morocco. [4

HUNTINGTON. 6 $3/4$ x 4 $3/16$". Cropped at foot, injuring some catchwords and signatures. Note by Kemble: "Collated & Perfect. J. P. K. 1798." The Kemble (sold, 1821), Devonshire (sold, January, 1914) copy. Inlaid and bound with Merry Wives, 1619, and other plays in Vol. 119. [5

HAMLET, 1605.

Second edition, later title. Differs from the preceding only in the date on the title.

COPIES.

BRITISH MUSEUM. 6 $7/8$ x 4 $7/8$". Last leaf lacking; cropped at foot, slightly injuring a few catchwords; ink stain on F$_4$ recto, G$_3$ recto, G$_4$ recto; some leaves soiled. The Garrick (bequeathed, January 7, 1779) copy. Bound in red morocco with Garrick's arms. Pressmark, C. 34. k. 2. [6

TRINITY COLLEGE, CAMBRIDGE. 7 $7/8$ x 5 $1/8$". Stamp on verso title. The Capell (presented, June, 1779) copy. Bound in brown calf with Henry IV, 1632, and other plays. Pressmark, S. 31. [7

HAMLET

HAMLET, 1611.

The | Tragedy | of | Hamlet | Prince of Denmarke. | By | VVilliam Shakespeare. | Newly imprinted and enlarged to almost as much | againe as it was, according to the true | and perfect Coppy. | [Smethwicke's device] | At London, | Printed for Iohn Smethwicke and are to be sold at his shoppe | in Saint Dunstons Church yeard in Fleetstreet. | Vnder the Diall. 1611.

Third edition. Title, 1 leaf; B-N^4; O^2; total, 51 leaves. Type-page, 6 $7/16$ x 4 $3/4$".
Catchwords: Bi, *Mar.;* Ci, But; Di, Being; Ei, You; Fi, tifull; Gi, O; Hi, *Enter;* Ii, May; Ki, The; Li, Let; Mi, Clambrin; Ni, My; Oi, O.

COPIES.

BALLIOL COLLEGE, OXFORD. 7 x 5 $1/4$". Title mounted. Note: "Extracted from a book of Plays, Arch. M.6.12, and bound April 1864. Donald M. Owen Librarian, Balliol." Bound in red morocco. [8

BODLEIAN. 7 $1/8$ x 4 $15/16$". Probably the Heber (June, 1834, No. 5470) copy. Purchased, 1834. Bound in russia, gilt tooling. Pressmark, Malone 866. [9

BOSTON PUBLIC. 6 $7/8$ x 4 $7/8$". The Nixon (May, 1818, No. 671), Heber (December, 1834, No. 2021), Barton (sold, May, 1873) copy. Bound in maroon morocco, by Lewis. [10

BRITISH MUSEUM. 6 $13/16$ x 4 $3/4$". Somewhat soiled. Large grease stain at lower outer corner at end of book. The Garrick (bequeathed, January, 1779) copy. Bound in red morocco, Garrick's arms on sides. Pressmark, C. 34. k. 4. [11

BRITISH MUSEUM. 6 $5/8$ x 4 $1/2$". Title lacking. Badly cropped. Old red stamp denoting purchase before 1840. Half bound. Pressmark, C. 59. [11*

DYCE COLLECTION. 7 x 4 $1/2$". Cropped at top, injuring headlines on D$_3$, Fi, F$_4$, G$_3$, H$_2$, H$_3$, Li. With "C. P. A. Dyce". The Dyce (bequeathed, 1869) copy. Bound in blue morocco extra, by Riviere. [12

EDINBURGH UNIVERSITY. 7 $1/4$ x 5 $1/2$". Title in facsimile; mended on inner margin throughout. The Halliwell (presented, 1872) copy. Bound in green levant morocco, by Bedford. [13

ELIZABETHAN CLUB. 7 x 5 $1/4$". Title rebacked on inner margin; cropped at foot, injuring two signatures. "for Marc Stapfer" on title; Huth book-plate. The Bandinel (August, 1861, No. 1264), Huth (November, 1911, No. 1203), Cochran (presented, December, 1911) copy. Bound in russia, gauffered edges. [14

FOLGER. 7 x 5 $1/4$". Figures in ink on verso N$_4$. The Jennens (collected, c. 1740, bequeathed, 1773, to W. P. A. Curzon, ancestor of Lord Howe), Howe (sold, December, 1907) copy. Bound in half blue morocco. [15

FOLGER. The Gott (sold through Sotheran, 1907) copy. Bound in red morocco, by Lewis. [16

FURNESS. 7 x 5". Cropped at foot, injuring a few signatures; Oi extended on outer margin; O$_2$ backed and mended on outer margin. Note by W. Tite on front fly-leaf. The Daniel (July, 1864, No. 1440), Tite (June, 1874, No. 2728) copy. Bound in red straight-grained morocco, with "G. D[aniel]" in gilt on front cover. [17

A CENSUS OF SHAKESPEARE QUARTOS

HUNTINGTON. 6 13/16 x 4 9/16". Title lacking; cropped top and foot. Signature of George Steevens; note: "Collated & Perfect, J. P. K., 1814"; and Roxburghe arms on Bi recto; notes by Steevens and numerous pencil marks. The Steevens (May, 1800, No. 1263), Roxburghe (May, 1812, No. 3864), Kemble (sold, 1821), Devonshire (sold, January, 1914) copy. Inlaid and bound in red levant morocco by Birdsall. [18

HUNTINGTON. 6 7/8 x 4 7/8". With signed autograph letter of Cobden Sanderson laid in. Book-plate of R. Hoe. The Pope (sold, June, 1895), Hoe (April, 1911, No. 2972) copy. Bound in brown morocco, elaborate gilt tooling, green silk doublures and fly-leaves, by Cobden Sanderson. [19

HUNTINGTON. 7 x 5 3/16". F4 in facsimile. Book-plate of E. D. Church. The Locker (sold, January, 1905), Church (sold, April, 1911) copy. Bound in red levant morocco, by Bedford. [20

TRINITY COLLEGE, CAMBRIDGE. 7 1/4 x 5 1/4". Title lacking; some leaves stained. The Capell (presented, June, 1779) copy. Bound in brown calf, with other Shakespeare plays. Pressmark, R. 19. 1. [21

WHITE. 6 5/8 x 5 1/8". Cropped top and foot, injuring some signatures and headlines; some corners extended. "Falconbridge, Toronto, 1885" on title; "Walter Townsend from W. G. Falconbridge 1894", and "Charles Young from Vernon, 1837" on fly-leaves. Purchased from Quaritch, December, 1896. Bound in brown straight-grained morocco, by Lewis. [22

HAMLET, n. d.

The | Tragedy | of | Hamlet | Prince of Denmarke. | Newly Imprinted and inlarged, according to the true | and perfect Copy lastly Printed. | By | William Shakespeare. | [Smethwicke's device] | London, | Printed by W. S. for Iohn Smethwicke, and are to be sold at his | Shop in Saint Dunstans Church-yard in Fleetstreet: | Vnder the Diall.

Fourth edition. A-N^4; total, 52 leaves. N4 blank. Type-page, 6 3/8 x 4 3/4".

Catchwords: A2, *Fran.;* Bi, Im-; Ci, The; Di, *Mar.;* Ei, My; Fi, Out; Gi, ous; Hi, *Ros.;* Ii, *Ham.;* Ki, *Quee.;* Li, And; Mi, they; Ni, And.

COPIES.

BODLEIAN. 7 x 5 1/16". Note by Malone facing title: "This edition of Hamlet was printed, I believe, in 1607, as was also I imagine the undated edition of Romeo & Juliet, for these two plays were entered on the Stationers books by John Smethwick Novr. 19, 1607. E. M. (P.S.) In the edition of 1604 the words following the title are- 'Newly imprinted and enlarged to almost as much againe as it was, according to the true and perfect coppie.'. (P.S.) This undated copy I have collated with the quarto of 1604, and have placed the variations at the bottom of the page. E. M. In the Edition of 1604 the play is entitled The Tragicall Historie of Hamlet, &c." At back of title, the title of 1604 is copied with note to Newly imprinted &c. "These words which I have underscored shew that there was an earlier edition than that of 1604, though it has hitherto been undiscovered. It was probably printed in 1602. See the Entries in the Stationers Books." The Malone

HAMLET

(presented, 1821) copy. Inlaid and bound in tree calf, yellow edges, with "E. M." on covers, with other plays in Vol. II of the collection. Pressmark, Malone, 34. [23

BOSTON PUBLIC. 7 x 5 ¼". Facsimile title by Harris. The Rodd (sold, September, 1843), Barton (sold, May, 1873) copy. Bound in red morocco, by Clarke and Bedford. [24

BRITISH MUSEUM. 7 ⅛ x 5". Small ink stain on N_2 verso and N_3 recto. On F_3 verso "The pangs of | office and" has been corrected to "The pangs of | dispis'd love", in an early hand. The Garrick (bequeathed, January, 1779) copy. Bound in red morocco, Garrick's arms on back. Pressmark, C. 34. k. 3. [25

BRITISH MUSEUM. 7 ¼ x 5 ¼". Small hole in B_3; soiled. The King George III (presented, 1823) copy. Inlaid and bound in half calf. Pressmark, C. 12. h. 14. [26

ELIZABETHAN CLUB. 7 1/16 x 5 3/16". Huth book-plate. Probably Sotheby (1868, No. 400). The Huth (November, 1911, No. 1204), Cochran (presented, December, 1911) copy. Bound in red levant morocco, by Bedford. [27

FOLGER. Cropped top and foot, injuring some headlines, signatures and catchwords; several leaves mended. Duplicate leaf B_2 pasted in at end. The Halliwell Rarities (sold, January, 1897, No. 62), Perry (sold, March, 1907) copy. Bound in red morocco, by Bedford. [28

FOLGER. The Warwick copy. [29

FOLGER. Title soiled and damaged. The Harford (May 6, 1907, No. 237) copy. Unbound. [30

FURNESS. 6 15/16 x 4 ½". Shakespeare's signature forged by W. H. Ireland on title; notes by W. Tite on fly-leaf; Roxburghe arms on verso title; book-plate of H. H. Furness. The S. Ireland (May, 1801, No. 473), Roxburghe (May, 1812, No. 3863, but see Huntington *infra*), Heber (June, 1834, No. 5469), Loscombe (July, 1854, No. 1041), Tite (July, 1874, No. 2727) copy. Bound in red morocco, with old calf sides having arms in gilt, set into later binding. [31

FURNESS. 7 x 5 ⅛". Lacking title, A_2, A_3; cropped at top, injuring several headlines; Di mended in margin. Book-plate of H. H. Furness. Purchased prior to 1880. Bound in dark blue morocco. [32

HUNTINGTON. 7 ⅜ x 5". N_4 blank and genuine. Roxburghe arms on verso title. The Roxburghe (May, 1812, No. 3863, but see Furness *supra*), Devonshire (sold, January, 1914) copy. Bound in orange morocco. [33

NEW YORK PUBLIC. 7 5/16 x 5 ¼". "July, 1834. From Wm. Pickering, Chancery Lane" on fly-leaf; Dramatis Personnae in old hand on verso title. The Pickering (sold, July, 1834), H. Stevens (sold, December, 1855), Lenox (incorporated as Lenox Library, 1870; New York Public, May, 1895) copy. Bound in purple morocco, by Clarke. [34

PERRY. 7 ⅛ x 5 ¼". Cropped at top, injuring a few headlines. The Mostyn (Sotheby, May, 1907, No. 482) copy. Unbound. [35

TRINITY COLLEGE, CAMBRIDGE. 7 ⅛ x 5 ⅛". N_4 blank and genuine. The Capell (presented, June, 1779) copy. Bound in brown calf, with other Shakespeare plays. Pressmark, R. 20. 1. [36

A CENSUS OF SHAKESPEARE QUARTOS

WHITE. 6 13/16 x 4 3/4". Cropped top and foot, injuring some headlines, cutting away some signatures and catchwords and injuring some last lines of text. Bookplate of W. H. Crawford. Probably the Sotheby (August 11, 1865, No. 133) copy. The Crawford (March, 1891, No. 2884), Quaritch (sold, April, 1897) copy. Bound in red levant morocco, by Bedford. [37

HAMLET, 1637.

The | Tragedy | of Hamlet | Prince of | Denmark. | Newly imprinted and inlarged, according to the true | amd perfect Copy last Printed. | By William Shakespeare. | [Smethwicke's device] | London, | Printed by R. Young for John Smethwicke, and are to be sold at his | Shop in Saint Dunstans Church-yard in Fleet-street, | under the Diall. 1637.

Fifth edition. A-N^4; total, 52 leaves. Type-page, 6 7/16 x 3 11/16".

Catchwords: A$_2$, *Fran.*; B$_1$, From; C$_1$, This; D$_1$, Such; E$_1$, Or; F$_1$, *Polo.*; G$_1$, *Ham.*; H$_1$, *Ham.*; I$_1$, *Ger.*; K$_1$, *Enter*; L$_1$, *King*; M$_1$, roare?; N$_1$, leave.

COPIES.

BODLEIAN. 7 x 5 1/8". Two wormholes in imprint, one ending at B$_1$, the other at C$_4$; D$_1$-D$_2$ outer top corner cut off. Early manuscript corrections on C$_3$ verso, C$_4$ recto and verso, D$_2$ recto, D$_3$ verso, etc. The Malone (presented, 1821) copy. Inlaid and bound with other plays in Vol. II. Pressmark, Malone, 33. [38

BOSTON PUBLIC. 7 3/16 x 5 7/16". B$_3$ mended in lower outer corner, some letters lacking; B$_1$ and C$_1$ mended in lower corners. The Barton (sold, May, 1873) copy. Bound in red morocco, some edges uncut, by Clarke and Bedford. [39

BRITISH MUSEUM. 7 3/16 x 5 1/2". Lower corner of title mended; flaws in margins of several leaves; D$_1$ and M$_3$, lower corner made up; in some cases the natural unevenness of the edges has been patched by the binder. The Garrick (bequeathed, January, 1779) copy. Bound in red morocco, Garrick's arms on back. Pressmark, C. 34. k. 5. [40

CAMBRIDGE UNIVERSITY. 7 x 4 7/8". Title backed and defective, lacking all of imprint. "E. C.[apell]" and scribblings on title; "J. W. Bruce" on fly-leaf; "Saml. Sandars M.A. Trinity College Cambridge, 1885"; Manuscript list of characters for Henry IV on last page. The Capell, C. D. Gardner (June, 1880, No. 1422), Sandars (bequeathed, 1894) copy. Bound in russia. Pressmark, SSS. 32. 23. [41

CRICHTON STUART. [42

DYCE COLLECTION. 6 3/4 x 5". "C.P. A. Dyce" on fly-leaf; "This copy was once the property of that valuable injured Editor, Lewis Theobald. See the collation and Remarks in his handwriting, passim. J. Boaden." on fly-leaf; Titles of 1605 and 1611 editions transcribed by Theobald on each side of Smethwicke's device; notes mostly on margin, few on interleaves. The Theobald (sold, October, 1744), Boaden (c. 1839), Dyce (bequeathed, 1869) copy. Interleaved and bound in half morocco. [43

HAMLET

DYCE COLLECTION. 7 7/16 x 5 5/16". Lower corner torn off B$_3$, I$_3$; upper corner torn off C$_2$, K$_2$, K$_3$; small piece from top of E$_1$, H$_3$, M$_1$; lower margin torn off E$_4$. "C.P. A. Dyce". The Dyce (bequeathed, 1869) copy. Bound in calf, lower edges untrimmed. [44

DYCE COLLECTION. 7 x 5 1/8". Cropped at top, injuring headlines on G$_2$ and N$_3$; corner of G$_2$ mended. "1659" and scribbles below a cut off name on title; outer margins extended on title; "Liber Johannis Brewer. 1659" on H$_4$ verso; "C.P. A. Dyce." The Dyce (bequeathed, 1869) copy. Bound in calf, with Othello, 1630. [45

EDINBURGH UNIVERSITY. 6 13/16 x 5". Title in facsimile; A$_2$ slightly mended; cropped at top throughout. The Halliwell (presented, 1872) copy. Bound in red levant morocco by Bedford. [46

ETON COLLEGE. 7 1/8 x 5 1/8". D$_2$ torn in headline. "5649" on title. The Storer (bequeathed, 1799) copy. Bound with other plays in Vol. IV. [47

FOLGER. 7 x 5". Title mended and stained; "Matthew Wighaloger his Booke" on title; A$_2$ mended. The Jennens (collected, c. 1740, bequeathed, 1773, to W. P. A. Curzon, the ancestor of Lord Howe), Howe (sold, December, 1907) copy. Bound in half blue morocco. [48

FOLGER. The Warwick copy. [49

FOLGER. The Kalbfleisch (sold, c. 1900) copy. Bound in dark green levant morocco, uncut, by David. [50

FOLGER. A$_2$ in facsimile. Dodd, Mead & Co. (sold December, 1899) copy. [51

FOLGER. Title and part of N$_4$ in facsimile. The Ellis (sold, 1899) copy. Bound in red morocco, by Bedford. [52

HUNTINGTON. 7 1/16 x 5 3/8". Leaves stabbed and mended on inner margins throughout. Church book-plate. The Pope (sold, October, 1895), Church (sold, April, 1911) copy. Bound in red levant morocco, red levant doublures, by Michel. [53

HUNTINGTON. 7 1/4 x 4 15/16". Small piece of title cut out at top. The Devonshire (sold, January, 1914) copy. Bound in orange morocco. [54

KINGSLEY. 7 x 4 7/8". Hoe book-plate. The Hoe (April, 1912, No. 2937) copy. Bound in red levant morocco, by Riviere. [55

MORGAN. 7 5/16 x 5 1/8". Title backed and mended; A$_2$, A$_3$, and F$_1$, mended in margins. J. P. Morgan book-plate. The Quaritch (sold, May, 1890), Irwin (sold, March, 1900) copy. Bound in maroon levant morocco, by Zaehnsdorf. [56

NEW YORK PUBLIC. 7 3/8 x 5 5/16". The H. Stevens (sold, December, 1855), Lenox (incorporated as Lenox Library, 1870; New York Public, May, 1895) copy. Bound in purple morocco, many leaves uncut at bottom, by Clarke. [57

PERRY. 7 1/4 x 5 3/16". The Hodgson (November 29, 1906, No. 96) copy. Unbound. [58

ROBINSON. 7 x 4 7/8". Title worn and soiled; 2 leaves mended in margins. "George Steevens" and "W.E.Burton" on title. Woodcut of arms of Charles I of England pasted on verso title. The Steevens (May, 1800, No. 1264), Burton (October, 1860, No. 4659), Phinney (bequeathed to his daughter, Mrs. Wirt Robinson) copy. Bound in yellow morocco. [59

A CENSUS OF SHAKESPEARE QUARTOS

TRINITY COLLEGE, CAMBRIDGE. 7 ¼ x 5 ¼″. The Capell (presented, June, 1779) copy. Bound in brown calf, with other Shakespeare plays. Pressmark, R. 21. 1. [60

WHITE. 7 ¼ x 5 ⅜″. Signatures C and D transposed by binder. The Pope (sold, June, 1895), Dodd, Mead & Co. (sold, January, 1897) copy. Bound in tan morocco, some leaves uncut at foot. [61

HAMLET, 1676.

Four Line Imprint.

The | Tragedy | of | Hamlet | Prince of Denmark. | As it is now Acted at his Highness the | Duke of York's Theatre. | By | William Shakespeare. | [Ornament] | London: | Printed by Andr. Clark, for J. Martyn, and H. Herringman, | at the Bell in St. Paul's Church-yard, and at the Blue | Anchor in the lower Walk of the New Exchange, 1676.

Sixth or seventh edition. 2 leaves without signatures; B-M^4; total, 46 leaves. Type-page, 7 ½ x 4 $\frac{15}{16}$″.
Catchwords: (A2), The; Bi, *Mar. O;* Ci, I think; Di, Doom'd; Ei, Your; Fi, *Pol.* My; Gi, the; Hi, I will; Ii, *Qu.* Mad; Ki, Dear; Li, the; Mi, Court.

∗ The two editions of this date are reset throughout, but with many of the same mistakes; we have not been able to determine which is the earlier. They can be distinguished at once by the title-pages, one edition having four lines of imprint while the other has five.

COPIES

BIRMINGHAM. 8 ⅜ x 6″. Purchased, 1883. Bound in boards, morocco back. [62

BODLEIAN. 8 $\frac{9}{16}$ x 6 $\frac{7}{16}$″. Title mended on inner margin; Di and Mi torn in margins; Blank corners of M4 cut off. "Purchd, 1828" on title. Purchased, 1828. Bound in half calf. Pressmark, Malone 770. [63

BRITISH MUSEUM. 8 $\frac{1}{16}$ x 6 $\frac{1}{16}$″. Title torn on inner margin and soiled; stabbed throughout on inner margin. Purchased, 1846. Bound in half morocco. Pressmark, 1344. f. 25. [64

BRITWELL LIBRARY. 8 ¼ x 6 ¼″. Title and last leaf soiled. Unbound. [65

FOLGER. Some margins mended; writing on verso title. The McKee (April, 1901, No. 2614) copy. Bound in dark blue morocco, by Bradstreet. [66

RICHARDSON. 8 $\frac{3}{16}$ x 6 ⅛″. M2 mended in corner. Bound in half morocco. [67

VICKERY. 8 ⅝ x 6 ½″. Book-plate of M. D. Phidson. Purchased, 1905. Bound in brown levant morocco, by Riviere. [68

WHITE. 8 ⅞ x 6 ⅝″. Bound in brown cloth in 1913. [69

HAMLET

HAMLET, 1676.

FIVE LINE IMPRINT.

The | Tragedy | of | Hamlet | Prince of Denmark. | As it is now Acted at his Highness the | Duke of York's Theatre. | By | William Shake-speare. | [Ornament] | London: | Printed by Andr. Clark, for J. Martyn, and H. Herring-|man, at the Bell in St. Paul's Church-Yard, and | at the Blue Anchor in the lower Walk of | the New Exchange, 1676.

Seventh or sixth edition. Collation and Catchwords the same as in the four-line imprint, except (A2) which has no catchword here. Type-page, 7 ½ x 3 ⅞".

COPIES

BOSTON PUBLIC. 8 ⁷⁄₁₆ x 6 ⅜". The Barton (sold, May, 1873) copy. Bound in half morocco. [70

BRITISH MUSEUM. 8 ⁷⁄₁₆ x 6 ¼". Badly foxed, edges very tender. "Thos. Jolley, 1807. Hamlet, 1676" on front fly-leaf; "Mary Griffith" on title. The Jolley (June, 1844, No. 608) copy, purchased, 1845. Bound in half morocco. Pressmark, 1344-f-30. [71

EDINBURGH UNIVERSITY. 8 ¼ x 6 ³⁄₁₆". Acquired prior to 1800. Bound in half calf with arms of University on sides. [72

HUNTERIAN MUSEUM, GLASGOW. Size not given. Slightly cropped at top. Bound with books by other authors. Pressmark, Co. 3, 34. [73

PERRY. 8 ⅜ x 5 ⅞". Last leaf mended. "Arthur Bigge" on fly-leaf and "Richard Beret" on "To the Reader" and last leaf; Book-plate of J. Brand. Probably the Bigge (March, 1714) copy. The Brand (May, 1807, No. 6448) copy. Bound in red levant morocco, by Stikeman. [74

UNIVERSITY OF MICHIGAN. 8 ⅝ x 6 ⁷⁄₁₆". Slightly browned. Purchased, 1897. Bound in boards. [75

HAMLET, 1676.

EDITION UNCERTAIN.

COPIES

CRICHTON STUART. [76

FOLGER. The Halliwell Rarities (sold, January, 1897, No. 101), Perry (sold, March, 1907) copy. Bound in half brown morocco. [77

FOLGER. The Warwick copy. [78

FOLGER. With both titles. The Roxburghe (May, 1812, No. 3865), Jonas (May, 1903) copy. [79

LINCOLN COLLEGE, OXFORD. 8 ½ x 6 ⅜". Cropped, title stained. Early marginalia; small heraldic device on first blank verso. Bound in brown leather. Pressmark, Q. v. 1. (1). [80

A CENSUS OF SHAKESPEARE QUARTOS

HAMLET, 1683.

The | Tragedy | of | Hamlet | Prince of Denmark. | As it is now Acted at his Highness the | Duke of York's Theatre. | By | William Shakespeare. | London: | Printed for H. Heringman and R. Bentley, at the Blew Anchor in | the New Exchange, and in Russell-street in Covent Garden. 1683.

Eighth edition. 2 leaves without signatures; B-M⁴; total, 46 leaves. Type-page, 7 5/16 x 4 1/8".

Catchwords: (A2), The; Bi, *Mar.* O; Ci, I think; Di, Doom'd; Ei, Your; Fi, *Pol.* My; Gi, the; Hi, I will; Ii, *Qu.* Mad; Ki, Dear; Li, the; Mi, *Court.*

COPIES

ADLER. 8 1/2 x 6 1/4". Bound in half blue morocco. [81

BIRMINGHAM. 8 1/2 x 6 1/2". Purchased, 1883. Bound in half roan. [82

BOSTON PUBLIC. 8 x 5 7/8". Cropped at top, injuring some headlines. Purchased, August 16, 1882. Bound in boards, morocco back. [83

BRITISH MUSEUM. 8 5/16 x 6 1/4". Title and A2 mended on lower inner margin. Purchased October 5, 1857. Bound in half morocco. Pressmark, 11762-f-4. [84

FOLGER. The Warwick copy. [85

FURNESS. 8 3/8 x 6 1/2". Book-plate of H. H. Furness. Probably the Tite (May, 1874, No. 2729) copy. Bound in calf, red edges. [86

KINGSLEY. 8 5/8 x 6 9/16". With manuscript list of actors including John Kemble and Mrs. Siddons on page containing "Dramatis Personae". Bound in brown morocco, some leaves uncut. [87

KINGSLEY. 8 3/8 x 6 3/16". The Poor (April, 1909, No. 969) copy. Bound in half morocco. [88

PERRY. 8 1/4 x 6 3/16". Book-plate of Sir William Horton. Bound in half calf, with other plays. [89

WHEATLEY. 8 1/2 x 6 1/4". Title mended in upper margin; headline of E4 cut into. The Sotheby (May 25, 1905, No. 643) copy. Bound in green levant morocco, some leaves uncut at bottom, by Riviere. [90

WHITE. 8 3/8 x 6 1/4". The Pickering (sold, December, 1898) copy. Bound for Mr. White, in half morocco. [91

WRENN, Estate of J. H. 8 3/16 x 6 1/16". Book-plate of John Henry Wrenn. Purchased, March 17, 1907. Bound in calf, by Riviere. [92

HAMLET, 1695.

FOUR LINE IMPRINT.

The | Tragedy | of | Hamlet | Prince of Denmark. | As it is now Acted at the Theatre Royal, | by their Majesties Servants. | By | William Shakespeare. | [Ornament] | London: | Printed for H. Herringman, and

[10]

HAMLET

R. Bentley; and sold | by R. Bentley, J. Tonson, T. Bennet, and F. Sanders. | MDCXCV.

Ninth edition, first or second issue. 2 leaves without signatures; B-L⁴, M¹; total, 43 leaves. Type-page, 7 ¾ x 4 ¾".

Catchwords: (A2), *The;* Bi, *Bar.;* Ci, Goes; Di, Upon; Ei, I; Fi, Twekes; Gi, *Ham.;* Hi, That; Ii, *Capt.;* Ki, The; Li, The; Mi, Of.

∗ There are two issues of this year differing in the title-pages; one has four lines in imprint, the other has only three. There are a number of differences in the text but apparently these were corrections in the press. We have not been able to determine which title-page is the earlier.

COPIES

BIRMINGHAM. 8 ½ x 6 ⅜". G4 cropped at top, injuring headline. Probably the Daniel (July, 1864, No. 1441) copy. The Sotheby (March 14, 1870, No. 568) copy. Bound in half calf, by Lewis. [93

BOSTON PUBLIC. 8 ⁹⁄₁₆ x 6 ⁵⁄₁₆". The Barton (sold, May, 1873) copy. Bound in half calf. [94

FURNESS. 8 ¼ x 6 ¹⁄₁₆". Book-plate of H. H. Furness. Purchased prior to 1880. Bound in boards. [95

FURNESS. 8 ½ x 6 ¼". Title, "To the Reader", and Mi lacking; cropped at top, injuring few headlines. Book-plate of H. H. Furness. Purchased prior to 1880. Bound in half morocco. [96

WHITE. 8 ⅝ x 6 ⅝". "J.B.Major" on title. The Sewell (January, 1897, No. 3445) copy. Bound in brown cloth for Mr. White, February, 1913. [97

HAMLET, 1695.

Three Line Imprint.

The | Tragedy | of | Hamlet | Prince of Denmark. | As it is now Acted at the Theatre Royal, | by their Majesties Servants. | By | William Shakespeare. | [Ornament] | London: | Printed for R. Bentley, in Russel-street in Covent-Garden. | MDCXCV.

∗ This differs from the other issue of the same year only in the imprint and in some corrections which were apparently made while the volume was in press.

COPIES

BRITISH MUSEUM. 8 ¾ x 6 ⁹⁄₁₆". Title ¼" short on lower margin. The Garrick (bequeathed January, 1779) copy. Bound in half red morocco, Garrick's arms on back. Pressmark, 644. i. 46. [98

BRITISH MUSEUM. 8 ⁵⁄₁₆ x 5 ⅞". Title and A2 lacking. Foxed, with writing on pp. 46 and 55. Bound in half morocco with other old plays. Pressmark, 841. d. 39. [99

A CENSUS OF SHAKESPEARE QUARTOS

PERRY. 8 ½ x 6 ⅜". Interleaved throughout with notes. Book-plate of F. A. Marshall; signed autograph letter of Furnival to Marshall about Hamlet laid in. The Marshall (June, 1890, No. 1173) copy. Bound in boards. [100

WHITE. 8 ¾ x 6 ½". With imprint torn, lacking four words and the date. Bound in brown cloth. [101

HAMLET, 1695.
Issue Uncertain.

COPIES

CRICHTON STUART. [102

FOLGER. The Warwick copy. [103

HAMLET, 1703.
"Barnardo" Edition.

The | Tragedy | of | Hamlet | Prince of Denmark. | As it is now Acted by Her Majesties | Servants. | By | William Shakespeare. | London. | Printed for Rich. Wellington, at the Dolphin and Crown in Pauls Church-| Yard, and E. Rumball in Covent-Garden. 1703. [6 lines of advertisements of books.]

Tenth or eleventh edition. 2 leaves without signatures; B-L^4; M^2; total, 44 leaves. M2 contains advertisements of books. Type-face, 7 ⅞ x 4 $\frac{11}{16}$".

Catchwords: (A2), The; Bi, *Bar.*]; Ci, Goes; Di, Upon; Ei, I; Fi, 'Twekes; Gi, *Ham.*; Hi, That; Ii, *'Capt.*; Ki, The; Li, The; Mi, Of.

*There are two editions of this year but the title-pages are so much alike that they can only be distinguished by a confrontation. The text is line for line the same but has differences in capitals, spelling and punctuation. We give the following differences but have not been able to decide which is earlier.

	Barnardo.	*Bornardo.*
Bi, last line.	*Barnardo.*	*Bornardo.*
Ci, line 7	*Wittenberg.*	*Witenberg.*
Di, line 25	*Rankly*	*Ranckly*
Ei, last line	*limbs*	*limde*
Gi, line 27.	*Trumpets sound*	*The Trumpet sounds*
Hi, next to last line.	*In noise so rude.*	*Tongue In noise so rude.*
Mi, line 35.	*Had it th'ability*	*Had he th' ability.)*

COPIES

ADLER. 8 ½ x 6 $\frac{5}{16}$". Somewhat stained. With M2. Bound in half calf. [104

BIRMINGHAM. 8 ⅝ x 6 ⅝". Purchased in 1883. Bound in boards, calf back. [105

BOSTON PUBLIC. 8 ⅝ x 6 $\frac{5}{16}$". The Barton (sold, May, 1873) copy. Bound in half calf. [106

HAMLET

BRITISH MUSEUM. 8 9/16 x 6 3/8". "Eliz. Dolben, 1691" and her book-plate inside front cover. Purchased. Bound in old stamped calf, rebacked, with other old plays. Pressmark, 841. c. 3. [107

COCK. 8 3/4 x 6 1/8". Two leaves slightly defective at foot. Purchased from a second-hand bookseller in Sweden. Bound in half leather. [108

FURNESS. 8 7/16 x 6 1/8". Badly foxed. Purchased prior to 1880. Bound in half calf. [109

FURNESS. 8 1/2 x 6 1/2". Cropped at top, injuring some headlines. Book-plate of H. H. Furness. The Pickering (sold prior to 1880) copy. Bound in half calf. [110

MONCKTON. 8 3/16 x 6 1/8". Few headlines cut into, slightly stained. Purchased at sale of Mrs. John Way, 1869. Bound with others in half calf. [111

NEW YORK PUBLIC. 8 3/4 x 6 1/2". Title rebacked and mended; cropped at top, injuring some headlines. The Myers (presented, 1899) copy. Bound with other plays. [112

PICKERING & CHATTO. 8 3/8 x 6 5/8". Cropped at top. Bound in half calf. [113

UNIVERSITY OF MICHIGAN. 8 3/8 x 6 1/4". Ei torn at bottom. The McMillan (presented, 1884) copy. Bound in half calf. [114

WHITE. 8 3/4 x 6". "E. Shaw" on title; note by John Genest on verso title. Purchased in a bound volume of plays from Pickering, March, 1898, and rebound separately in half morocco, December, 1912. [115

WHITE. 8 9/16 x 6 1/2". The Sewell (January, 1897, No. 3448) copy. Bound in half morocco. [116

HAMLET, 1703.

"Bornardo" Edition.

BOSTON PUBLIC. 8 1/8 x 6 1/4". The Barton (sold, May, 1873) copy. Bound with other Shakespeare plays. [117

KINGSLEY. 8 3/8 x 6 1/4". Poor book-plate. The Poor (February, 1909, No. 638) copy. Bound in red levant morocco, by Riviere. [118

YALE UNIVERSITY. 8 9/16 x 6 5/16". Purchased, 1912. Bound in calf. [119

HAMLET, 1703.

Edition Uncertain.

COPY

FOLGER. The Warwick copy. [120

HENRY IV, PART 1

UNDESCRIBED EDITION.

KNOWN ONLY FROM A FRAGMENT CONSISTING OF SHEET C, 4 LEAVES.

FOLGER. 7 ¼ x 5 ⁵⁄₁₆″. C₁-C₄, 4 leaves only. Note by Halliwell: "The reason of these leaves being clumsily mended and unskillfully inserted arises from my considering them to be so precious that I would not trust them out of my own hands, the binders merely supplying the cover. There can be little doubt but that they are a portion of the first and hitherto unknown edition of the First Part of Henry 4th, published by Wise early in the year 1598. . . . These leaves were found at Bristol some years ago in the binding of a copy of Thomas' Rules of the Italian Grammar. Quarto, 1567. J. O. Halliwell, May 25th, 1867." The Halliwell Rarities (sold, January, 1897, No. 19), Perry (sold, March, 1907) copy. Bound in red morocco. [121

HENRY IV, 1598.

The | History of | Henrie the | fourth; | With the battell at Shrewsburie, | betweene the King and Lord | Henry Percy, surnamed | Henrie Hotspur of | the North. | With the humorous conceits of Sir | Iohn Falstalffe. | [Short's device] | At London, | Printed by P.S. for Andrew Wise, dwelling | in Paules Churchyard, at the signe of | the Angell. 1598.

First described edition. A-K⁴; total, 40 leaves. Type-page, 6 ⁵⁄₁₆ x 3 ⅜″.
Catchwords: A₂, Which; B₁, *Prin.;* C₁, O the; D₁, *Hot;* E₁, *Prin.;* F₁, And; G₁, Through; H₁, The; I₁, And; K₁, hot.

COPIES

BRITISH MUSEUM. 7 ¼ x 5 ⅛″. Lacking all of E₄ except a piece 3 ½ x 1″ at foot of lower inner margin; lacking K₄; corners of title and many other leaves made up. Inserted at end is the following letter: "Sir, In my lodgings at Hawick I lately found this play. Observing it to be the first edition, I begged it of my Landlord, although incompleat, on your account. If it should not be of use to you, I shall still be pleased with my intentions; But if it is, I shall be better pleased; and most of all if that use be such as may entertain or benefit the public; in which I see you smilingly concur with me. I am with the highest esteem Sir, your unknown but most obedient humble servant Humani Nihil . . . To David Garrick Esq. July, 26, 1757." The Garrick (bequeathed, January, 1779) copy. Bound in red morocco. Pressmark, C. 34. k. 5*. [122

HUNTINGTON. 6 ½ x 4 ¼". Cropped at top, injuring many headlines. Note by Sixth Duke of Devonshire: "Collated and Perfect. D. 1827". The Bunbury (exchanged, 1823), Payne & Foss (sold, 1823), Devonshire (sold, January, 1914) copy. Inlaid and bound with Hamlet, 1603, and other plays in Vol. 542. [123

TRINITY COLLEGE, CAMBRIDGE. 7 ⅛ x 5 ¼". Worm-holes in A1-B3. The Capell (presented, June, 1779) copy. Bound in brown calf, with Hamlet, n. d. Pressmark, R. 20. 4 [124

HENRY IV, 1599.

The | History of | Henrie the | Fourth; | With the battell at Shrews-burie, | betweene the King and Lord Henry | Percy, surnamed Henry Hot-|spur of the North. | With the humorous conceits of Sir | Iohn Falstalffe. | Newly corrected by W. Shake-speare. | [Device] | At London, | Printed by S.S. for Andrew Wise, dwelling | in Paules Church-yard, at the signe of | the Angell. 1599.

Second edition. A-K^4; total, 40 leaves. Type-page, 6 ½ x 3 ⅝".

Catchwords: A2, Which; B1, *Prin.;* C1, O the; D1, *Hot.;* E1, *Prin.;* F1, And; G1, Through; H1, The; I1, And; K1, hot.

COPIES

BODLEIAN. 6 13/16 x 5". Malone's note: "This is the second edition of this play, which I have collated with the first printed in 1598." The Malone (presented, 1821) copy. Inlaid and bound in tree calf, yellow edges, with "E.M." on covers, with other plays in Vol. VII. of the collection. Pressmark, Malone, 38. [125

BRIDGEWATER HOUSE. 7 ⅜ x 5 ⅛". Acquired prior to 1649 when it was catalogued by John, Second Earl of Bridgewater. Bound in morocco with arms of the Marquis of Stafford afterwards the First Duke of Sutherland, by Murton. [126

BRITISH MUSEUM. 7 ⅛ x 5". "Geo. Steevens" on title. The Steevens (May, 1800, No. 1265), King George III (presented, 1823) copy. Bound in half red morocco. Pressmark, C. 12. g. 12. [127

BRITISH MUSEUM. 6 ¾ x 4 ¾". Cropped at top, injuring first "THE" of title, headpiece of A2, and many headlines; many leaves mended at top or foot; title and several leaves stained. The Garrick (bequeathed, January, 1779) copy. Bound in red morocco, Garrick's arms on sides. Pressmark, C. 34. k. 6. [128

CRICHTON STUART. [129

ELIZABETHAN CLUB. 7 ⅝ x 5 9/16". I1-K4 remargined; blank corners extended and mended throughout. Huth book-plate. The Halliwell (Sotheby, May, 1857, No. 875), Huth (November, 1911, No. 1195), Cochran (presented, December, 1911) copy. Bound in red morocco, some leaves uncut, by Bedford. [130

FOLGER. The Roxburghe (May, 1812, No. 3832) copy. [131

HUNTERIAN MUSEUM, GLASGOW. Size not given. Bound with Henry IV, Part 2, 1600, and works by other authors. Pressmark, Co. 3. 27. [132

HENRY IV

HUNTINGTON. 6 ⅞ x 4 ⅜". Cropped at top, injuring some headlines; some corners damaged, F3-G4 injured in lower part, a few letters in facsimile. "Collated & Perfect. J.P.K. 1798" and "This is the second edition of this Play. Mr. Malone has collated this edition with the first, printed in 1598, and the marginal variations found here, with the date of 1598, are transcribed from his copy of the Quarto 1599, which he obliged me with. J.P.K. Jany. 1st. 1804." The Kemble (sold, 1821), Devonshire (sold, January, 1914) copy. Inlaid and bound with Henry IV, Part 2, 1600, and other plays in Vol. 305. [133

HUNTINGTON. 6 13/16 x 4 15/16". I2 to K4 in facsimile; upper portion of title torn, injuring some letters; cropped at top, injuring nearly all headlines. Locker and Church book-plates. The Heber (June, 1834, No. 5455) Halliwell (Sotheby, April, 1864, No. 671), Lettsom (November, 1865, No. 957), Tite (May, 1874, No. 2734), Locker (sold, January, 1905), Church (sold, April, 1911) copy. Bound in red morocco, by Tuckett. [134

TRINITY COLLEGE, CAMBRIDGE. 7 x 5 ⅛". The Capell (presented, June, 1779) copy. Bound in brown calf, with other plays. Pressmark, S. 37. 4 [135

HENRY IV, 1604.

The | History of | Henrie the fourth, | With the battell at Shrewsburie, | betweene the King, and Lord | Henry Percy, surnamed Henry Hot-|spur of the North. | With the humorous conceits of Sir | Iohn Falstalffe. | Newly corrected by W. Shake-|speare. | [Ornament] | London | Printed by Valentine Simmes, for Mathew Law, and | are to be solde at his shop in Paules Churchyard, | at the signe of the Fox. | 1604.

Third edition. A-K⁴; total, 40 leaves. Type-page, 6 5/16 x 3 ⅝".
Catchwords: A2, Which; B1, *Prince;* C1, lacking; D1, *Hot.;* E1, *Prin.;* F1, And; G1, Through; H1, The; I1, And; K1, hot.

COPIES

BODLEIAN. 7 3/16 x 4 ⅜". C1 lacking; small bit of text transferred (perhaps by paste) from verso I2 to recto I3. Scribbling on recto D1. The Malone (presented, 1821) copy. Inlaid and bound in tree calf, yellow edges, with "E.M." on covers, with other plays in Vol. V of the collection. Pressmark, Malone, 36. [136

TRINITY COLLEGE, CAMBRIDGE. 7 ¼ x 5 ¾". Title, B1, D2, D3, K1-K4, lacking; edges frayed. With "Elisabeth Copinger" on E1. The Capell (presented, June, 1779) copy. Bound in brown calf, with other plays. Pressmark, R. 23. 8. [137

HENRY IV, 1608.

The | History of | Henry the fourth, | With the battell at Shrewseburie, | betweene the King, and Lord | Henry Percy, surnamed Henry | Hotspur of the North. | With the humorous conceites of Sir | Iohn Falstalffe. | Newly corrected by W. Shake-speare. | [Ornament] | London, | Printed for Mathew Law, and are to be sold at | his shop in Paules Church-yard, neere vnto S. | Augustines gate, at the signe of | the Foxe. 1608.

Fourth edition. A-K^4; total, 40 leaves. Type-page, 6 7/16 x 3 3/8".

Catchwords: A2, Which; Bi, *Prince;* Ci, O,; Di, *Hot.;* Ei, *Prince;* Fi, And; Gi, Through; Hi, The; Ii, And; Ki, hote.

COPIES

BODLEIAN. 6 13/16 x 4 3/4". "George Steevens" and Roxburghe arms on title; Heber stamp on fly-leaf. Heber's notes: "Very scarce. There are 3 preceding eds. 1598-1599-1604. Same copy bt. by I. Reid at G. Steevens sale for £1-7-0. Roxburghe sale, £2-5-0." "This ed. was unknown to G. Steevens when he printed H. IV. among the 20 plays. Not in Capell's colln. see his Cat. of Shakespeariana p. 218 where he refers for its existence to Mr. Bowle's copy (the same as present) Steevens bot. many of Bowle's books of White. See Steevens ed. of Shakespeare in 15 vols. Vol. I p. 442, note** where he distinctly states the present, formerly Mr. Bowle's, to be the only copy known." The Bowle (January 19, 1790), White, Steevens (May, 1800, No. 1266), Reed, Roxburghe (May, 1812, No. 3833), Heber (June, 1834, No. 3456) copy. Bound in half red morocco. Pressmark, Malone, 868. [138

BRITISH MUSEUM. 6 7/8 x 5". Inner margin and lower corner of title restored; slip pasted on fly-leaf with note in Halliwell's writing: "This is *one* of only two perfect copies known. It is not in the Capell or in any other collection except the Bodleian, which has the single copy that passed through the various sales to Heber's time. So extremely rare is it that I gladly gave Garrett of Newcastle £25 for an *imperfect* copy. The present is in a perfect genuine state, not made up in any way." The Halliwell (sold, November 9, 1858) copy. Bound in crimson morocco. Pressmark, C. 34. k. 7. [139

CRICHTON STUART. [140

FOLGER. K4 in facsimile. "John Cooper, 1688", "Mr. Thomas Middleton Esq. of Silkswoorth" both in old handwriting. The Warwick copy. [141

HUNTINGTON. 6 7/8 x 4 3/4". Cropped at foot, last figure of date in imprint difficult to read. The Devonshire (sold, January, 1914) copy. Bound in crimson morocco, by Birdsall. [142

PERRY. 6 13/16 x 4 3/4". Ei, E3, E4, injured in lower corner, a few letters lacking; cropped at top, injuring a few headlines. List of Dramatis Personae in old hand inserted between Ai and A2. Belonged to family of Carrington, Missenden Abbey prior to 1800. The Carrington (Sotheby, July, 1905, No. 381) copy. Bound in boards. [143

WHITE. 7 3/16 x 5 1/4". Title backed and mended; A2 mended on inner margin; Di and K4 extended on outer upper corner; H4 extended on lower inner corner; inner upper corners extended throughout. The Perkins (July, 1889, No. 1698) copy. Bound in red morocco with arms of F. Perkins in gilt on covers. [144

HENRY IV, 1613.

The | History of | Henrie the fourth, | With the Battell at Shrwseburie, betweene | the King, and Lord Henrie Percy, sur-|named Henrie Hotspur

HENRY IV

of the North. | VVith the humorous conceites of Sir | *Iohn Falstaffe.* | Newly corrected by W. Shake-speare. | [White's device] | London, | Printed by W.W. for Mathew Law, and are to be sold | at his shop in Paules Church-yard, neere vnto S. | Augustines Gate, at the signe of the Foxe. | 1613.

Fifth edition. A-K^4; total, 40 leaves. Type-page, 6 ⅜ x 3 ⅝".

Catchwords: A2, which; B1, *Prince;* C1, O,; D1, *Hot.;* E1, *Prince.;* F1, And; G1, Through; H1, The; I1, And; K1, I.

COPIES

BODLEIAN. 7 x 4 ⅞". G3 torn, affecting lines 4, 3, 2, from foot of recto and last 11 lines of verso; print torn off middle of last line on K3 recto. The Malone (presented, 1821) copy. Inlaid and bound in tree calf, yellow edges, with "E.M." on covers, with other plays in Vol. I of the collection. Pressmark, Malone, 32. [145

BRITISH MUSEUM. 6 ¾ x 4 ¾". Cropped at foot, injuring signatures and catchwords on A2, A3, E3. "George Steevens" on title and Roxburghe arms on verso. The Steevens (May, 1800, No. 1267), Roxburghe (May, 1812, No. 3834), Halliwell (sold, November 9, 1858) copy. Bound in red morocco. Pressmark, C. 34. k. 9. [146

BRITISH MUSEUM. 6 $^{15}\!/_{16}$ x 5 ⅝". K4 lacking and supplied in pen facsimile on 2 leaves of tracing paper; A1-C2 very tender, some corners restored; outer margin of E3 patched. An early hand has added divisions into scenes. Note by Halliwell pasted opposite title: "This copy wanting the last leaf (sic) should be preserved with my other copy, which is perfect, on account of the curious variations in sheet H. which in this one was evidently corrected after the other was struck off. . . ." The Halliwell (sold, November 9, 1858) copy. Bound in blue straight-grained morocco. Pressmark, C. 34. k. 8. [147

ELIZABETHAN CLUB. 7 $^{1}\!/_{16}$ x 4 $^{15}\!/_{16}$". K1 mended in lower portion; some leaves stained. "This copy belonged to the late Mr. Windus, & was purchased at his sale, March, 1868 by Lilly for ——. I obtained it, April 1870 by exchange with Wm. Harrison of Samlesbury Hall. J. O. H.[alliwell]". Huth book-plate. The Windus (March, 1868, No. 908), Harrison (exchanged, April, 1870), Halliwell, Huth (November, 1911, No. 1196), Cochran (presented, December, 1911) copy. Bound in red morocco, by Hayday. [148

FOLGER. 6 ¾ x 4 ⅞". Cropped at foot, injuring some catchwords. The Pope (sold, December, 1895), Hoe (April, 1911, No. 2973) copy. Bound in orange levant morocco, elaborately inlaid and tooled sides and back; orange levant morocco doublure, silk fly-leaves, by Riviere. [149

FOLGER. Size not given. I4 mended; a few leaves stained. The Jennens (collected c. 1740, bequeathed, 1773, to W. P. A. Curzon, ancestor of Lord Howe), Howe (sold, December, 1907) copy. Bound in half blue morocco. [150

HUNTINGTON. 7 x 4 $^{15}\!/_{16}$". A1 and K4 remargined; some leaves soiled. The Devonshire (sold, January, 1914) copy. Bound in half olive morocco. [151

HUNTINGTON. 6 ⅞ x 5 $^{3}\!/_{16}$". I4 extended in upper portion with headlines in facsimile. With Locker and Church book-plates. The Tite (May, 1874, No. 2736), Locker (sold, January, 1905), Church (sold, April, 1911) copy. Bound in red levant morocco, by Bedford. [152

NEW YORK PUBLIC. 6 ⅝ x 4 ⁹⁄₁₆″. Notes on verso title and throughout book, probably by George Steevens; "Geo. Steevens" on title; "A. Dyce" on fly-leaf. The Steevens, Dent (April, 1827, No. 1035), Thorpe (1827-1839), Loscombe (June, 1854, No. 1043), H. Stevens (sold, December, 1855), Lenox (incorporated as Lenox Library, 1870; New York Public, May, 1895) copy. Bound in red morocco, by Hering. [153

TRINITY COLLEGE, CAMBRIDGE. 7 ¼ x 5 ¼″. Upper corner torn off K₂, and wormholes. Collated throughout in Capell's hand with the edition of 1608. The Capell (presented, June, 1779) copy. Bound with other plays in brown calf. Pressmark, R. 21. 2. [154

HENRY IV, 1622.

The | Historie | of | Henry the Fourth. | With the Battell at Shrewse-burie, betweene | the King, and Lord Henry Percy, surnamed | Henry Hotspur of the North. | With the humorous conceits of Sir | Iohn Fal-staffe. | Newly corrected. | By William Shake-speare. | [Ornament] | London, | ¶Printed by T.P. and are to be sold by Mathew Law, dwelling | in Pauls Church-yard, at the Signe of the Foxe, neere | S. Austines gate, 1622.

Sixth edition. A-K⁴; total, 40 leaves. Type-page, 6 ½ x 3 ⅝″.

Catchwords: A₂, Which; B₁, *Prince;* C₁, O.; D₁, *Hot.;* E₁, *Prince.;* F₁, And; G₁, Through; H₁, The; I₁, And; K₁, I.

COPIES

BODLEIAN. 7 ⅛ x 5 ³⁄₁₆″. Heber stamp on fly-leaf. The Heber (June, 1834, No. 5458) copy. Bound in half morocco. Pressmark, Malone, 869. [155

BOSTON PUBLIC. 7 ¹⁄₁₆ x 5 ⅛″. The Halliwell (May, 1857, No. 869), Barton (sold, May, 1873) copy. Bound in brown morocco, by Bedford. [156

BRITISH MUSEUM. 6 ¹³⁄₁₆ x 5″. Paper darkened, a little stained and tender; title slightly cropped at top and foot. Pencil reference to English Theater; "2107" on verso title. The King George III (presented, 1823) copy. Bound in half morocco. Pressmark, C. 12. g. 21. [157

CRICHTON STUART. [158

DYCE COLLECTION. 7 ⁷⁄₁₆ x 5 ¹³⁄₁₆″. Stained; G-K, foxed; F₁-F₄ much cleaned. "C.P. A. Dyce". The Dyce (bequeathed, 1869) copy. Bound in red morocco. [159

EDINBURGH UNIVERSITY. 6 ¾ x 4 ⅞″. Title and K₄ in facsimile; cropped at top and foot, injuring some headlines and signature-marks. The Halliwell (presented, 1872) copy. Bound in half levant morocco, by Bedford. [160

FOLGER. Size not given. The Gott (sold through Sotheran, 1907) copy. Bound in red morocco, by Lewis. [161

FOLGER. The Warwick copy. [162

FOLGER. Size not given. Date on title in facsimile. Probably the Utterson (April, 1852, No. 1697), Tite (May, 1874, No. 2737), Kershaw (July, 1877, No. 1229), Gaisford (April, 1890, No. 1744) copy. Bound in red morocco. [163

HENRY IV

HUNTINGTON. 7 x 5 1/16". Church book-plate. The Griswold (sold, August, 1889), Church (sold, April, 1911) copy. Bound in red levant morocco. [164

PERRY. 6 13/16 x 4 13/16". Title mended on upper margin, injuring top word; several leaves mended in upper margin. Bound in red levant morocco, by Riviere. [165

TRINITY COLLEGE, CAMBRIDGE. 7 1/8 x 5 1/2". Dramatis Personae on verso title in old hand. The Capell (presented, June, 1779) copy. Bound in brown calf, with other plays. Pressmark, S. 27. 4. [166

HENRY IV, 1632.

The | Historie | of | Henry the Fourth: | VVith the battell at Shrewesbury, be-|tweene the King, and Lord Henry Percy, | surnamed Henry Hotspur of | the North. | With the humorous conceits of Sir | Iohn Falstaffe. | Newly corrected, | By William Shake-speare. | London, | Printed by Iohn Norton, and are to bee sold by | William Sheares, at his shop at the great South doore | of Saint Pauls-Church; and in Chancery-Lane, | neere Serieants-Inne. 1632.

Seventh edition. A-K^4; total, 40 leaves. Type-page, 6 1/2 x 3 11/16".

Catchwords: A2, Which; Bi, *Prince;* Ci, O, the; Di, *Ser.;* Ei, *Prince.;* Fi, And; Gi, Through; Hi, The; Ii, And; Ki, I am.

* Line for line reprint of 1622 edition.

COPIES

BOSTON PUBLIC. 7 7/8 x 5 7/8". The Barton (sold, May, 1873) copy. Bound in red morocco, entirely uncut, by Lewis. [167

BRITISH MUSEUM. 7 x 4 3/4". An old "6" and modern "8" on title; list of characters in old hand on verso; scribbles on several leaves. The Garrick (bequeathed, January, 1779) copy. Bound in red morocco, Garrick's arms on back. Pressmark, C. 34. k. 10. [168

EDINBURGH UNIVERSITY. 6 7/16 x 4 3/4". Cropped at top, injuring some headlines; K2-K4 extended at fore edge and foot. The Halliwell (presented, 1872) copy. Bound in red morocco, by Bedford. [169

EDINBURGH UNIVERSITY. 7 1/8 x 4 3/4". Acquired prior to 1800. Bound in green straight-grained morocco with arms of University on sides. [170

FOLGER. 7 1/4 x 5". The Jennens (collected c. 1740, bequeathed, 1773, to W. P. A. Curzon, ancestor of Lord Howe), Howe (sold, December, 1907) copy. Bound in half blue morocco. [171

FOLGER. From the library of a German noble whose ancestor bought plays in England 150 years ago. The Sotheby (July 13, 1909, No. 323) copy. Bound with other plays. [172

FOLGER. The Warwick copy. [173

FOLGER. Portion of K4 in facsimile. [174

A CENSUS OF SHAKESPEARE QUARTOS

TRINITY COLLEGE, CAMBRIDGE. 7 ⅛ x 5 ¼". Capell book-plate on verso title. The Capell (presented, June, 1779) copy. Bound in brown calf, with other Shakespeare plays. Pressmark, S. 31. 1. [175

WHITE. 7 x 5". "Geo. Steevens," on title; Signature and book-plate of John F. Marsh. The Steevens (May, 1800, No. 1268), Marsh (May, 1882, No. 2406), Libbie (April 2, 1890, No. 1018), Libbie (April 28, 1891, No. 858) copy. Bound in light brown levant morocco. [176

HENRY IV, 1639.

The | Historie | of | Henry the Fourth: | VVith the Battell at | Shrewsbury, betweene the King, | and Lord Henry Percy, surnamed | Henry Hotspur of the | North. | VVith the humorous conceits of Sir | Iohn Falstaffe. | Newly corrected, | By | VVilliam Shake-speare. | London, | Printed by John Norton, and are to be sold by | Hugh Perry, at his shop next to Ivie-bridge | in the Strand, 1639.

Eighth edition. A-K^4; total, 40 leaves. Type-page, 6 ⅜ x 3 11/16".

Catchwords: A2, Which; Bi, *Prince;* Ci, O, the; Di, *Ser.;* Ei, *Prince.;* Fi, And; Gi, Through; Hi, The; Ii, And; Ki, I.

∗ Line for line reprint of 1632 edition.

COPIES

ALINGTON. 7 1/16 x 5 ⅛". Title a little stained. Few manuscript notes. Previously belonged to the Booth family. Bound in boards. [177

BODLEIAN. 6 13/16 x 4 13/16". Cropped at top, cutting off top of "THE" in title and several headlines; two holes burnt in middle of title; A2 has corner cut off; wormhole runs through several leaves. Owner's name (?) dated "1720" obliterated from title. The Malone (presented, 1821) copy. Inlaid and bound with other plays in Vol. II. Pressmark, Malone, 33. [178

BOSTON PUBLIC. 7 ⅜ x 5 ¼". Title and last portion foxed. Probably the Burton (October 8, 1860, No. 4617) copy. The Barton (sold, May, 1873) copy. Bound in half calf. [179

BRITISH MUSEUM. 7 x 5 1/16". Two copies of title, the first added with pieces out and clumsily restored, the second lacking lower third; Ai-A4 inner margin made up; Ai-Bi, Di, D2 mended at top; D4, G4, I3, mended in corners. Red stamp, "10 Feb. 1859" over yellow crown at end to show some leaves purchased to complete book; "Richard Hawkins" at end; "Eliz. Mary Croussmaker, her book 1746" on second title. The Garrick (bequeathed, January, 1779) copy. Bound in red morocco, Garrick's arms on sides. Pressmark, C. 34. k. 11. [180

CRICHTON STUART. [181

EDINBURGH UNIVERSITY. 6 13/16 x 4 9/16". The Halliwell (presented, 1872) copy. Bound in brown straight-grained morocco, by Bedford. [182

ETON COLLEGE. 7 ⅛ x 5 ⅛". I2 mended in margin. The Storer (bequeathed, 1799) copy. Bound in sprinkled calf, with Romeo, 1637, and other plays in Vol. I. [183

HENRY IV

FOLGER. Several leaves slightly mended. Book-plate of John Kershaw. The Corser (February, 1871, No. 417), Kershaw (July, 1877, No. 1230), Halliwell Rarities (sold, January, 1897, No. 26), Perry (sold, March, 1907) copy. Bound in brown levant morocco, by Bedford. [184

FOLGER. Halliwell's note: "By far the largest copy I ever saw." Probably the Halliwell (Sotheby, April 12, 1864, No. 670) copy. The Warwick copy. Bound in morocco, by Bedford. [185

FOLGER. McKee copy? [186

FURNESS. $7\,9/16 \times 5\,5/16''$. Lower margins torn. Book-plate of H. H. Furness. The A. R. Smith (sold, February, 1874) copy. Bound in half leather, with arms on covers, many leaves uncut at bottom. [187

FURNESS. $6\,15/16 \times 4\,11/16''$. Title, Ii, Ki-K4, lacking; cropped at top, injuring some headlines; stained. Book-plate of H. H. Furness. Purchased prior to 1880. Bound in cloth. [188

GUILDHALL LIBRARY, LONDON. $7 \times 4\,7/8''$. A4 mended in lower margin; G3 lower margin frayed. Acquired prior to 1859. Bound in red morocco, by Hayday. [189

HUNTINGTON. $7\,1/4 \times 5\,1/16''$. Upper corner of K2 mended, stained and dirty. With stamp, "Bibliotheca Heberiana, 5459". The Heber (June, 1834, No. 5459), Devonshire (sold, January, 1914) copy. Bound in half red morocco. [190

HUNTINGTON. $7\,5/16 \times 5\,1/4''$. Church book-plate. The Griswold (sold, August, 1889), Church (sold, April, 1911) copy. Bound in red levant morocco. [191

MORGAN. $7 \times 5\,1/4''$. Cropped at top, injuring two headlines. Morgan book-plate. The Lettsom (November, 1865, No. 956), Tite (May, 1874, No. 2738), Asay (sold, December, 1881), Irwin (sold, March, 1900) copy. Bound in red levant morocco. [192

NEW YORK PUBLIC. $6\,15/16 \times 5''$. Ci mended in blank margins. The H. Stevens (sold, December, 1855), Lenox (incorporated as Lenox Library, 1870; New York Public, May, 1895) copy. Bound in green morocco, by Bedford. [193

TRINITY COLLEGE, CAMBRIDGE. $7\,1/8 \times 5\,1/8''$. Stained. The Capell (presented, June, 1779) copy. Bound in brown calf, with Spenser's Complaints, etc. Pressmark, S 29. 4. [194

WHITE. $6\,11/16 \times 5\,1/16''$. Cropped at top, injuring some headlines. The Sewell (January, 1897, No. 3434) copy. Bound in brown levant morocco, by Hammond. [195

HENRY IV, 1700.

K. Henry IV. | With the | Humours | of | Sir John Falstaff. | A | Tragi-Comedy. | As it is Acted at the | Theatre in Little-Lincolns-Inn-Fields | by | His Majesty's Servants. | Revived, with Alterations. | Written Originally by Mr. Shakespear. | London, | Printed for R.W. and Sold by John Deeve at Bernards-Inn-Gate | in Holborn, 1700.

Ninth edition. Title, 1 leaf; B-G4; H3; total, 28 leaves. Type-page, $7\,9/16 \times 4\,5/8''$.

A CENSUS OF SHAKESPEARE QUARTOS

Catchwords: Bi, Such; Ci, *Enter;* Di, *[Exeunt.* | Scene; Ei, *Prin.;* Fi, Which; Gi, *[Exeunt omnes.* | Scene; Hi, Making.

*This edition was abridged but not altered by Thomas Betterton.

COPIES

ADLER. 8 ⅜ x 6 ¼". Spotted. Bound in boards. [196

BIRMINGHAM. 8 $\frac{7}{16}$ x 5 ¼". Title mended on outer blank margin; H3 mended. Some notes on margins; book-plates of Frederick Perkins and F. A. Marshall. The Perkins (July, 1889, No. 1712), Marshall (July, 1890, No. 1177) copy. Bound in half calf. [197

BODLEIAN. 8 $\frac{9}{16}$ x 6 $\frac{5}{16}$". Title torn; cropped at top, injuring some headlines; H2 and H3 torn on inner margins. The Malone (presented, 1821) copy. Bound with other old plays in calf. Pressmark, Malone 73. [198

BODLEIAN. 8 ½ x 6". Few headlines cut into. The Malone (presented, 1821) copy. Bound with other old plays in calf. Pressmark, Malone 111. [199

BOSTON PUBLIC. 8 $\frac{7}{16}$ x 6 ⅝". Probably the Jolley (June, 1844, No. 594) copy. The Barton (sold, May, 1873) copy. Bound in half morocco. [200

BRITISH MUSEUM. 8 ⅜ x 6". Worn on all edges. The King George III (presented, 1823) copy. Bound in half morocco. Pressmark, 163. h. 69. [201

BRITISH MUSEUM. 8 $\frac{1}{16}$ x 6 ⅛". Title mended in several places; cropped top and foot, injuring some headlines, signatures and catchwords. The Garrick (bequeathed, January, 1779) copy. Bound in half morocco, Garrick's arms on back. Pressmark, 644. f. 51. [202

BRITISH MUSEUM. 8 $\frac{9}{16}$ x 6 $\frac{7}{16}$". Purchased. Bound with Hamlet, 1703, and other old plays. Pressmark, 841. c. 3. [203

FOLGER. The Warwick copy. [204

HARVARD UNIVERSITY. 8 ½ x 6 ¼". Title lacking; H3 torn in lower outer corner, injuring a few letters. The Drew (presented, February, 1903) copy. Bound in cloth. [205

HUNTINGTON. 8 ⅜ x 6 ½". Cropped at top, injuring one headline. The Kemble (sold, 1821), Devonshire (sold, January, 1914) copy. Bound with other plays in Vol. 140. [205*

MORGAN. 8 ⅜ x 6 ⅜". Morgan book-plate. The Irwin (sold, March, 1900) copy. Bound in red levant morocco, by Pratt for Mr. Irwin. [206

NEW YORK PUBLIC. 8 ¾ x 6 ½". "Tho. Corbin" on top of title. The Myers (presented, 1899) copy. Bound with other plays. [207

UNIVERSITY OF MICHIGAN. 8 $\frac{13}{16}$ x 6 ⅝". The Sotheby (June 27, 1906, No. 439) copy. Bound in half morocco, by Holland. [208

WHEATLEY. 8 $\frac{7}{16}$ x 6 ⅜". The Pickering (sold c. 1905) copy. Unbound. [209

WRENN, Estate of J. H. 8 $\frac{11}{16}$ x 6 ¾". Book-plate of J. H. Wrenn. Purchased, April 7, 1905. Bound in polished calf, by Riviere. [210

HENRY IV, PART 2

HENRY IV, PART 2, 1600.
Sheet E, 4 Leaves.

The | Second part of Henrie | the fourth, continuing to his death | and coronation of Henrie | the fift. | With the humours of sir Iohn Fal-|staffe, and swaggering | Pistoll. | As it hath been sundrie times publikely | acted by the right honourable, the Lord | Chamberlaine his seruants. | Written by William Shakespeare. | [Ornament] | London | Printed by V.S. for Andrew Wise, and | William Aspley. | 1600.

First edition, first issue. A-K^4; L^2; total, 42 leaves. L2 blank. Type-page, 6 ⅛ x 3 ½".

Catchwords: A2, I; Bi, *Iohn;* Ci, *Hostesse.;* Di, eate; Ei, *Boy.;* Fi, and; Gi, *Mow.;* Hi, and; Ii, I; Ki, Into; Li, First.

COPIES

BODLEIAN. 6 ¾ x 4 ¾". Bi-B4, Li, lacking; cropped at top, cutting off top of "THE" in title and headlines in sheet A; piece torn from blank margin of title and from Ci-C4, injuring from 7 to 17 lines of text. On A2 recto, "Goe to the Emmot O thou slugard and learne of hir". Malone's note facing title: "In this copy signature E has only the ordinary quantity of leaves, namely four. The publisher finding he had omitted somewhat, cancelled the two latter (viz. E3 & E4) reprinted them in a different manner and added a fifth in order to get in the omitted lines. This is the only difference between the copies. See the other copy with the additional leaf in Vol. V. In a copy of the play which belonged to Samuel Tysen Esqr. and was sold with his collection in Dec. 1801 is written in the titlepage, in the handwriting of Shakespeare's times, '11 December 1610. price v d.'" The Malone (presented, 1821) copy. Inlaid and bound in tree calf, yellow edges, with "E.M." on covers, with other plays in Vol. IV. Pressmark, Malone 35. [211

BRITISH MUSEUM. 6 ¾ x 4 15/16". Sheet E, 4 leaves, only. Halliwell's note: "There is only one early edition of this play but some copies have an enlarged sheet E, with an additional scene, consisting of six leaves. The fact clearly is that, as originally published, sheet E contained only four leaves. The error was found out, & in copies issued afterwards the sheet was altered. There are two copies in the Museum, but both have the enlarged sheet. The present genuine copy of the original sheet is taken from a duplicate in my collection." The Halliwell (sold, November 9, 1858) copy. Bound in red morocco. Pressmark, C. 34. k. 13. [212

HUNTERIAN MUSEUM, GLASGOW. Bound with Henry IV, Pt. 1, 1599, and works by other authors. Pressmark, Co. 3. 27. [213

HUNTINGTON. $6\,13/16 \times 4\,3/8''$. Cropped at top, injuring "THE" on title and some headlines. "Collated & Perfect. J.P.K. 1798." The Kemble (sold, 1821), Devonshire (sold, January, 1914) copy. Inlaid and bound with Henry IV, 1599, and other plays in Vol. 305. [214

HUNTINGTON. $6\,13/16 \times 4\,7/8''$. Lower corner of E_4 is extended with ends of 15 lines in facsimile; upper margins of A_2, A_3, E_i-E_4 are extended, headlines in facsimile. Note by Halliwell on front fly, dated 1866; few stage directions in old hand; book-plates of Locker and Church. The Heber (December, 1834, No. 2019), Halliwell (sold, c. 1866), Tite (May, 1874, No. 2735), Locker (sold, January, 1905), Church (sold, April, 1911) copy. Bound in red levant morocco, by Bedford. [215

PERRY. $6\,13/16 \times 4\,3/4''$. Title lacking; cropped at top, injuring some headlines. "William Penn" (the Admiral) on D_2. The Penn (owned c. 1670), Carrington family (owned prior to 1800), George Carrington (Sotheby, July, 1905, No. 382) copy. Bound in boards. [216

TRINITY COLLEGE, CAMBRIDGE. $7 \times 4\,3/4''$. Title a little torn at foot. The Capell (presented, June, 1779) copy. Bound in brown calf, with other plays. Pressmark, S. 35. 3. [217

HENRY IV, PART 2, 1600.

Sheet E, 6 Leaves.

First edition, second issue. Title same as first issue.
Collation: A-D^4; E^6; F-K^4; L^2; total, 44 leaves.
Catchwords same as first issue.

＊When the first issue was finished the printer discovered that he had omitted something in Act 3, he therefore canceled E_3 and E_4 and reprinted them adding E_5 and E_6 to contain the omitted matter.

COPIES

BODLEIAN. $7\,3/16 \times 4\,3/8''$. B_3, C_3, D_3, stained; small tear in K_4. The Malone (presented, 1821) copy. Inlaid and bound with Henry IV, 1604, and other plays in Vol. V. Pressmark, Malone 36. [218

BRIDGEWATER HOUSE. $7\,1/4 \times 5\,1/8''$. Acquired prior to 1649 when it was catalogued by John, Second Earl of Bridgewater. Bound in green morocco with arms of the Marquis of Stafford, by Murton. [219

BRITISH MUSEUM. $6\,3/4 \times 4\,5/8''$. With two stubs left from the cancelled leaves in sheet E. "George Steevens" on title. Pencil reference to "English Theatre." The Steevens (May, 1800, No. 1269 or 1270), King George III (presented, 1823) copy. Bound in half morocco. Pressmark, C. 12. g. 20. [220

BRITISH MUSEUM. $7\,1/16 \times 4\,15/16''$. Inner margin of title strengthened a little; wide lower margins, some headlines slightly cropped. The Garrick (bequeathed, January, 1779) copy. Bound in red morocco, with Garrick's arms on sides. Pressmark, C. 34. k. 12. [221

HENRY IV

ELIZABETHAN CLUB. 6¾ x 5″. Title mended; A2, A3, E1-E6 extended on outer margin; L1, L2 mended on inner margin; cropped at top, injuring some headlines; L2 blank and genuine. Huth book-plate. The Halliwell (May, 1857, No. 872), Huth (November, 1911, No. 1197), Cochran (presented, December, 1911) copy. Bound in red morocco, by Bedford. [222

HUNTINGTON. 6½ x 4 5/16″. Cropped at top, injuring some headlines. Note by Duke of Devonshire: "This copy differs from Kemble's Vol. 305, having the scene between the king & Council Sheet E3, 4, 5. Collated & Perfect. D. 1827". The Bunbury (exchanged, 1823), Payne & Foss (sold, 1823), Devonshire (sold, January, 1914) copy. Inlaid and bound with Hamlet, 1603 and other plays in Vol. 542. [223

HUNTINGTON. 6 11/16 x 4 ⅞″. Leaves stabbed on inner margin throughout book. Church book-plate. The Locker (Sotheby, April, 1904, No. 1182), Church (sold, April, 1911) copy. Bound in red levant morocco, by Bedford. [224

WHITE. 7 x 5 ⅛″. With lines 18 and 20 on verso F4 not in the other White copy. With notes by Heber and his stamp on fly-leaf. The Heber (June, 1834, No. 5460), Perkins (July, 1889, No. 1694) copy. Bound in red morocco, arms of F. Perkins in gilt on covers. [225

WHITE. 6½ x 4 9/16″. A2, A3, E1-E6, and L1 in facsimile; cropped at top, injuring some headlines. Probably the Sotheby (August, 1821), Heber (June, 1834, No. 5460*), Rodd (1837, No. 4158) copy. The Crawford (March, 1891, No. 2888) copy. Bound in red levant morocco, by Bedford. [226

HENRY IV, PART 2, 1600.
Issue Uncertain.
COPY.

CRICHTON STUART. Probably Steevens (May, 1800, No. 1269), Bute (bequeathed) copy. [227

HENRY V.

HENRY V, 1600.

The | Cronicle | History of Henry the fift, | With his battell fought at Agin Court in | France. Togither with Auntient | Pistoll. | As it hath bene sundry times playd by the Right honorable | the Lord Chamberlaine his seruants. | [Creede's device] | London | Printed by Thomas Creede, for Tho. Milling-|ton, and Iohn Busby. And are to be | sold at his house in Carter Lane, next | the Powle head. 1600.

First edition. A-G^4; total, 28 leaves. G$_2$ is wrongly marked G$_3$; G$_4$ is blank. Type-page, 6 ⅛ x 3 ⅜".

Catchwords: A$_2$, *Bish;* B$_1$, *Nim.* I; C$_1$, Question; D$_1$, Will; E$_1$, Which; F$_1$, The; G$_1$, And.

COPIES.

BODLEIAN. 6 15/16 x 4 ⅞". Stained. The Malone (presented, 1821) copy. Inlaid and bound with Henry IV, 1613, and other plays in Vol. I. Pressmark, Malone, 32. [228

BRITISH MUSEUM. 7 3/16 x 4 ¾". Wide lower margins but some a little mended; title-page backed. The King George III (presented, 1823) copy. Bound in crimson morocco. Pressmark, C. 12. g. 22. [229

ELIZABETHAN CLUB. 7 1/16 x 5 ¼". Stabbed throughout on inner margins. "15. 7. 6. Sale by Sotheby, 1821" in Heber's hand and Heber's stamp on front fly-leaf; G$_4$ genuine but partly lacking; Huth book-plate. The Heber (June, 1834, No. 5461), Daniel (July, 1864, No. 1431), Huth (November, 1911, No. 1208), Cochran (presented, December, 1911) copy. Bound in vellum. [230

HUNTINGTON. 7 x 5". With names of "J. ffleming. 1695", "Gower, 1704" and "George Steevens," and scribbling on several leaves; "Collated & Perfect. J. P. K. 1804" The Steevens (May, 1800, No. 1271), Kemble (sold, 1821), Devonshire (sold, January, 1914) copy. Inlaid and bound with Lear, 1608, and other plays in Vol. 375. [231

HUNTINGTON. 7 x 5 ¼". B$_4$-G$_3$ in facsimile; B$_1$-B$_3$ have some words in facsimile. Locker and Church book-plates. The Tite (May, 1874, No. 2739), Locker (sold, January, 1905), Church (sold, April, 1911) copy. Bound in red levant morocco, by Bedford. [232

TRINITY COLLEGE, CAMBRIDGE. 6 ½ x 4 ¾". Cropped at top, injuring title-page and most headlines. The Capell (presented, June, 1779) copy. Bound in brown calf, with other plays. Pressmark, W. 5. 5. [233

A CENSUS OF SHAKESPEARE QUARTOS

HENRY V, 1602.

The | Chronicle | History of Henry the fift, | With his battell fought at Agin Court | in France. Together with Auntient | Pistoll. | As it hath bene sundry times playd by the Right honorable | the Lord Chamberlaine his seruants. | [Creede's device] | London | Printed by Thomas Creede, for Thomas | Pauier, and are to be sold at his shop in Cornhill, | at the signe of the Cat and Parrets neare | the Exchange. 1602.

Second edition. A-F^4; G^2; total, 26 leaves. Type-page, 6 ⅛ x 4 ⅜".

Catchwords: A2, *Bish.*; Bi, At; Ci, *Exe.*; Di, Or; Ei, No; Fi, *Flew;* Gi, Come.

COPIES.

HUNTINGTON. 6 ½ x 4 ⅜". "Collated & Perfect. D. 1827". The Bunbury (exchanged, 1823), Payne & Foss (sold, 1823), Devonshire (sold, January, 1914) copy. Inlaid and bound with Hamlet, 1603, and other plays in Vol. 542. [234

TRINITY COLLEGE, CAMBRIDGE. 7 x 4 ¾". Collated throughout by Capell with editions of 1600 and 1608. The Capell (presented, June, 1779) copy. Bound in brown calf, with other Shakespeare plays. Pressmark, S. 35. 2. [235

HENRY V, 1608 [1619].

The | Chronicle History | of Henry the fift, vvith his | battell fought at Agin Court in | France. Together with an-|cient Pistoll. | As it hath bene sundry times playd by the Right Honou-|rable the Lord Chamberlaine his | Seruants. | [Heb Ddieu device] | Printed for T. P. 1608. [Thomas Pavier, 1619]

Third edition. A-G^4; total, 28 leaves. Type-page, 6 1/16 x 3 5/16". G4 blank.

Catchwords: A2, *Bysh.*; Bi, *Nim.*; Ci, Question; Di, At; Ei, Thinke; Fi, *Enter;* Gi, *Har.*

COPIES.

BIRMINGHAM. 7 x 5 7/16". With manuscript notes by J. O. Halliwell. The George Smith (July, 1867, No. 2578), Halliwell (presented, April, 1867) copy. Bound in red levant morocco, by Bedford. [236

BODLEIAN. 6 ⅞ x 5 ⅛". Large piece torn off Gi, 23 lines of text lacking; small piece of paper transferred from Di recto to C4 verso; E3 and E4 torn in blank margins; badly stained. Note in old hand on F4: "Cleopatra and marks antomie". The Malone (presented, 1821) copy. Inlaid and bound with other plays in Vol. I. Pressmark, Malone, 32. [237

BOSTON PUBLIC. 7 5/16 x 5 ⅜". Gi extended on margin. The Rodd (sold, 1842), Barton (sold, May, 1873) copy. Bound in blue straight-grained morocco. [238

BRITISH MUSEUM. 7 9/16 x 5 ⅞". Some rust holes in Sheet B. The Garrick (bequeathed, January, 1779) copy. Bound in red morocco, Garrick's arms on sides. Pressmark, C. 34. k. 14. [239

HENRY V

BRITISH MUSEUM. 7 x 4 13/16″. Title strengthened near inner margin. Scribbles on title. The King George III (presented, 1823) copy. Rebound in brown morocco, 1905. Pressmark, C. 12. g. 33. [240

BRITWELL LIBRARY. 7 1/8 x 5 1/4″. F2 mended in blank margin. Fountaine Walker book-plate. The Jadis (March, 1828, No. 165), Corser (February, 1871, No. 404), Kinnear, Walker (May, 1893, No. 447) copy. Bound in red morocco with Kinnear arms on covers, red morocco doublure and silk fly-leaves, by Lewis. [241

CRICHTON STUART. [242

DODD. 7 1/16 x 5 3/8″. G4 blank and genuine. Lower corner of title mended with date in facsimile; upper corner of Gi mended with parts of 22 words on verso in facsimile. The Locker (sold, January, 1905) copy. Bound in tan straight-grained morocco. [243

DYCE COLLECTION. 7 1/16 x 5 1/8″. Title very brown. The Dyce (bequeathed, 1869) copy. Bound in red morocco extra, by Murton. [244

EARLE. 6 13/16 x 4 13/16″. The Thomas (sold, 1909), Rosenbach (sold, June, 1910) copy. Bound in red levant morocco, by Riviere. [245

EDINBURGH UNIVERSITY. 6 7/8 x 5 1/8″. Di mended in lower margin; title brown from exposure. "E. C."[apell] on title. The Capell, Halliwell (presented, 1872) copy. Bound in brown morocco. [246

ELIZABETHAN CLUB. 7 7/16 x 5 1/2″. G4 blank and genuine. Title extended in outer blank margin. Huth book-plate. The Huth (November, 1911, No. 1209), Cochran (presented, December, 1911) copy. Bound in red levant morocco, by Bedford. [247

ETON COLLEGE. 7 1/8 x 5 3/16″. "J. Payne" on title; Di torn. The Payne (c. 1787), Storer (bequeathed, 1799) copy. Bound with other plays in Vol. IV. [248

FOLGER. The Jennens (collected, c. 1740, bequeathed, 1773, to W. P. A. Curzon, ancestor of Lord Howe), Howe (sold, December, 1907) copy. Bound in half blue morocco. [249

FOLGER. Size not given. The Gott (sold through Sotheran, 1907) copy. Bound in half red morocco, by Lewis. [250

FOLGER. The Warwick copy. [251

FOLGER. The Griswold (probably sold, August, 1889) copy. [252

FOLGER. Hole in one leaf. The Foster (June, 1894, No. 27), Jonas (sold, May, 1903) copy. Bound in morocco, by Riviere. [253

FURNESS. 7 1/4 x 5 5/16″. Note on verso title signed "E. C."[apell] and his manuscript corrections in red ink throughout the book. Book-plate of H. H. Furness. The Capell, Halliwell (Sotheby, May, 1856, No. 336), Kinsman (sold, July, 1872) copy. Bound in green levant morocco, gilt tooling, blue silk doublures and fly-leaves. [254

FURNESS. 6 5/8 x 4 7/8″. C3, D3, Gi-G4 lacking. Title mended and backed. Presentation inscription from J. O. Halliwell to H. H. Furness. The Halliwell (presented, January, 1871) copy. Bound in old half calf. [255

HUNTINGTON. 7 1/8 x 5 5/16″. G4 blank and genuine. Church book-plate. The Church (sold, January, 1911) copy. Bound in dark green morocco. [256

A CENSUS OF SHAKESPEARE QUARTOS

HUNTINGTON. 6 7/8 x 4 13/16". "Collated & Perfect. J. P. K. 1798". The Kemble (sold, 1821), Devonshire (sold, January, 1914) copy. Inlaid and bound with other plays in Vol. 305. [257

JOHN CARTER BROWN LIBRARY. 7 1/16 x 5". Acquired prior to 1871. Bound in red levant morocco, by De Coverly. [258

MORGAN. 7 3/16 x 5 1/4". G3 mended. Morgan book-plate. The Asay (sold, December, 1881), Irwin (sold, March, 1900) copy. Bound in old rose levant morocco, somewhat faded, by Bedford. [259

MURRAY. 7 1/4 x 5 5/16". Book-plate of John Murray, Newstead, Wimbledon Park. Acquired prior to 1892. Bound in calf. [260

NEW YORK PUBLIC. 7 3/16 x 5 1/4". G4 blank and genuine. With "January 1835, from W. P. 2" on fly-leaf. The H. Stevens (sold, December, 1855), Lenox (incorporated as Lenox Library, 1870; New York Public, May, 1895) copy. Bound in maroon morocco. [261

PERRY. 7 x 5 1/4". The Gwynne, Count Goertz-Wrisberg (sold, August, 1902), Quaritch (sold, October, 1902) copy. Bound in old calf with "Edward Gwynne" in gilt on covers and white label on back "Plays und Pamphlets of Shakespeare", the volume contains six genuine and three spurious plays. [262

TERRY. 6 5/8 x 4 1/2". Roxburghe arms on verso title. The Roxburghe (May, 1812, No. 3839), Pope (sold, June, 1895), Hoe (April, 1911, No. 2970), G. D. Smith (sold, March, 1915) copy. Bound in brown levant morocco, dark green doublure, elaborate gilt tooling and edges, by Michel. [263

TRINITY COLLEGE, CAMBRIDGE. 7 1/2 x 5 5/8". G4 blank and genuine. The Capell (presented, June, 1779) copy. Bound in brown calf, with other plays. Pressmark, Q. 12. 2. [264

WHITE. 6 13/16 x 4 3/4". Di mended in lower inner margin; some headlines cut into. Note on fly: "Bought of Messrs Boone for £10. Transferred to Mr. Cosens at cost price March, 1864." The Cosens (November, 1890, No. 4062), Quaritch (sold, December, 1890) copy. Bound in red levant morocco, by Riviere. [265

JULIUS CAESAR.

JULIUS CAESAR, 1684.

Julius Caesar. | A | Tragedy. | As it is Now Acted, | At The | Theatre Royal. | Written | By William Shakespeare. | [Ornament] | London, | Printed by H. H. Jun. for Hen. Heringman and R. Bentley in | Russel-street in Covent-Garden, and sold by Joseph Knight and | Francis Saunders at the Blew Anchor in the Lower Walk of the | New Exchange in the Strand. 1684.

First edition. Title, 1 leaf; B-H⁴; I², total, 31 leaves. Type-page, 8 x 4 ⅝″.

Catchwords: Bi, Surgeon; Ci, Thy; Di, And; Ei, My; Fi, Cry; Gi, To; Hi, *Cassi*.

COPIES.

BOSTON PUBLIC. 8 ¼ x 6 ⅜″. Cropped at top, injuring some headlines. The Barton (sold, May, 1873) copy. Bound in half morocco. [266

BRITISH MUSEUM. 8 ⁵⁄₁₆ x 6 ¼″. Last leaf cropped at top, injuring headline. Purchased, 1856. Bound in brown morocco. Pressmark, 11763. e. 21. [267

BRITWELL LIBRARY. 8 ⁹⁄₁₆ x 6 ½″. Title and Bi torn in lower inner corner. "Catherine Clapcott" on title. Unbound. [268

EDINBURGH UNIVERSITY. 8 ⁵⁄₁₆ x 6″. I₂ verso stained; cropped at top, injuring two or three headlines. The Halliwell (presented, 1872) copy. Bound in half morocco. [269

FOLGER. The Warwick copy. [270

PERRY. 8 ¼ x 6 ¹⁄₁₆″. Book-plate of Sir William Horton, Chaderton. Bound in old half calf, with other plays. [271

WHEATLEY. 8 ¹¹⁄₁₆ x 6 ⁷⁄₁₆″. Title mended on inner margin; H₂ injured in headline. Purchased from Pickering & Chatto. Bound in green levant morocco, by Riviere. [272

WHITE. 8 ⅝ x 6 ⅜″. Title and Bi mended in margins. The Bangs (November 10, 1898, No. 402) copy. Bound in half morocco. [273

WRENN, Estate of J. H. 8 ⅜ x 6 ½″. Purchased prior to May 25, 1903. Bound in polished calf, by Riviere. [274

A CENSUS OF SHAKESPEARE QUARTOS

JULIUS CAESAR, n. d.

There were four undated editions of this play issued between the first edition, 1684, and the sixth, 1691. They differ so slightly that errors in pagination are here given as well as the usual collation, to enable an owner to determine which edition he has. The four editions are all reset throughout and confrontation shows many differences not easy to describe. The editions were probably issued in the order here assigned to them.

Julius Caesar. | A | Tragedy. | As it is Now Acted | At The | Theatre Royal. | Written By | William Shakespeare. | [Ornament] | London, | Printed by H. H. Jun. for Hen Herringman and R. Bentley in | Russel-street, in Covent Garden, and sold by Joseph Knight and | Francis Saunders at the Blew Anchor in the Lower Walk of the | New-Exchange in the Strand.

Second edition. Collation: A-H^4; total, 32 leaves. Type-page, 8 ½ x 6 ¼".

Catchwords: A$_2$, *Cobl.* Nay; B$_i$, Sleek-; C$_i$, *Brut;* D$_i$, *Caes:* What; E$_i$, He; F$_i$, Then; G$_i$, *Bru.;* H$_i$, *Cass.*

Pagination: 1, 4-18, 91, 20-27, 18, 29, 20, 31-40, 33-48, 57, 50, 51, 60, 61, 54, 55, 64.

COPIES.

ADLER. 8 x 5 $^{15}/_{16}$". Cropped at top, injuring a few headlines; stained. Bound in half morocco. [275

BRITISH MUSEUM. 8 ¼ x 6". Badly foxed; title mended, injuring one letter of imprint; A$_4$ extended on inner margin; H$_4$ extended on lower outer corner, a few words injured. Purchased. Bound in half calf, with Macbeth, 1687. Pressmark, 642. e. 18(1). [276

BRITWELL LIBRARY. 8 $^9/_{16}$ x 6 $^5/_{16}$". Unbound. [277

EDINBURGH UNIVERSITY. 8 $^5/_{16}$ x 6 $^3/_{16}$". Foxed. "1-6" on title. The Halliwell (presented, 1872) copy. Bound in half morocco. [278

ELIZABETHAN CLUB. 8 $^9/_{16}$ x 6 $^5/_{16}$". Huth book-plate. The Huth (November, 1911, No. 1206), Cochran (presented, December, 1911) copy. Bound in red levant morocco, some edges uncut at bottom, by Bedford. [279

VICKERY. 8 $^{11}/_{16}$ x 6 ½". The Sotheby (May 25, 1905, No. 634) copy. Bound in green levant morocco, by Riviere. [280

WHEATLEY 8 $^7/_{16}$ x 6 $^5/_{16}$". Foxed. Purchased from Pickering & Chatto. Bound in red morocco, by Riviere. [281

JULIUS CAESAR, n. d.

Julius Caesar. | A | Tragedy. | As it is now Acted | At The | Theatre Royal. | Written By | William Shakespeare. | [Ornament] | London. | Printed by H. H. Jun. for Hen. Herringman, and R. Bentley in | Russel-street in Covent-Garden, and sold by Joseph Knight and | Francis Saunders at the Blew-Anchor in the Lower Walk of the | Nuw-Exchange in the Strand.

JULIUS CAESAR

Third edition. A-H⁴; total, 32 leaves. Page numbers 46 and 47 are exchanged. Type-page, 7 ¾ x 3 ⅝".

Catchwords: A2, *Cobl.*Nay; Bi, Sleek-; Ci, Brutus; Di, *Culp.*; Ei, He; Fi, Then; Gi, *Bru-;* Hi, *Cassi.*

COPIES.

HUNTINGTON. 8 ⁷⁄₁₆ x 6 ³⁄₁₆". Church book-plate. The Sotheby (March 16, 1903, No. 1265), Dodd, Mead & Co. (sold, June, 1904), Church (sold, January, 1911) copy. Bound in brown levant morocco, by Riviere. [282

SCHIFF. 8 ⅝ x 6 ⁵⁄₁₆". Title extended at top. The Brooks (sold, November, 1913), Hellman (sold, December, 1913) copy. Bound in panelled calf, by Ramage. [283

WHITE. 8 ⅝ x 6 ⁷⁄₁₆". The Jarvis (sold, March, 1892) copy. Bound in boards, morocco back. [284

YALE UNIVERSITY. 8 ½ x 6 ⅛". Bound with other old plays. [285

JULIUS CAESAR, n. d.

Julius Caesar: | A | Tragedy. | As it is now Acted | At The | Theatre Royal. | Written By | William Shakespeare. | [Ornament] | London, | Printed by H. H. Jun. for Hen. Herringman, and R. Bentley in | Russel-street in Covent-Garden, and sold by Joseph Knight and | Francis Saunders at the Blew-Anchor in the Lower Walk of the | New-Exchange in the Strand.

Fourth edition. A-H⁴; total, 32 leaves. Page 15 is wrongly numbered 51. Type-page, 7 ¹⁵⁄₁₆ x 3 ⅝".

Catchwords: A2, *Cobl.*Nay; Bi, Sleek-; Ci, Brutus; Di, *Cal.*; Ei, He; Fi, Then; Gi, *Bru.;* Hi, *Cassi.*

COPIES.

ADLER. 8 ⅞ x 6 ¼". C2-Di lacking; title torn, a few letters injured; H4 badly mended, many words injured; some leaves extended and mended. Purchased from Pickering. Bound in half calf. [286

BIRMINGHAM. 8 ½ x 6 ⅛". A few headlines cut into. Purchased, 1881. Bound in red morocco. [287

BOSTON PUBLIC. 8 ⁷⁄₁₆ x 6 ³⁄₁₆". Sheet A foxed; two leaves cropped at top, injuring headlines. "Eliza Hulme, 1813" on title. The Hulme (c. 1813), Barton (sold, May, 1873) copy. Bound in half calf. [288

KINGSLEY. 8 ⅛ x 6 ⅛". Headlines cropped; the first few leaves have some words corrected and directions written in. Purchased, London, 1912. Bound in red morocco, by Bradstreet. [289

LIBRARY OF CONGRESS. 9 x 7". Much worn and foxed, mended and covered with crepeline, each leaf mounted; writing on title. Purchased, 1877. Bound in half morocco. [290

NEW YORK PUBLIC. 8 11/16 x 6 5/16". Title and several leaves mended in upper blank margins; A2, A3, Hi, H4, mended in upper portions, a few letters lacking. The Lenox (incorporated as Lenox Library, 1870; New York Public, May, 1895) copy. Bound in olive green levant morocco, by Bedford. [291

WALLACE. 8 3/8 x 6 5/8". Washed, a few margins mended. The Allis (March 25, 1912, No. 736) copy. Bound in red levant morocco, by Pratt. [292

WHEATLEY. 8 11/16 x 6 3/8". Ci trimmed. Unbound. [293

WHITE. 8 3/4 x 6 3/16". "John Genest, Dec. 12, 1815" on title and his notes in book. The Genest (1815), Pickering (sold in volume with other Shakespeare plays, March 26, 1898) copy. Rebound for Mr. White, February, 1913, in half morocco, by Walters. [294

WRENN, Estate of J. H. 6 9/16 x 8 5/8". Presented by Edmund Gosse. Bound in red levant morocco, by Riviere. [295

JULIUS CAESAR, n. d.

Julius Caesar: | A | Tragedy, | As it is now Acted | At The | Theatre-Royal. | Written By | William Shakespeare. | [Ornament] | London: | Printed by H. H. Jun' for Hen. Herringman and R. Bentley in | Russel street in Covent-garden, and sold by Joseph Knight and | Francis Saunders, at the Blue Anchor in the Lower Walk of | the New-Exchange in the Strand.

Fifth edition. A-G^4; H^2; total, 30 leaves. Page 3, line 3 "Enter Murellus". Type-page, 7 15/16 x 4 1/4".

Catchwords: A2, What; Bi, *Bru.;* Ci, [*Aside,* | *Cass.;* Di, And; Ei, And; Fi, ACT; Gi, And; Hi, I shall.

COPIES.

BIRMINGHAM. 8 5/8 x 6 3/4". Purchased, 1892. Bound in boards. [296

FOLGER. Manuscript notes in old handwriting. The Herman (Sotheby, January 23, 1885), Halliwell Rarities (sold, January, 1897, No. 118), Perry (sold, March, 1907) copy. Bound in mottled calf, by Riviere. [297

WHITE. 8 3/4 x 6 1/2". Title slightly mended. The Pickering (sold, September, 1892) copy. Bound in calf. [298

JULIUS CAESAR.

BELONGING TO ONE OF THE UNDATED EDITIONS.

COPIES.

CRICHTON STUART. [299

CRICHTON STUART. [300

FOLGER. The Warwick copy. [301

FOLGER. [302

FOLGER. [303

JULIUS CAESAR

JULIUS CAESAR, 1691.

Julius Caesar. | A | Tragedy. | As it is now Acted | At The | Theatre Royal. | Written by | William Shakespeare. | [Ornament] | London, | Printed for Henry Herringman, and Richard Bentley | at the Post-House, in Russel-street, Covent-|Garden, 1691.

Sixth edition. A-H^4; total, 32 leaves. A1 blank; title, A2. Type-page, 7 ¾ x 4 ⅝".
Catchwords: A3, Sir,; B1, Is; C1, Upon; D1, *Caius;* E1, *Cask.;* F1, Al; G1, Dash; H1, *Cass.*

COPIES.

ADLER. 8 ⅜ x 6 ¼". A4 lacking; title cropped, injuring top line; some leaves stained; wormhole through some margins. Purchased from Voynich. Bound in blue levant morocco. [304

BIRMINGHAM. 8 ½ x 6 ½". A3 mended in upper corner; D3 cut close at foot; D4 torn in upper corner, injuring a few letters. The Harrison of Samlesbury (January, 1881, No. 927) copy. Bound in boards, leather back. [305

BODLEIAN. 8 ⅝ x 6 ¼". A1 blank and genuine. Purchased, 1866. Bound in half calf. Pressmark, Malone, 962. [306

BOSTON ATHENAEUM. 8 ½ x 6 ¼". Purchased prior to 1870. Bound with collection of old plays. [307

BOSTON PUBLIC. 8 ⅝ x 6 ⅜". The Barton (sold, May, 1873) copy. Bound in half calf. [308

BRITISH MUSEUM. 8 9/16 x 6 ⅜". Foxed. Bound with Hamlet, 1703, and other plays. Pressmark, 841. c. 3. [309

BRITWELL LIBRARY. 8 ½ x 6 ½". A1 blank and genuine. Unbound. [310

BROOKS. 8 9/16 x 6 1/16". Bound in half brown morocco. [311

FOLGER. The Halliwell Rarities (sold, January, 1897, No. 105), Perry (sold, March, 1907) copy. Bound in half brown morocco. [312

FOLGER. The Warwick copy. [313

FURNESS. 8 ¼ x 6 3/16". The Kershaw (July, 1877, No. 1240) copy. Bound in red levant morocco, by Bedford. [314

KINGSLEY. 7 15/16 x 5 ¾". Cropped at foot, injuring signatures and catchwords; H4 recto, lacking last line and mended. The Voynich (sold, 1908) copy. Bound in brown morocco. [315

PERRY. 8 ⅝ x 6 ⅞". With "J. W. Major" on fly-leaf. Unbound. [316

PICKERING & CHATTO. 8 ⅛ x 6". Cropped at top and foot, injuring some headlines. The Sotheby (May 25, 1905, No. 633) copy. Bound in half calf. [317

UNIVERSITY OF MICHIGAN. 8 x 5 ⅞". One line of text cropped at foot. The Halliwell (Sotheby, July, 1889, No. 901) copy. Bound in half morocco, by Bedford. [318

VALENTINE. [319

WHITE. 8 ½ x 6 ⅜". The Pickering (sold, September, 1892) copy. Bound in half calf. [320

KING LEAR.

KING LEAR, 1608.

M. William Shak-speare: | His | True Chronicle Historie of the life and | death of King Lear and his three | Daughters. | With the vnfortunate life of Edgar, sonne | and heire to the Earle of Gloster, and his | sullen and assumed humor of | Tom of Bedlam: | As it was played before the Kings Maiestie at Whitehall vpon | S. Stephans night in Christmas Hollidayes. | By his Maiesties seruants playing vsually at the Gloabe | on the Bancke-side. | [Okes' device] | London, | Printed for Nathaniel Butter, and are to be sold at his shop in Pauls | Church-yard at the signe of the Pide Bull neere | St. Austins Gate. 1608.

First edition. Title, 1 leaf; B-L⁴; total, 41 leaves. Type-page, 6 ⅜ x 3 ⅝".

Catchwords: Bi, *Bast.;* Ci, *Glost.;* Di, sooth; Ei, *Kent;* Fi, Effects; Gi, Is; Hi, *Corn.;* Ii, With; Ki, your; Li, My.

COPIES.

BODLEIAN. 6 ⅞ x 5 ⅛". L₄ lacking; slight tear at foot of Ei; L₃ verso soiled. The Malone (presented, 1821) copy. Inlaid and bound with other plays in Vol. IV. Pressmark, Malone, 35. [321

BODLEIAN. 7 x 4 ⁵⁄₁₆". Title lacking. Cropped at top, injuring some headlines. The Malone (presented, 1821) copy. Inlaid and bound with other plays in Vol. VI. Pressmark, Malone, 37. [322

BRITISH MUSEUM. 6 ¹⁵⁄₁₆ x 4 ¾". Lower margins of some leaves broken; F₂ has signature and catchword cropped; K₂ lower corner mended; C₂ verso, D₃ verso, F₃ recto, cropped on front margin, injuring some stage directions. Printed description by Halliwell inserted on fly-leaf: "First edition. A perfect and genuine copy. Only three perfect copies of this first edition have, to my knowledge, been sold by auction during the last thirty years, two in Heber's collection & the present one. Both of Heber's copies are now in America, one in the collection of Mr. Lenox, the other in that of Mr. Barton. It is almost the only first edition not in the Daniel collection." Unfortunately there is no copy of the Pide Bull edition in the Barton (now the Boston Public) Library; there is a copy of the other edition of 1608 which Winsor described as Heber, No. 2016, but there is a manuscript note in the book itself to the effect that Winsor was wrong. Probably the Loscombe (June, 1854, No. 1046) copy. Bound in purple morocco. Pressmark, C. 34. k. 18. [323

BRITISH MUSEUM. 7 1/8 x 5″. Title lacking and supplied in facsimile; rest of copy soiled and occasionally stained; "Thomas Middleton, John Cooper, Richard from Mary. John Cooper, 1688, 1667" on verso L4; some manuscript corrections. Halliwell's note on fly-leaf: "Purchased of Garrett of Newcastle for £20 J. O. H. This copy of the first edition of Lear, wanting the title, should be preserved with my perfect copy, on account of its containing an extraordinary number of curious textual variations, although both copies are evidently printed from the same forms. . . ." The Halliwell (sold, November 9, 1858) copy. Bound in purple morocco. Pressmark, C. 34. k. 17. [324

FOLGER. The Gott (sold through Sotheran, 1907) copy. Bound in red morocco, by Lewis. [325

FOLGER. C1-L2, a fragment only. Many leaves mended and several headlines cropped. The Halliwell Rarities (sold, January, 1897, No. 750), Perry (sold, March, 1907) copy. Bound in green morocco, by Tuckett. [326

HUNTINGTON. 7 1/2 x 5 1/8″. Stage directions on C2 verso and D3 verso slightly cut; corner of B1 damaged; stabbed throughout. "Collated & Perfect, J. P. K. 1804"; "George Steevens"; "Edw. Palmer"; "There is another copy of this Play printed for Nathaniel Butter, 4to, 1608. Vol. 119". The Steevens (May, 1800, No. 1277 or 1278?), Kemble (sold, 1821), Devonshire (sold, January, 1914) copy. Inlaid and bound with other plays in Vol. 375. [327

NEW YORK PUBLIC. 7 3/16 x 5 3/16″. Title mended; L4 mended and backed; manuscript notes throughout. The Heber (June, 1834, No. 5450), H. Stevens (sold, December, 1855), Lenox (incorporated as Lenox Library, 1870; New York Public, May, 1895) copy. Bound in purple straight-grained morocco, by Clarke. [328

TRINITY COLLEGE, CAMBRIDGE. 7 x 4 7/8″. Notes by Capell: "Collated with another old 4° printed likewise by Thomas Creede, but for Tho. Millington and John Busby—anno 1600. E. C."; "Added in black the principal variations of the 4° of 1608. E. C." Capell book-plate on verso title. The Capell (presented, June, 1779) copy. Bound in brown calf, with other plays. Pressmark, S. 35. 1. [329

WHITE. 7 1/8 x 5 3/8″. With sheets C, E, F, G, corrected and D, H, K, uncorrected. The Mostyn (Sotheby, May 31, 1907, No. 481) copy. Bound in red levant morocco, by Club Bindery, 1908. [330

KING LEAR, 1608 [1619].

M. VVilliam Shake-speare, | His | True Chronicle History of the life | and death of King Lear, and his | three Daughters. | With the vnfortunate life of Edgar, | sonne and heire to the Earle of Glocester, and | his sullen and assumed humour of Tom | of Bedlam. | As it was plaid before the Kings Maiesty at White-Hall, vp-|pon S. Stephens night, in Christmas Hollidaies. | By his Maiesties Seruants, playing vsually at the | Globe on the Banck-side. | [Heb Ddieu device] | Printed for Nathaniel Butter. | 1608. [1619]

KING LEAR

Second edition. A-L⁴; total, 44 leaves. Type-page, 6 3/16 x 4 3/4″.
Catchwords: A2, Bast.; Bi, *Fran.*; Ci, daughter; Di, thunders; Ei, Thou; Fi, The; Gi, *Kent;* Hi, *Old;* Ii, With; Ki, *Cor.*; Li, Come.

COPIES.

BODLEIAN. 7 7/16 x 5 1/2″. Pinprickt pattern on title. The Malone (presented, 1821) copy. Inlaid and bound with other plays in Vol. IV. Pressmark, Malone, 35. [331

BOSTON PUBLIC. 7 7/16 x 5 1/8″. Title foxed, wormhole mended in a few leaves. The Barton (sold, May, 1873) copy. Bound in brown straight-grained morocco, by Lewis. [332

BRITISH MUSEUM. 7 1/4 x 5 1/4″. Ii-L4, wormhole in outer margin; grease stain throughout. The King George III (presented, 1823) copy. Bound in half morocco. Pressmark, C. 12. g. 27. [333

BRITISH MUSEUM. 7 5/8 x 5 3/4″. Title and A2 mended in outer margin; small stain on E2, Ii-I3; tender throughout. The Garrick (bequeathed, January, 1779) copy. Bound in red morocco, Garrick's arms on sides. Pressmark, C. 34. k. 19. [334

BRITISH MUSEUM. 7 1/6 x 5 1/4″. Title and Bi lacking; A2, A3, remargined, sides and foot; L4 corner mended. Manuscript title supplied. Presented. Bound in red morocco. Pressmark, C. 34. k. 20. [335

CARRINGTON. Size not given. With "George Steevens" on title-page. The Steevens (May, 1800, No. 1277), Carrington (offered and bought in at Sotheby's, July 28, 1905, No. 383) copy. Inlaid and bound in half morocco. [336

EDINBURGH UNIVERSITY. 6 11/16 x 5″. F4 in facsimile. Title extended on inner margin; A2, A3, extended on lower and outer margin; A4 extended on upper corner, a few words in facsimile; Ci extended on lower inner corner, a few words in facsimile; Fi mended in center, a few letters lacking; wormhole mended in lower margin through most of book. Probably the Sotheby (August 11, 1865, No. 144) copy. The Halliwell (presented, 1872) copy. Bound in red morocco, by Bedford. [337

ELIZABETHAN CLUB. 7 3/16 x 5 1/4″. A2 mended in lower margin, catchword lacking; a few leaves stained. Huth book-plate. Probably the Freeling (November, 1836, No. 2076), Thorpe (sold, 1837, No. 1861), Puttick (April 16, 1849, No. 322) copy. The Huth (November, 1911, No. 1198), Cochran (presented, December, 1911) copy. Bound in blue morocco, by Lewis. [338

ETON COLLEGE. 7 1/16 x 5 1/8″. B3 torn. The Storer (bequeathed, 1799) copy. Bound with other plays in Vol. III. [339

FOLGER. The Jennens (collected, c. 1740, bequeathed, 1773, to W. P. A. Curzon, ancestor of Lord Howe), Howe (sold, December, 1907) copy. Bound in half blue morocco. [340

FOLGER. The Halliwell Rarities (sold, January, 1897, No. 39), Perry (sold, March, 1907) copy. Bound in blue morocco, by Lewis. [341

FOLGER. The Warwick copy. [342

FOLGER. The Griswold (probably sold, August, 1889) copy. [343

A CENSUS OF SHAKESPEARE QUARTOS

FURNESS. 6 ¾ x 5". Title mended and backed, five letters lacking; cropped at top, injuring some headlines; A2 mended in lower margin. Manuscript notes by Capell. The Capell, Kinsman (sold, July, 1872) copy. Bound in green levant morocco, blue silk doublures and fly-leaves. [344

HUNTINGTON. 7 x 4 ⅞". Some headlines cropped. Two Birket Foster bookplates. The Daniel (July, 1864, No. 1437), Foster (June, 1894, No. 26), Sotheby (December 14, 1906, No. 393), Sabin (sold, 1908), Halsey (sold, December, 1915) copy. Bound in green morocco, with "G. D.[aniel]" in gilt on front cover, by Lewis. [345

HUNTINGTON. 6 ⅝ x 4 5/16". Cropped at top and foot, injuring some headlines and signatures. "Collated & Perfect. J. P. K. 1798." The Kemble (sold, 1821), Devonshire (sold, January, 1914) copy. Inlaid and bound with other plays in Vol. 119. [346

HUNTINGTON. 7 3/16 x 5 5/16". Ki-K4 extended on outer margin. Locker and Church book-plates. The Locker (sold, January, 1905), Church (sold, April, 1911) copy. Bound in red levant morocco, by Bedford. [347

MORGAN. 7 1/16 x 5 3/16". Ives book-plate; list of Dramatis Personae in manuscript on verso title. The Perkins (July, 1889, No. 1700), Ives (March, 1891, No. 888), Van Antwerp (July, 1907, No. 198), Quaritch (sold, 1907) copy. Bound in red levant morocco, with Perkins's arms on covers, by Lewis. [348

MURRAY. 7 x 5 ¼". Stain on margin of H3-I2. Book-plate of John Murray, Newstead, Wimbledon Park; label of Tudor Exhibition, London, 1889. Acquired prior to 1889. Bound in brown levant morocco, elaborately tooled, by Hayday. [349

NEW YORK PUBLIC. 7 ⅛ x 5 ⅜". C4, B2, B3, F4, extended on outer and lower margins; B4-C3 extended in lower corner. The H. Stevens (sold, December, 1855), Lenox (incorporated as Lenox Library, 1870; New York Public, May, 1895) copy. Bound in brown morocco, by Bedford. [350

PERRY. 7 x 5 ¼". The Gwynne, Goertz-Wrisberg (sold, August, 1902), Quaritch (sold, October, 1902) copy. Bound in old calf, with "Edward Gwynne" on covers, in volume containing six genuine and three spurious plays. [351

PICKERING & CHATTO. 6 ¾ x 4 7/16". Six leaves in facsimile; cropped on fore edge. The Fitzgerald (June, 1907, No. 233) copy. Bound in green levant morocco, by Larkins. [352

SHAKESPEARE BIRTHPLACE LIBRARY. 7 1/16 x 5 ¼". Some scribbles on title. The Hussey (May, 1906, No. 380), Quaritch (sold, 1906) copy. Bound in red morocco, by Riviere. [353

TERRY. 6 ¾ x 5 1/16". Hoe book-plate. The Pope (sold, June, 1895), Hoe (January, 1912, No. 3035), G. D. Smith (sold, March, 1915) copy. Bound in brown levant morocco, maroon doublure elaborately tooled, in green morocco case, by David. [354

TRINITY COLLEGE, CAMBRIDGE. 7 ½ x 5 ⅝". Last leaf torn. The Capell (presented, June, 1779) copy. Bound in brown calf, with other plays. Pressmark, Q. 11. 4. [355

WHITE, A. T. 7 1/16 x 5". A2 and A3 mended on upper margins; A4 extended on lower margin and mended; Ii-I4 extended on outer margins, a few letters in facsimile. Book-plate of W. H. Crawford. Probably the Utterson (April, 1852, No. 1693), Sotheby (1856, No. 259) copy. The Crawford (March, 1891, No. 2892) copy. Bound in red levant morocco, by Bedford. [356

KING LEAR

WHITE, W. A. 7 x 5 ¼″. A1-A3 extended in outer margin; K4 mended in upper portion, lacking part of one word in headline. Signature and book-plate of John F. Marsh. The Marsh (May, 1882, No. 2409) copy, purchased August, 1887. Bound in brown levant morocco. [357

KING LEAR, 1608.
Edition Unknown.
COPY.

CRICHTON STUART. [358

KING LEAR, 1655.

M. William Shake-speare, | His | True Chronicle History of the life | and death of King Lear, and his | three Daughters. | With the Vnfortunat life of Edgar, | sonne and heire to the Earle of Glocester, and | his sullen assumed humour of Tom | of Bedlam. | As it was plaid before the Kings Maiesty at Whit-Hall, vp-|on S. Stephens night, in Christmas Hollldaies [sic]. | By his Maiesties Servants playing vsually at the | Globe on the Bank-side. | [Ornament] | London. | Printed by Jane Bell, and are to be sold at the East-end | of Christ-Church. 1655.

Third edition. A-L^4; total, 44 leaves. Type-page, 6 ¼ x 3 $^{13}/_{16}$″.

Catchwords: A2, [Bast.; Bi, Fran.; Ci, daughter; Di, thunders; Ei, Thou; Fi, The; Gi, Kent; Hi, Old; Ii, With; Ki, Cor.; Li, Come.

COPIES.

BIRMINGHAM. 6 ¾ x 5″. Purchased, March, 1884. Bound in red levant morocco, by Hammond. [359

BOSTON PUBLIC. 7 ¼ x 5 ¼″. Title and several margins mended. Jolley book-plate. The Jolley (June, 1844, No. 610), Halliwell (Sotheby, May, 1857, No. 873), Barton (sold, May, 1873) copy. Bound in half brown morocco, uncut at bottom, two leaves misplaced by binder. [360

BRIDGEWATER HOUSE. 7 $^3/_{16}$ x 5 $^1/_{16}$″. Two headlines cropped. Bound in half calf. [361

BRITISH MUSEUM. 7 ⅛ x 5 $^3/_{16}$″. Title mended, some writing on title. On A2, "Frances Wolfreston her book." The H. Stevens (sold, April 1, 1857) copy. Rebound in brown morocco, 1897. Pressmark, C. 34. k. 54. [362

CRICHTON STUART. [363

EDINBURGH UNIVERSITY. 7 ⅛ x 5 $^3/_{16}$″. Title tender and mended; cropped at top, injuring a few headlines; uncut at foot. The Halliwell (presented, 1872) copy. Bound in light brown levant morocco, by Bedford. [364

ETON COLLEGE. 7 $^1/_{16}$ x 5 ⅛″. Title torn; cropped at top, injuring some headlines; L2 torn in lower outer corner, injuring signature mark; some leaves heavily inked. The Storer (bequeathed, 1799) copy. Bound with other plays in Vol. III. [365

FOLGER. Probably the C. D. Gardner (June, 1880, No. 1425) copy. The Halliwell Rarities (sold, January, 1897, No. 193), Perry (sold, March, 1907) copy. Bound in calf, panelled sides. [366

FOLGER. Title and Li in facsimile. [367

FURNESS. 7 1/16 x 5". Title in facsimile. Note by Halliwell on fly-leaf. The Tite (May, 1874, No. 2746), Kershaw (July, 1877, No. 1231) copy. Bound in red levant morocco, by Bedford. [368

HUNTINGTON. 7 1/4 x 5 3/16". Cropped at top, injuring some headlines; leaves stabbed on inner margins throughout. Church book-plate. The Simes (July, 1886, No. 1535), Griswold (sold, August, 1889), Church (sold, April, 1911) copy. Bound in purple morocco. [369

NEW YORK PUBLIC. 7 x 5 1/8". Title mended in margin. The H. Stevens (sold, December, 1855), Lenox (incorporated as Lenox Library, 1870; New York Public, May, 1895) copy. Bound in red morocco, by Bedford. [370

TRINITY COLLEGE, CAMBRIDGE. 7 1/8 x 5 1/8". Stained. The Capell (presented, June, 1779) copy. Bound in brown calf, with other plays. Pressmark, S. 21. 4. [371

WHITE. 7 5/16 x 5 1/2". The Quaritch (sold, September, 1892) copy. Bound in brown levant morocco, gilt border, by Hayday. [372

LOVE'S LABORS LOST.

LOVE'S LABORS LOST, 1598.

A | Pleasant | Conceited Comedie | Called, | Loues labors lost. | As it was presented before her Highnes | this last Christmas. | Newly corrected and augmented | By W. Shakespere | [Ornament] | Imprinted at London by W. W. | for Cutbert Burby. | 1598.

First edition. A-I^4; K^2; total, 38 leaves. Type-page, 6 3/8 x 3 1/2".

Catchwords: A2, To; Bi, *Ber.*; Ci, *Prin.*; Di, a man; Ei, *Enter*; Fi, The; Gi, *Dull*; Hi, *Queene*; Ii, *Bero.*; Ki, To.

COPIES.

BODLEIAN. 7 3/16 x 5 1/16". Title mended, small hole in the margin of Ci; Ki and K2 stained. The Malone (presented, 1821) copy. Inlaid and bound in tree calf, yellow edges, with "E. M." on covers, with other plays in Vol. III of the collection. Pressmark, Malone, 34. [373

BRIDGEWATER HOUSE. 7 1/8 x 4 7/8". Acquired prior to 1649, when it was catalogued by John, Second Earl of Bridgewater. Bound in green morocco, with arms of Marquis of Stafford, by Murton. [374

BRITISH MUSEUM. 7 11/16 x 5 3/16". Wormholes in upper and lower margins through nearly the entire book. Bibliotheca Heberiana stamp. The Bindley (February, 1819, No. 2041), Heber (June, 1834, No. 5448), Daniel (July, 1864, No. 1428) copy. Purchased, August, 1864. Bound in marbled paper covers, in green morocco case. Pressmark, C. 34. l. 14. [375

EDINBURGH UNIVERSITY. 6 13/16 x 4 7/8". Cropped at top. "No. 4" in old hand on title. The Drummond (presented, 1627) copy. Bound in green morocco, arms of Edinburgh University on covers. [376

FOLGER. A2-A4 in facsimile. The Sotheby (August 11, 1865, No. 136), Halliwell Rarities (sold, January, 1897, No. 21), Perry (sold, March, 1907) copy. Bound in blue levant morocco, by Bedford. [377

FOLGER. The Gott (sold through Sotheran, 1907) copy. Bound in red morocco, by Lewis. [378

HUNTINGTON. 7 1/4 x 5 1/8". Church book-plate. The Locker (sold, January, 1905), Church (sold, April, 1911) copy. Bound in brown morocco, Kinnear arms on sides. [379

A CENSUS OF SHAKESPEARE QUARTOS

HUNTINGTON. 6 11/16 x 4 1/16". Cropped at foot, injuring some signatures and catchwords. "Collated & Perfect. J. P. K. 1804". The Kemble (sold, 1821), Devonshire (sold, January, 1914) copy. Inlaid and bound with other plays in Vol. 375. [380

TRINITY COLLEGE, CAMBRIDGE. 7 x 5 1/8". The Capell (presented, June, 1779) copy. Bound in brown calf, with other plays. Pressmark, S. 37. 3. [381

WHITE. 7 x 4 7/8". Cropped at top, injuring some headlines; K2 mended in upper outer corner, some letters lacking. The Perkins (July, 1889, No. 1690) copy. Bound in red morocco, Perkins's arms in gilt on covers. [382

LOVE'S LABORS LOST, 1631.

Loues Labours lost. | A VVittie and | Pleasant | Comedie, | As it was Acted by his Maiesties Seruants at | the Blacke-Friers and the Globe. | Written | By William Shakespeare. | [Smethwicke's device] | London, | Printed by W. S. for Iohn Smethwicke, and are to be | sold at his Shop in Saint Dunstones Church-|yard vnder the Diall. | 1631.

Second edition. A-I^4; K^2; total, 38 leaves. Type-page, 6 5/8 x 3 3/4".

Catchwords: A2, *Longaiull;* Bi, *apprehended;* Ci, *Nau.;* Di, *Enter;* Ei, *Nath.;* Fi, *As;* Gi, *Ped.;* Hi, *Qu.;* Ii, *Qu.;* Ki, *Enter.*

COPIES.

BODLEIAN. 7 1/2 x 5 7/16". F3 verso, "Actus Quartus" corrected to "Quintus" in old hand. The Malone (presented, 1821) copy. Inlaid and bound with other plays in Vol. II. Pressmark, Malone, 33. [383

BOSTON PUBLIC. 7 x 5 1/4". Title extended at foot and sides; C4, D2 remargined; K2 rebacked; Ki mended on outer margin. Note by Halliwell on flyleaf: "My duplicate copy, sold in May, 1856, fetched £9". The Halliwell (Sotheby, May, 1857, No. 879), Barton (sold, May, 1873) copy. Bound in maroon morocco. [384

BRITISH MUSEUM. 7 1/8 x 5 3/16". Title soiled. The King George III (presented, 1823) copy. Inlaid and bound in half morocco. Pressmark, C. 12. L. 11. [385

BRITISH MUSEUM. 6 13/16 x 4 7/8". Cropped at top, injuring many headlines. The Garrick (bequeathed, January, 1779) copy. Bound in green straight-grained morocco, with Garrick's arms on sides, by Tuckett for the Museum. Pressmark, C. 34. k. 21. [386

CRICHTON STUART. [387

DODD. 7 x 5". Title slightly mended in margin; C2 mended at foot, six words of last line in facsimile; K2 mended in margin. Book-plates of Francis Redhead Yorke Cheney and R. Hoe. The Cheney, Hoe (April, 1911, No. 2976) copy. Bound in green levant morocco, by Bedford. [388

DYCE COLLECTION. 7 9/16 x 5 1/4". Title very brown. "C.P. A. Dyce". The Dyce (bequeathed, 1869) copy. Bound in calf. [389

LOVE'S LABORS LOST

EDINBURGH UNIVERSITY. 7 1/8 x 4 7/8". A1-A4, K1, K2 badly stained. Book-plate of William Holgate. Probably the Rhodes (1825, No. 2085) copy. The Holgate (June, 1846), Windus (March, 1868, No. 911), Halliwell (presented, 1872) copy. Bound in red morocco, by Hayday. [390

ETON COLLEGE. 7 1/8 x 5 1/4". "5653" on title; note probably by Storer on verso title; K2 backed and some catchwords cropped. The Storer (bequeathed, 1799) copy. Bound with Midsummer Night's Dream, 1600, and other plays, in Vol. II. [391

FOLGER. The Halliwell (May, 1856, No. 333), Tite (May, 1874, No. 2749), Kershaw (July, 1877, No. 1232), Quaritch (sold, March, 1879), Halliwell Rarities (sold, January, 1897, No. 33), Perry (sold, March, 1907) copy. Bound in half green morocco. [392

FOLGER. Fragment only, lacking A2-C4, G4, H1, H2, I4-K2. The Sotheby (April 18, 1904, No. 771) copy. [393

FOLGER. Title and last leaf defective, some headlines cropped. The [Kean] Sotheby (June 23, 1898, No. 137), Jonas (sold, May, 1903) copy. Bound in morocco, by Riviere. [394

FOLGER. The Pickering (sold, 1903) copy. [395

HUNTINGTON. 7 1/16 x 5 3/8". Stabbed throughout on inner margin. Church book-plate. The Griswold (sold, August, 1889), Church (sold, April, 1911) copy. Bound in red levant morocco, with Griswold's arms on front cover, by Bedford. [396

MORGAN. 7 1/16 x 4 7/8". The Quaritch (sold, June, 1890), Irwin (sold, March, 1900) copy. Bound in red levant morocco, by Zaehnsdorf. [397

NEW YORK PUBLIC. 7 3/16 x 5 1/4". The H. Stevens (sold, December, 1855), Lenox (incorporated as Lenox Library, 1870; New York Public, May, 1895) copy. Bound in red morocco, by Bedford. [398

PICKERING & CHATTO. 7 5/16 x 5 5/16". Title mended in margins; extended and mended on upper margins, some letters of headlines in facsimile. The Sotheby (July, 1903, No. 492) copy. Bound in red levant morocco, by Riviere. [399

PRIVATE OWNER, NO. 1. 6 15/16 x 4 7/8". Date cut off imprint. Bound in leather, c. 1680, when it came into the possession of the family of the present owner. [400

TRINITY COLLEGE, CAMBRIDGE. 7 1/8 x 5 1/4". The Capell (presented, June, 1779) copy. Bound in brown calf, with other plays. Pressmark, S. 31. 5. [401

WHITE. 7 x 5". Title and K2 backed and extended; cropped at top, injuring some headlines; K1 extended on outer and inner margins. The C. D. Gardner (June, 1880, No. 1426), Sewall (January, 1897, No. 3432) copy. Bound in old rose levant morocco. [402

WHITE. 6 15/16 x 4 3/4". Cropped at foot, injuring a few signatures. Book-plate of James Forbes. The Cosens (November, 1890, No. 4067), Daly (March, 1900, No. 2992) copy. Bound in sprinkled calf. [403

MACBETH.

MACBETH, 1673.

Macbeth: | A | Tragedy. | Acted | At the | Dukes-Theatre. | [Ornament] | London, | Printed for William Cademan at the Popes-|Head in the New Exchange, in the | Strand. 1673.

First edition. 2 leaves without signatures; B-I^4; K^2; total, 36 leaves. Type-page, 7 ½ x 4 ½".

Catchwords: (A2), Macbeth,; B1, 'Gainst; C1, And; D1, *Macb.*This; E1, *Ross;* F1, But; G1, Some-; H1, Than; I1, *Ang.;* K1, *Enter.*

COPIES.

BIRMINGHAM. 7 ⅞ x 5 ¾". Cropped at top, injuring some headlines. Purchased, 1880. Bound in boards. [404

BODLEIAN. 8 ⅜ x 6 ¼". Title and list of Persons Names, backed. Purchased, 1878. Bound in half blue morocco. Pressmark, Malone, 1010. [405

BRITISH MUSEUM. 8 ¼ x 5 ¾". Title torn in margins; D3 stained with red ink; K2 mended in lower margin. Purchased, 1846. Bound in half morocco. Pressmark, 1344. f. 32. [406

DYCE COLLECTION. 8 ¼ x 6 ¼". Corner last leaf mended. "1-6" at top of title; "pr. Shakespear" after "London" on title. The Dyce (presented, 1869) copy. Bound in half mottled calf, red label. [407

FOLGER. The Sotheby (July 18, 1900, No. 1071) copy. Bound with other plays in old calf, uncut. [408

FURNESS. 8 3/16 x 6 7/16". Cropped at foot, injuring some signatures. Purchased prior to 1880. Bound in boards, leather back. [409

WHITE. 8 ½ x 6 ⅛". K2 mended in margin. The [Jonas] Sotheby (March 15, 1911, No. 526) copy. Bound in sprinkled calf. [410

MERCHANT OF VENICE.

MERCHANT OF VENICE, 1600.

The most excellent | Historie of the Merchant | of Venice. | VVith the extreame crueltie of Shylocke the Iewe | towards the sayd Merchant, in cutting a iust pound | of his flesh: and the obtayning of Portia | by the choyse of three | chests. | As it hath beene diuers times acted by the Lord | Chamberlaine his Seruants. | Written by William Shakespeare. | [Ornament] | At London, | Printed by I. R. for Thomas Heyes, | and are to be sold in Paules Church-yard, at the | signe of the Greene Dragon. | 1600.

First edition. A-I^4; K^2; total, 38 leaves. Type-page, 6 ¼ x 3 ¾″.

Catchwords: A2, Vayling; Bi, worth; Ci, or,; Di, *Clawne;* Ei, *That;* Fi, *Bass.;* Gi, *Baltha.;* Hi, cannot; Ii, *Enter;* Ki, for.

COPIES.

BODLEIAN. 6 ¾ x 4 9/16″. F4, small piece torn from outer blank margin; Ki, K2, stained. "S^6" on top of title. The Malone (presented, 1821) copy. Inlaid and bound with Henry IV, 1599, and other plays in Vol. VII. Pressmark, Malone, 38. [411]

BOSTON PUBLIC. 6 ¾ x 4 ⅞″. Title mended in margins. The Heber (December, 1834, No. 2014), Barton (sold, May, 1873) copy. Bound in brown levant morocco, gilt tooling, by Lewis. [412]

BRIDGEWATER HOUSE. 7 ⅛ x 4 ⅞″. Acquired prior to 1649, when it was catalogued by John, Second Earl of Bridgewater. Bound in green morocco, with arms of the Marquis of Stafford, by Murton. [413]

BRITISH MUSEUM. 7 3/16 x 4 ⅞″. Roxburghe arms on verso title. The Roxburghe (May, 1812, No. 3813), King George III (presented, 1823) copy. Bound in half morocco. Pressmark, C. 12. g. 11. [414]

BRITISH MUSEUM. 6 ⅞ x 5 3/16″. A3, D3, D4, K2 mended in margins; slightly soiled. The King George III (presented, 1823) copy. Bound in half morocco. Pressmark, C. 12. g. 32. [415]

BRITISH MUSEUM. 6 11/16 x 4 ¾″. Title darkened; cropped at top, injuring many headlines. On back of title is list of early plays in manuscript and on early fly-leaf bound in at end is another list. The Garrick (bequeathed, January, 1779) copy. Bound in green morocco, with Garrick's arms on sides, by Tuckett for the Museum. Pressmark, C. 34. k. 22. [416]

CRICHTON STUART. With L. Theobald's signature and notes. The Theobald, Steevens (May, 1800, No. 1279), Bute copy. Inlaid. [417

DYCE COLLECTION. 7 ⅝ x 5 ⅛". Rust hole in title and K$_2$; small piece cut from lower corner of D$_2$; some lower margins slightly stained. The Dyce (bequeathed, 1869) copy. Bound in blue morocco, by Murton. [418

ELIZABETHAN CLUB. 6 ¾ x 4 $\frac{9}{16}$". Somewhat stained. Huth book-plate and note, probably by H. Huth, on fly-leaf: "Mr. Gardner's copy, a very bad one, sold at Sotheby's in July, 1854, for ——. This copy cost me —— See my cash-book, 28 Oct. 1854". The Huth (November, 1911, No. 1214), Cochran (presented, December, 1911) copy. Bound in brown straight-grained morocco, by Murton. [419

FOLGER. Title, A$_2$, A$_4$, F$_4$, in facsimile; A$_3$ mended and a few words are lacking. Malone's note: "This copy was given to me by Dr. Farmer and the words on the first page are his handwriting. For the title-page I am answerable." The Farmer (May, 1798, No. 7855), Malone (Sotheby, November, 1818), Sotheby (August 11, 1865, No. 134). Halliwell Rarities (sold, January, 1897, No. 752), Perry (sold, March, 1907) copy. Inlaid and bound in half brown morocco, by Bedford. [420

FOLGER. The Warwick copy. [421

FOLGER. The Jadis (March, 1828, No. 162), Daniel (July, 1864, No. 1432) copy. Bound in green morocco, by Lewis. [422

HUNTINGTON. 6 ¾ x 4 $\frac{5}{16}$". F$_2$ mutilated; rust hole in E$_3$. Note on page opposite title as to rarity of this edition. "Collated & Perfect. J. P. K. 1798". The Kemble (sold, 1821), Devonshire (sold, January, 1914) copy. Inlaid and bound with Richard II, 1597, and other plays in Vol. 120. [423

HUNTINGTON. 6 $\frac{11}{16}$ x 4 $\frac{7}{16}$". Cropped at top, injuring some headlines. Locker and Church book-plates. The J. D. Gardner (July, 1854, No. 2195), Tite (June, 1874, No. 2752), Locker (sold, January, 1905), Church (sold, April, 1911) copy. Bound in red morocco, elaborately panelled sides, by Hayday. [424

NEW YORK PUBLIC. 6 ¾ x 5". Note by Heber on fly-leaf: "There is a Copy in Capells Coll. Trin. Coll . . . in the Br. Mus . . . in the Library of Geo. III (Roxb. copy). The D. of Grafton's copy of this ed. (1815, sold for) 9. 9. 0. The Roxburghe copy of this ed (1812) sold for £ 10. 0. 0. Mr. Bindley's . . . (1819) . . . 22. 1. 0." The Heber (June, 1834, No. 5446), H. Stevens (sold December, 1855), Lenox (incorporated as Lenox Library, 1870; New York Public, May, 1895) copy. Bound in purple straight-grained morocco. [425

TRINITY COLLEGE, CAMBRIDGE. 7 x 5 ⅛". The Capell (presented, June, 1779) copy. Bound with other plays in brown calf. Pressmark, S. 30. 4. [426

WHITE. 7 ⅛ x 5 $\frac{5}{16}$". The Mostyn (Sotheby, May 31, 1907, No. 478) copy. Bound in red levant morocco, by Club Bindery. [427

MERCHANT OF VENICE, 1600 [1619].

The | Excellent | History of the Mer-|chant of Venice. | With the extreme cruelty of Shylocke | the Iew towards the saide Merchant, in cut-|ting a iust pound of his flesh. And the obtaining | of Portia, by the choyse

MERCHANT OF VENICE

of | three Caskets. | Written by W. Shakespeare. | [Heb Ddieu device] | Printed by J. Roberts, 1600. [1619]

Second edition. A-K^4; total, 40 leaves. Type-page, 6 ¼ x 3 ⅝″.

Catchwords: A2, *Salar.;* B1, to; C1, Yea; D1, What; E1, Which; F1, *With;* G1, Ile; H1, You; I1, Comes; K1, *Enter.*

COPIES.

BODLEIAN. 7 $\frac{7}{16}$ x 5 ½″. The Malone (presented, 1821) copy. Inlaid and bound with Midsummer Night's Dream, Roberts, 1600, and other plays in Vol. IV. Pressmark, Malone, 35. [428

BOSTON PUBLIC. 7 ⅜ x 5 ¼″. Title mended in upper margin. The Rodd (sold, September 22, 1843), Barton (sold, May, 1873) copy. Bound in green morocco, by Lewis. [429

BRITISH MUSEUM. 7 $\frac{9}{16}$ x 5 $\frac{15}{16}$″. Blue chalk mark on title; B3 torn in lower corner. The Garrick (bequeathed, January, 1779) copy. Bound in red straight-grained morocco, tooled sides, Garrick's arms on sides, many leaves uncut. Pressmark, C. 34. k. 23. [430

BRITISH MUSEUM. 7 x 5 ⅜″. Lower corners of sheets E-K papered over in most leaves. Numerous signatures on verso K4; note on recto K4: "This copy was used by S. I." Probably the Ireland (May 7, 1801, No. 466) copy. The King George III (presented, 1823) copy. Bound in half morocco. Pressmark, C. 12. g. 31. [431

EDINBURGH UNIVERSITY. 6 ⅞ x 5 $\frac{1}{16}$″. C1-C4, G1-G4, K2-K4 in facsimile; title extended in lower corner; A2, A3, extended upper and outer margins, injuring headlines. Halliwell's note: "This copy has a few leaves of text in facsimile, I gave Mr. Lacy £20 for an unbound copy wanting several leaves, I think the present copy, but I am not sure. *As a rule, I do not retain** the original when I have a satisfactory lithographic FS. but an exception is made in this instance on account of the water-marks.
*This was a rule I was *commencing* to make, but did not keep long in that mind." The Halliwell (presented, 1872) copy. Bound in red levant morocco, by Bedford. [432

ELIZABETHAN CLUB. 6 $\frac{15}{16}$ x 5 ⅛″. Huth book-plate. The Huth (November, 1911, No. 1213), Cochran (presented, December, 1911) copy. Bound in red morocco, by Bedford. [433

ETON COLLEGE. 7$\frac{1}{16}$ x 4 $\frac{15}{16}$″. Some interleaves. The Storer (bequeathed, 1799) copy. Bound with other plays in Vol. II. [434

FOLGER. 7 ⅛ x 5 ¼″. Some early manuscript notes in margins. The Jennens (collected, c. 1740, bequeathed, 1773, to W. P. A. Curzon, ancestor of Lord Howe), Howe (sold, December, 1907) copy. Bound in half blue morocco. [435

FOLGER. The Warwick copy. [436

FOLGER. The Griswold (probably sold, August, 1889) copy. [437

FURNESS. 7 ⅛ x 5 $\frac{9}{16}$″. With manuscript titles of Heyes, 1600, and 1637, editions of Merchant of Venice in Capell's handwriting inserted at end and Capell's notes throughout. The Capell, Kinsman (sold, July, 1872) copy. Bound in green levant morocco, blue silk doublures and fly-leaves. [438

A CENSUS OF SHAKESPEARE QUARTOS

HUNTINGTON. 6 ⅞ x 5 ⅛". F1 mended in lower blank margin. Locker manuscript notes and book-plate. The Locker (sold, January, 1905), Dodd, Mead & Co. (sold, April, 1905), Halsey (sold, December, 1915) copy. Bound in red levant morocco, by Bedford. [439

HUNTINGTON. 7 3/16 x 5 ¼". Church book-plate. The Church (sold, April, 1911) copy. Bound in red levant morocco, by Bedford. [440

HUNTINGTON. 7 ⅛ x 5". Long quotation from Stationers' Register on page opposite title by Kemble and "Collated & Perfect. J. P. K. 1798"; "This Edition is not so rare as that printed for Thomas Heyes, of the same date. See Vol. 120 of my collection. J. P. K." The Kemble (sold, 1821), Devonshire (sold, January, 1914) copy. Inlaid and bound with other plays in Vol. 119. [441

MORGAN. 7 x 5 3/16". Birket Foster book-plate. The Foster (June, 1894, No. 24), Sotheby (December 14, 1906, No. 389), Thomas (sold, January, 1910) copy. Bound in red morocco, gilt gauffered edges. [442

NEW YORK PUBLIC. 7 ⅛ x 5 ¼". The H. Stevens (sold, December, 1855), Lenox (incorporated as Lenox Library, 1870; New York Public, May, 1895) copy. Bound in purple morocco. [443

PERRY. 7 x 5 ¼". The Gwynne, Goertz-Wrisberg (sold, August, 1902), Quaritch (sold, October, 1902) copy. Bound in old calf, with "Edward Gwynne" on covers, in volume containing six genuine and three spurious plays. [444

SHAKESPEARE BIRTHPLACE LIBRARY. 7 1/16 x 5 ¼". The Hussey (May, 1906, No. 377), Quaritch (sold, 1906) copy. Bound in red morocco, by Riviere. [445

SHAKESPEARE BIRTHPLACE LIBRARY. 7 ⅛ x 5 ¼". C1 and C4 in facsimile; stained on margin. The Haggard (Sotheby, 1867, No. 211) copy. Bound in old russia. [446

TRINITY COLLEGE, CAMBRIDGE. 7 ½ x 5 ⅝". The Capell (presented, June, 1779) copy. Bound in brown calf, with other plays. Pressmark, Q. 11. 5. [447

TROWBRIDGE. 7 ¼ x 5 5/16". K3 and K4 in facsimile; I4, K1, K2, extended on outer margins; G4 extended on lower outer corner. The Richmond (sold February, 26, 1896) copy. Bound in brown morocco. [448

VALENTINE. [449

WHITE, A. T. 6 ¾ x 4 ⅝". A3 extended in margin and mended; cropped at top, injuring some headlines. Signature and book-plate of John F. Marsh. The Marsh (May, 1882, No. 2410), Quaritch (sold, 1887) copy. Bound in brown straight-grained morocco, with Kinnear arms in gilt on covers. [450

MERCHANT OF VENICE, 1637.

The most excellent | Historie of the Merchant | of Venice. | VVith the extreame crueltie of Shylocke | the Iewe towards the said Merchant, in | cutting a just pound of his flesh: and the ob-|taining of Portia by the choice | of three Chests. | As it hath beene divers times acted by the | Lord Chamberlaine his Servants. | Written by William Shakespeare. | [Orna-

MERCHANT OF VENICE

ment] | London, | Printed by M. P. for Laurence Hayes, and are to be sold | at his Shop on Fleetbridge. 1637.

Third edition, earlier title. A-I^4; total, 36 leaves. Type-page, 6 ⅜ x 3 ⅞".

Catchwords: A2, To; B1, *Ner.*; C1, *Gobbo;* D1, But; E1, *Sol.* And; F1, I got; G1, *Loren.*Yet; H1, *Por.* Have; I1, But.

COPIES.

BODLEIAN. 7 1/16 x 4 ¾". Title backed. "purch. 1828" on title. Purchased, 1828. Bound in half morocco. Pressmark, Malone, 769. [451

BOSTON PUBLIC. 7 ¼ x 5 ¼". A2 and I4 mended on margins. The Barton (sold, May, 1873) copy. Bound in blue levant morocco, gilt tooling. [452

BOSTON PUBLIC. 6 ⅞ x 4 ⅝". Title worn with margins cut close; cropped at top, injuring some headlines; stained and foxed. The Barton (sold, May, 1873) copy. Bound in half calf. [453

BRITISH MUSEUM. 7 x 4 ⅞". Cropped at top, injuring some headlines. On verso title are names of actors added in manuscript. The Garrick (bequeathed, January, 1779) copy. Bound in red straight-grained morocco, Garrick's arms on back. Pressmark, C. 34. k. 24. [454

CRICHTON STUART. [455

EDINBURGH UNIVERSITY. 7 ⅛ x 5 ¼". Title, A3-B2, B4-D3, extended in corners; A2, B3, extended on front margin; E4 extended on lower margin. "Tho. Malbons Booke, 1639" and scribbles on title; "Tho. Malbone 1639" on verso I4. The Halliwell (presented, 1872) copy. Bound in red morocco by Tuckett. [456

ETON COLLEGE. 6 15/16 x 5". Cropped at top, injuring some headlines; D1 torn; a few leaves uncut at foot. The Storer (bequeathed, 1799) copy. Interleaved and bound with other plays in Vol. II. [457

FOLGER. All leaves mended in corners. Probably Corser (February, 1871, No. 399), Craufurd (July, 1876, No. 1037), Kershaw (July, 1877, No. 1239) copy. The Halliwell Rarities (sold, January, 1897, No. 8), Perry (sold, March, 1907) copy. Bound in red morocco, by Lewis. [458

FOLGER. 7 x 5". The Hoe (January, 1912, No. 3038) copy. Bound in red levant morocco, by Chambolle-Duru. [459

FOLGER. 7 ⅛ x 5". Title and two leaves soiled. The Sotheby (June 20, 1904, No. 631) copy. Bound in red morocco, silk doublures. [460

FOLGER. The Warwick copy. [461

FURNESS. 7 x 5 ¾". Title in facsimile. "Bought of Mr. Halliwell, £10-10-0 1867" in Tite's handwriting. The Halliwell (sold, 1867), Tite (May, 1874, No. 2754) copy. Bound in red levant morocco, by Bedford. [462

HUNTINGTON. 6 ½ x 5 ¼". Cropped at top, injuring many headlines. With duplicate stamp of Lenox Library, and Church book-plate. The New York Public Library (duplicate sale, May, 1906, No. 212), Church (sold, April, 1911) copy. Bound in green morocco, by Bedford. [463

NEW YORK PUBLIC. 7 x 5 ¼". The H. Stevens (sold, December, 1855), Lenox (incorporated as Lenox Library, 1870; New York Public, 1895) copy. Bound in olive morocco, some lower edges uncut, by Bedford. [464

A CENSUS OF SHAKESPEARE QUARTOS

SHAKESPEARE BIRTHPLACE LIBRARY. 6 ⅞ x 4 ½″. Title mended on inner margin; cropped on fore edge and foot throughout. The Corney (Sotheby, 1871, No. 2948), A. R. Smith (sold, 1872) copy. Bound in half calf. [465

TRINITY COLLEGE, CAMBRIDGE. 7 ⅛ x 5 ⅛″. F4 mutilated in lower margin. The Capell (presented, June, 1779) copy. Bound in brown calf, with other plays. Pressmark, S. 31. 3. [466

WHITE. 7 ⅛ x 5 ⅛″. Title in facsimile. Probably the Jolley (June, 1844, No. 599) copy. The Crawford (March, 1891, No. 2898) copy. Bound in red levant morocco, by Bedford. [467

MERCHANT OF VENICE, 1652.

The most excellent | Historie | of the | Merchant of Venice: | With the extreame cruelty of Shylocke | the Jew towards the said Merchant, in cutting a | just pound of his flesh: and the obtaining | of Portia by the choyce of three Chests. | As it hath been diverse times acted by the | Lord Chamberlaine his Servants. | Written by William Shakespeare. | [Ornament] | London: | Printed for William Leake, and are to be solde at his shop at the | signe of the Crown in Fleetstreet, between the two | Temple Gates. 1652.

Third edition, later title. A-I⁴; total, 36 leaves. Ci is wrongly marked Bi in some copies. Type-page, 6 ⅜ x 3 ¹⁵⁄₁₆″.

Catchwords: A2, To; Bi, *Ner.;* Ci, *Gobbo;* Di, But; Ei, *Sol.* And; Fi, I got; Gi, *Loren.* Yet; Hi, *Por.* Have; Ii, But.

＊This differs from the quarto of 1637 only in the title. On the back of this are "The Actors Names" and a list of books "Printed and solde by William Leake".

COPIES.

BRITISH MUSEUM. 7 ³⁄₁₆ x 5 ³⁄₁₆″. Slightly stained. The Garrick (bequeathed, January, 1779) copy. Bound in red straight-grained morocco. Pressmark, C. 34. k. 26. [468

BRITISH MUSEUM. 7 ¹⁄₁₆ x 5″. Cropped at top, injuring headlines on F2, F3, I3. "8907, 6495, 2215, Richard Warner, 1749" on title. The Garrick (bequeathed, January, 1779) copy. Bound in red straight-grained morocco, Garrick's arms on back, some leaves uncut at foot. Pressmark, C. 34. k. 25. [469

CRICHTON STUART. [470

EDINBURGH UNIVERSITY. 7 ¼ x 5 ¼″. A4 extended on upper margin. Halliwell's note: "Perfect. Although a late edition, this is one of the very rarest of the Shakespeare quartos. No copy has occurred for sale for very many years & only four or five are known to exist." The Halliwell (presented, 1872) copy. Bound in red levant morocco, several leaves uncut at foot, by Bedford. [471

ETON COLLEGE. 7 ¹⁄₁₆ x 5″. Worn. The Storer (bequeathed, 1799) copy. Interleaved and bound in sprinkled calf, with Richard III, 1634, and other plays in Vol. III. [472

MERCHANT OF VENICE

FOLGER. Di mended in lower corner, injuring catchword. The Jennens (collected, c. 1740, bequeathed, 1773, to W. P. A. Curzon, ancestor of Lord Howe), Howe (sold, December, 1907) copy. Bound in half blue morocco. [473

FOLGER. The Halliwell Rarities (sold, January, 1897, No. 65), Perry (sold, March, 1907) copy. Bound in half olive green morocco. [474

FOLGER. The Jonas (sold, May, 1903) copy. [475

MORGAN. 6 7/8 x 5 3/8". Title extended on inner margin; A_2, A_3, extended on upper margin; E_4, F_1, F_2, mended in margins, a few letters injured; I_3 and I_4 partially remargined and mended. The Brooks (sold, 1910) copy. Bound in old boards, marbled paper. [476

NEW YORK PUBLIC. 7 3/8 x 5 1/4". The H. Stevens (sold, December, 1855), Lenox (incorporated as Lenox Library, 1870; New York Public, 1895) copy. Bound in purple straight-grained morocco, by Clarke. [477

PERRY. 7 1/4 x 5 3/8". Title stained, blank margins torn. The Carrington (Sotheby, July, 1905, No. 379) copy. Bound in old boards, some leaves uncut at foot. [478

SHAKESPEARE MEMORIAL LIBRARY. 6 7/8 x 4 3/4". Title, A_2, A_3, mended in outer margin injuring a few words; A_4, H_2-I_4 extended on outer margin; B_1-C_4, G_1, G_4 mended on outer margin; E_1 mended in lower margin. Halliwell's note: "One of the rarest, if not the rarest, of the later Shakespeare quartos, but I have had the good luck, since this was bound to buy a nicer copy from Mr. Jarvis". The [Halliwell] Sotheby (July, 1889, No. 905) copy. Bound in brown levant morocco, by Bedford for Halliwell. [479

TRINITY COLLEGE, CAMBRIDGE. 7 1/4 x 5 3/8". The Capell (presented, June, 1779) copy. Bound in brown calf, with other plays. Pressmark, S. 27. 5. [480

WHITE. 7 3/8 x 4 5/8". Book-plate of Edward Whittaker Hennell. The Christie (December 5, 1906, No. 180) copy. Bound in red levant morocco, some leaves uncut at foot. [481

MERRY WIVES OF WINDSOR.

MERRY WIVES OF WINDSOR, 1602.

A | Most pleasaunt and | excellent conceited Co-|medie, of Syr Iohn Falstaffe, and the | merrie Wiues of Windsor. | Entermixed with sundrie | variable and pleasing humors, of Syr Hugh | the Welch Knight, Iustice Shallow, and his | wise Cousin M. Slender. | With the swaggering vaine of Auncient | Pistoll, and Corporall Nym. | By William Shakespeare. | As it hath bene diuers times Acted by the right Honorable | my Lord Chamberlaines seruants. Both before her | Maiestie, and elsewhere. | [Ornament] | London | Printed by T. C. for Arthur Iohnson, and are to be sold at | his shop in Powles Church-yard, at the signe of the | Flower de Leuse and the Crowne. | 1602.

First edition. A-G^4; total, 28 leaves. A1 blank except for signature; title, A2. Type-page, 6 1/16 x 3 1/4".

Catchwords: A3, The; B1, *Host.;* C1, Weele; D1, *Enter;* E1, *Sir;* F1, *Enter;* G1, The.

COPIES.

BODLEIAN. 7 1/16 x 4 13/16". A1 lacking; small rust hole in G1-G3. The Malone (presented, 1821) copy. Inlaid and bound with other plays in Vol. VII. Pressmark, Malone, 38. [482

BRITISH MUSEUM. 7 5/8 x 5 5/16". A1 lacking. Slight stain on top of title and A3; rust hole on A4 and D3. Bibliotheca Heberiana stamp on fly-leaf and Heber's note: "Bindleys sale Pt. III n. 2045" inside cover; Huth book-plate and Huth Bequest stamp. The Bindley (1819, No. 2045), Heber (June, 1834, No. 5443), Daniel (July, 1864, No. 1436), Huth (bequeathed, April, 1911) copy. Bound in marbled paper covers, lower edges uncut, with written label, "Merry Wives of Windsor, 1602". Pressmark, Huth, 48. [483

HUNTINGTON. 6 3/4 x 4 7/8". A1 lacking. Gaisford and Church book-plates. The Gaisford (April, 1890, No. 1741), Locker (sold, January, 1905), Church (sold, April, 1911) copy. Bound in red levant morocco, by Bedford. [484

HUNTINGTON. 6 9/16 x 4 5/16". A1 and G3 lacking; many headlines cropped or cut away; some pages damaged. The Bunbury (exchanged, 1823), Payne & Foss (sold, 1823), Devonshire (sold, January, 1914) copy. Inlaid and bound with Hamlet, 1603, and other plays in Vol. 542. [485

TRINITY COLLEGE, CAMBRIDGE. 6 ⅝ x 4 ¾". With A1. Wormhole in margin of B1-G4. The Capell (presented, June, 1779) copy. Bound in brown calf, with other plays. Pressmark, W. 5. 5. **[486**

MERRY WIVES OF WINDSOR, 1619.

A | Most pleasant and ex-|cellent conceited Comedy, | of Sir Iohn Falstaffe, and the | merry VViues of VVindsor. | VVith the swaggering vaine of An-|cient Pistoll, and Corporall Nym. | Written by W. Shake-speare. | [Heb Ddieu device] | Printed for Arthur Johnson, 1619.

Second edition. A-G⁴; total, 28 leaves. Type-page, 6 ⅛ x 3 ⅜".
Catchwords: A2, The; B1, who; C1, *Shal.;* D1, Throw; E1, *Mis:;* F1, Ile; G1, *Fent.*

COPIES.

BALLIOL COLLEGE, OXFORD. 7 9/16 x 5 ⅝". Title mounted, some corners injured and mended. Note on title: "Thomas Skynner 1621"; note: "Extracted from a book of plays, Arch M. 6. 12., and bound April 1864. Donald M. Owen librarian, Balliol." Bound in red morocco. **[487**

BODLEIAN. 7 ½ x 5 ½". Hole in margin B2 and B3; G1 mended in margin; pinprickt pattern on title. The Malone (presented, 1821) copy. Inlaid and bound with other plays in Vol. IV. Pressmark, Malone, 35. **[488**

BOSTON PUBLIC. 7 1/16 x 5 ¼". Title mended in lower portion, date in fac-simile; wormholes mended on inner portions of some leaves. The Rodd (sold, December, 1846), Barton (sold, May, 1873) copy. Bound in green straight-grained morocco, by Lewis. **[489**

BRITISH MUSEUM. 7 ¼ x 5 1/16". Slight damp stain throughout. The King George III (presented, 1823) copy. Bound in half morocco. Pressmark, C. 12. g. 24. **[490**

BRITISH MUSEUM. 7 ½ x 5 ⅞". Title browned; A4 mended in inner margin; B2, B3, B4, stained; D4 corner mended. The Garrick (bequeathed, January, 1779) copy. Bound in green straight-grained morocco, Garrick's arms on sides. Pressmark, C. 34. k. 27. **[491**

CLAWSON. 7 ½ x 5 ¼". "B. Kelley, 1774" on fly-leaf; Dramatis Personnae in old handwriting on verso title; Hoe book-plate. The Kelley (1774), Pope (sold, June, 1895), Hoe (November, 1912, No. 2893), G. D. Smith (sold, 1914) copy. Bound in red levant morocco starred, inlaid with green, tan and brown in floral design, gilt tooling, doublure of same design on blue levant morocco starred, in green levant case, by Riviere. **[492**

CRICHTON STUART. **[493**

DODD. 7 1/16 x 5 ¼". The Hussey (Sotheby, May 28, 1906, No. 381) copy. Bound in red levant morocco, by Club Bindery, 1906. **[494**

DYCE COLLECTION. 7 x 5 ⅛". Writing inked out on F1 verso and F2 recto; scribbling on title; "C.P. A. Dyce". The Dyce (bequeathed, 1869) copy. Bound in red morocco extra, by Murton. **[495**

MERRY WIVES OF WINDSOR

ELIZABETHAN CLUB. $6\,^{15}/_{16}$ x $4\,\frac{7}{8}''$. Huth book-plate. The Huth (November, 1911, No. 1205), Cochran (presented, December, 1911) copy. Bound in red straight-grained morocco. [496

FOLGER. $7\,\frac{1}{8}$ x $5\,\frac{1}{4}''$. A few leaves stained. The Jennens (collected, c. 1740, bequeathed, 1773, to W. P. A. Curzon, ancestor of Lord Howe), Howe (sold, December, 1907) copy. Bound in half blue morocco. [497

FOLGER. The Gott (sold through Sotheran, 1907) copy. Bound in half red morocco, by Lewis. [498

FOLGER. Lower corner of two leaves torn. The Sotheby (March 16, 1903, No. 1263) copy. Bound in morocco. [499

FOLGER. Title damaged. The Warwick copy. [500

FOLGER. The Quaritch (sold, 1895), Jonas (sold, May, 1903) copy. Bound in morocco, by Riviere. [501

HUNTINGTON. $7\,^{1}/_{16}$ x $5''$. With note written on the inlay: "This is the second Edition of the Merry Wives of Windsor which I have collated with the first printed in 1602. J. P. Kemble." "Collated & Perfect. J. P. Kemble. 1792." The Kemble (sold, 1821), Devonshire (sold, January, 1914) copy. Inlaid and bound with other plays in Vol. 119. [502

HUNTINGTON. $7\,^{3}/_{16}$ x $5\,\frac{3}{8}''$. Locker and Church book-plates. The Locker (sold, January, 1905), Church (sold, April, 1911) copy. Bound in red straight-grained morocco, by Bedford. [503

MORGAN. 7 x $5''$. The Pierce (sold, September, 1891), Irwin (sold, March, 1900) copy. Bound in blue levant morocco, brown levant morocco doublure, gilt tooling, by Motte. [504

NEW YORK PUBLIC. $7\,^{1}/_{16}$ x $5\,\frac{3}{8}''$. Manuscript corrections in old hand throughout. The H. Stevens (sold, December, 1855), Lenox (incorporated as Lenox Library, 1870; New York Public, 1895) copy. Bound in red morocco, gilt tooling, by Mackenzie. [505

PERRY. 7 x $5\,\frac{1}{4}''$. The Gwynne, Goertz-Wrisberg (sold, August, 1902), Quaritch (sold, October, 1902) copy. Bound in old calf with "Edward Gwynne" on covers, in volume containing six genuine and three spurious plays. [506

QUARITCH. $7\,\frac{1}{8}$ x $4\,\frac{7}{8}''$. Ci mended in lower margin. The Winans copy. Bound in red levant morocco, by Bedford. [507

QUARITCH. $6\,\frac{5}{8}$ x $4\,\frac{7}{8}''$. Bound in red levant morocco, by Riviere. [508

SHAKESPEARE BIRTHPLACE LIBRARY. $7\,^{3}/_{16}$ x $5\,^{3}/_{16}''$. G_2-G_4 extended in margins; D_2 mended in margin. The Van Antwerp (March, 1907, No. 199), Quaritch (sold, January, 1908) copy. Bound in red morocco, by Bedford. [509

SHAKESPEARE MEMORIAL LIBRARY. 7 x $5\,\frac{1}{4}''$. Title, B_2, B_3, in facsimile; A_2-B_i, B_4-E_4 extended in lower corner; G_i-G_4 stained and mended in margin. The Halliwell (Sotheby, July, 1889, No. 906) copy. Bound in red levant morocco, by Bedford. [510

TRINITY COLLEGE, CAMBRIDGE. $7\,\frac{1}{2}$ x $5\,\frac{5}{8}''$. C_2 torn at top. The Capell (presented, June, 1779) copy. Bound in brown calf, with other plays. Pressmark, Q. 11. 2. [511

A CENSUS OF SHAKESPEARE QUARTOS

TROWBRIDGE. 6 ⅞ x 5″. The Ives (March, 1891, No. 891) copy, purchased, March 10, 1896. Bound in red levant morocco, green levant morocco doublure, by Lortic. [512

WHITE. 6 ⅝ x 4 ⅝″. "George Steevens" on title; Roxburghe arms on verso title. The Steevens (May, 1800, No. 1282), Roxburghe (May, 1812, No. 3804), Perkins (July, 1889, No. 1705) copy. Bound in red morocco, Perkins's arms in gilt on covers. [513

WINDSOR CASTLE. 7 ¼ x 5 ⅝″. Unbound. [514

MERRY WIVES OF WINDSOR, 1630.

The | Merry VVives | of Windsor. | With the humours of Sir Iohn Falstaffe, | As also the swaggering vaine of Ancient | Pistoll, and Corporall Nym. | Written by William Shake-Speare. | Newly corrected. | [Ornament] | London: | Printed by T. H. for R. Meighen, and are to be sold | at his Shop, next to the Middle-Temple Gate, and in | S. Dunstans Church-yard in Fleet-street, | 1630.

Third edition. A-K⁴; total, 40 leaves. K⁴ blank. Type-page, 6½ x 3 ½″.

Catchwords: A2, *Shal.;* Bi, *Slender.;* Ci, Gentleman; Di, any; Ei, water; Fi, *Master;* Gi, I; Hi, *Mist;* Ii, of; Ki, *Euens.*

COPIES.

BODLEIAN. 7 ⁷⁄₁₆ x 5 ½″. Small piece off lower margin of I3. The Malone (presented, 1821) copy. Inlaid and bound with other plays in Vol. II. Pressmark, Malone, 33. [515

BOSTON PUBLIC. 7 ¹⁄₁₆ x 5 ¹⁄₁₆″. Wormhole through some leaves; manuscript notes at sides in old handwriting. The Barton (sold, May, 1873) copy. Bound in half red calf. [516

BRIDGEWATER HOUSE. 7 ⅛ x 5 ⅛″. Cropped at top, injuring some headlines. Acquired prior to 1649 when it was catalogued by John, Second Earl of Bridgewater. Bound in calf, with arms of the Marquis of Stafford, by Murton. [517

BRITISH MUSEUM. 7 x 4 ¾″. Soiled and a few small tears and mends. The Garrick (bequeathed, January, 1779) copy. Bound in red straight-grained morocco, Garrick's arms on back. Pressmark, C. 34. k. 28. [518

CRICHTON STUART. The Steevens copy. [519

EDINBURGH UNIVERSITY. 6 ⅞ x 4 ¹¹⁄₁₆″. Cropped at foot, injuring some signatures and catchwords. "George Steevens" on title; Roxburghe arms on verso; "Thos. Jolley, 1812" on fly-leaf and Jolley book-plate inside cover; Halliwell's notes: "This was the Roxburghe copy. . . . This ed. is very much rarer that the previous one of 1619. For ten copies of ed. 1619 not more than one of ed. 1630 can be found." The Steevens (May, 1800, No. 1283), Roxburghe (May, 1812, No. 3805), Jolley (June, 1844, No. 601), Halliwell (presented, 1872) copy. Bound in half calf. [520

MERRY WIVES OF WINDSOR

FOLGER. Title soiled and mended. Cropped at top, injuring some headlines; a few stains. Manuscript cast of actors including Betterton and Mrs. Bracegirdle on verso title. The Jennens (collected, c. 1740, bequeathed, 1773, to W. P. A. Curzon, ancestor of Lord Howe), Howe (sold December, 1907) copy. Bound in half blue morocco. [521

MURRAY. 6 ½ x 4 ¾". Cropped at top and foot, injuring headlines, signatures and catchwords. G_3 torn at foot. "J. Mitford" and note on front fly-leaf. The Mitford (April, 1860, No. 3496) copy. Bound in half roan. [522

NEW YORK PUBLIC. 6 $^{15}/_{16}$ x 5 $^1/_{16}$". Title cropped at top, injuring first line of print, mended in lower portion; a few headlines shaved. The H. Stevens (sold December, 1855), Lenox (incorporated as Lenox Library, 1870; New York Public, 1895) copy. Bound in green morocco. [523

TRINITY COLLEGE, CAMBRIDGE. 6 ⅞ x 5 ¼". K_4 blank and genuine. The Capell (presented, June, 1779) copy. Bound in brown calf with other plays. Pressmark, T. 7. 6. [524

A MIDSUMMER NIGHT'S DREAM.

A MIDSUMMER NIGHT'S DREAM, 1600.

[Ornament] | A | Midsommer nights | dreame. | As it hath beene sundry times pub-|lickely acted, by the Right honoura-|ble, the Lord Chamberlaine his | seruants. | Written by William Shakespeare. | [Fisher's device] | ¶Imprinted at London, for Thomas Fisher, and are to | be soulde at his shoppe, at the Signe of the White Hart, | in Fleetestreete. 1600.

First edition. A-H⁴; total, 32 leaves. Type-page, 6 x 3 ¼".

Catchwords: A2, A-; Bi, But; Ci, In; Di, How; Ei, Hit; Fi, Then; Gi, *Egeus;* Hi, Pat.

COPIES.

BODLEIAN. 6 13/16 x 4 11/16". C2, hole in line 3 from end; C3, lower half torn off; F2, small hole, line 10 from end. "George Steevens" on title. The Steevens (May, 1800, No. 1284), Malone (presented, 1821) copy. Inlaid and bound with other plays in Vol. VII. Pressmark, Malone, 38. [525

BOSTON PUBLIC. 7 ¼ x 5 1/16". The Heber (December, 1834, No. 2012), Barton (sold, May, 1873) copy. Bound in brown morocco, gilt tooling, by Lewis. [526

BRIDGEWATER HOUSE. 7 3/16 x 4 ⅞". Acquired prior to 1649 when it was catalogued by John, Second Earl of Bridgewater. Bound in morocco, with arms of the Marquis of Stafford, by Murton. [527

BRITISH MUSEUM. 6 5/16 x 4 ¼". Cropped at top, injuring many headlines; soiled, stained and mended in many small places. Purchased probably before 1840. Bound in yellow morocco, by Tuckett for the Museum. Pressmark, C. 34. k. 29. [528

ELIZABETHAN CLUB. 7 ⅝ x 5 ¼". Wormhole in lower blank margin of some leaves. Bibliotheca Heberiana stamp on fly-leaf: "Bindley's sale, Pt. III, 2040, Feb. 1819" in Heber's hand, inside front cover; Huth book-plate. The Bindley (February, 1819, No. 2040), Heber (June, 1834, No. 5442), Daniel (July, 1864, No. 1434), Huth (November, 1911, No. 1212), Cochran (presented, December, 1911) copy. Bound in paper covers, uncut. [529

FOLGER. The Gott (sold through Sotheran, 1907) copy. Bound in red morocco, by Lewis. [530

A CENSUS OF SHAKESPEARE QUARTOS

HUNTINGTON. 6 ⅝ x 4 ⅜". C2, C3, H2, H3, lacking; cropped at top, injuring some headlines. The Bunbury (exchanged, 1823), Payne & Foss (sold, 1823), Devonshire (sold, January, 1914) copy. Inlaid and bound with Hamlet, 1603, in Vol. 542. [531

TRINITY COLLEGE, CAMBRIDGE. 7 ⅛ x 5 ⅝". Title torn in outer margin. Note by Theobald on title: "Collated with the other Old Quarto, with the same Title, printed by James Roberts in 1600. L. T." The collations are entered in the margins. The Theobald (sold, October, 1744), Capell (presented, June, 1779) copy. Bound in brown calf, with other old plays. Pressmark, S. 27. 3. [532

A MIDSUMMER NIGHT'S DREAM, 1600 [1619].

[Ornament] A | Midsommer nights | dreame. | As it hath beene sundry times pub-|likely acted by the Right Honoura-|ble, the Lord Chamberlaine his | seruants. | Written by William Shakespeare. | [Device] | Printed by Iames Roberts, 1600. [William Jaggard for Thomas Pavier, 1619]

Second edition. A-H^4; total, 32 leaves. Type-page, 5 ⅞ x 3 ⅜".

Catchwords: A2, A-; B1, But; C1, In; D1, How; E1, Hit; F1, Then; G1, For; H1, Pat.

COPIES.

BODLEIAN. 7 ½ x 5 ½". The Malone (presented, 1821) copy. Inlaid and bound with other plays in Vol. IV. Pressmark, Malone, 35. [533

BOSTON PUBLIC. 7 x 5 ¼". The Bright (March, 1845, No. 5102), Barton (sold, May, 1873) copy. Bound in brown morocco, by Mackenzie. [534

BRITISH MUSEUM. 7 9/16 x 5 15/16". F3 mended in lower margin. The Garrick (bequeathed, 1779) copy. Bound in straight-grained yellow morocco, Garrick's arms on sides. Pressmark, C. 34. k. 30. [535

BRITISH MUSEUM. 7 ⅛ x 5 ¼". Sheet H stained in outer half. Early signatures of Edward Nedham and H. Cleaveland. The King George III (presented, 1823) copy. Bound in half morocco. Pressmark, C. 12. g. 30. [536

BRITWELL LIBRARY. 7 3/16 x 5 5/16". "George Steevens" on title; Gaisford book-plate. The Steevens, Tite (May, 1874, No. 2760), Craufurd (July, 1876, No. 1034), Gaisford (April, 1890, No. 1739) copy. Bound in green morocco, by Mackenzie. [537

CRICHTON STUART. [538

DODD. 6 15/16 x 5 5/16". Title extended in outer corners. Manuscript note on margin of F2. The Sotheby (December 6, 1905, No. 927) copy. Bound in brown morocco. [539

EDINBURGH UNIVERSITY. 6 15/16 x 5". C2-D4 in facsimile; G4 mended. The Halliwell (presented, 1872) copy. Bound in red levant morocco, by Bedford. [540

ELIZABETHAN CLUB. 7 x 5 ⅛". Three leaves stained. The Cochran (presented, December, 1911) copy. Bound in green levant morocco, by Riviere. [541

A MIDSUMMER NIGHT'S DREAM

ETON COLLEGE. 7 1/16 x 5 1/4". The Storer (bequeathed, 1799) copy. Bound in sprinkled calf, with Love's Labours Lost, 1631, and other plays in Vol. II. [542

FOLGER. 7 1/8 x 5 1/8". Some 18th century readings from Theobald and Hanmer on margins. The Jennens (collected, c. 1740, bequeathed, 1773, to W. P. A. Curzon, ancestor of Lord Howe), Howe (sold, December, 1907) copy. Bound in half blue morocco. [543

FOLGER. The Gott (sold through Sotheran, 1907) copy. Bound in red morocco, by Lewis. [544

FOLGER. Cropped at top, injuring some headlines. The Crawford (March, 1891, No. 2889), Jonas (sold, May, 1903) copy. Bound in morocco, by Riviere. [545

HUNTINGTON. 7 1/4 x 5 1/4". The Sabin (sold, 1908), Halsey (sold, December, 1915) copy. Bound in red levant morocco, by Riviere. [546

HUNTINGTON. 7 1/16 x 4 7/8". Cropped at top, injuring some headlines. Note opposite title: "Fisher's Edition of A Midsummer Nights dreame is, Mr. Malone thinks, preferable to Robert's which appears to have been followed in the folio 1623." "Collated & Perfect. J. P. K. 1798." The Kemble (sold, 1821), Devonshire (sold, January, 1914) copy. Inlaid and bound with other plays in Vol. 119. [547

HUNTINGTON. 7 1/16 x 5 1/4". Holgate, Ives and Church book-plates. The Holgate (June, 1846, No. 821), Windus (March, 1868, No. 905), Ives (March, 1891, No. 887), Church (sold, April, 1911) copy. Bound in red morocco, by Hayday. [548

LIBRARY OF CONGRESS. 6 11/16 x 4 9/16". Slightly foxed. Nos. "927" and "2105" apparently from old catalogues, appear in book. Purchased in 1876. Bound in red morocco, gilt tooling, gilt gauffered edges. [549

MORGAN. 6 5/8 x 4 1/2". "George Steevens" on title; Roxburghe arms on verso title. The Steevens (May, 1800, No. 1285), Roxburghe (May, 1812, No. 3811), Hanrott (February, 1834, No. 2695), Thorpe (1834), Assay (sold, December, 1881), Irwin (sold, March, 1900) copy. Bound in maroon morocco, Kinnear arms in gilt on covers. [550

MURRAY. 6 3/4 x 5 1/4". Cropped at top, injuring type-ornament on title and some headlines; H4 mended in lower margin. Book-plate of John Murray, label of Tudor Exhibition, 1889-1890. Probably the Loscombe (June, 1854, No. 1048) copy. Bound in olive morocco. [551

NEW YORK PUBLIC. 7 1/8 x 5 1/4". The H. Stevens (sold, December, 1855), Lenox (incorporated as Lenox Library, 1870; New York Public, May, 1895) copy. Bound in purple straight-grained morocco, by Clarke. [552

PERRY. 7 x 5 1/4". The Gwynne, Goertz-Wrisberg (sold, August, 1902), Quaritch (sold, October, 1902) copy. Bound in old calf, with "Edward Gwynne" on covers, in volume containing six genuine and three spurious plays. [553

SHAKESPEARE BIRTHPLACE LIBRARY. 7 1/16 x 5 1/16". Title, A2, A3, mended in corners; B4 remargined on fore edge. The Locker (sold, January, 1905), Dodd, Mead & Co. (sold, April, 1905), Van Antwerp (March, 1907, No. 196), Quaritch (sold, January, 1908) copy. Bound in red morocco, by Bedford. [554

TRINITY COLLEGE, CAMBRIDGE. 7 1/2 x 5 5/8". The Capell (presented, June, 1779) copy. Bound in brown calf, with other old plays. Pressmark, Q. 11. 3. [555

A CENSUS OF SHAKESPEARE QUARTOS

WHITE. 6 11/16 x 5 1/8". Cropped at top, injuring some headlines. The Perkins (July, 1889, No. 1695) copy. Bound in red morocco, Perkins's arms in gilt on covers. [556

A MIDSUMMER NIGHT'S DREAM, 1600.
Edition Unknown.
copy.

FOLGER. Bought at Sotheby (February, 1903). [557

MUCH ADO ABOUT NOTHING.

MUCH ADO ABOUT NOTHING, 1600.

[Ornament] Much adoe about | Nothing. | As it hath been sundrie times publikely | acted by the right honourable, the Lord | Chamberlaine his seruants. | Written by William Shakespeare. | [Ornament] | London | Printed by V. S. for Andrew Wise, and | William Aspley. | 1600.

First edition. A-I^4; total, 36 leaves. Type-page, 6 $\frac{5}{16}$ x 3 $\frac{7}{16}$".

Catchwords: A2, *Leo.;* B1, *Claudio;* C1, *Bene.;* D1, Con-; E1, Beleeue; F1, none; G1, A; H1, And; I1, *Bene.*

COPIES.

BODLEIAN. 6 $\frac{3}{4}$ x 4 $\frac{5}{16}$". The Malone (presented, 1821) copy. Inlaid and bound with other plays in Vol. VII. Pressmark, Malone, 38. [558

BOSTON PUBLIC. 6 $\frac{15}{16}$ x 4 $\frac{3}{4}$". Every leaf cut round and inlaid, very brittle and torn in some cases. "George Steevens" on title and his notes on verso title and on inlays. The Steevens (May, 1800, No. 1286), Bright (March, 1845, No. 5104), Barton (sold, May, 1873) copy. Bound in half morocco. [559

BRIDGEWATER HOUSE. 7 $\frac{3}{16}$ x 4 $\frac{7}{8}$". Acquired prior to 1649 when it was catalogued by John, Second Earl of Bridgewater. Bound in morocco, with arms of the Marquis of Stafford, by Murton. [560

BRITISH MUSEUM. 7 $\frac{1}{4}$ x 5". Spot on D$_3$, D$_4$; D$_4$ mended at foot. The King George III (presented, 1823) copy. Bound in half morocco. Pressmark, C. 12. g. 29. [561

BRITISH MUSEUM. 7 x 5". I$_4$ lacking; Title, A$_2$-A$_4$, I$_1$-I$_3$ mended; soiled throughout. The Garrick (bequeathed, January, 1779) copy. Bound in green straight-grained morocco, by Tuckett for the Museum. Pressmark, C. 34. k. 31.
[562

BRITWELL LIBRARY. 6 $\frac{3}{4}$ x 4 $\frac{3}{4}$". Gaisford book-plate. The Gaisford (April, 1890, No. 1740) copy. Bound in brown morocco, by Bedford. [563

DYCE COLLECTION. 6 $\frac{7}{8}$ x 4 $\frac{3}{4}$". "Coll. perfect. A. Dyce" "Read N͞o. 5th 88 Sam Moore" on title; list of characters on verso title. The Dyce (presented, 1869) copy. Bound in blue morocco. [564

EDINBURGH UNIVERSITY. 7 1/16 x 4 7/8". Title and I4 in facsimile; A2, A3, Bi-B4 mended; A4 extended in lower outer corner, catchwords in facsimile; F2-H3, Ii-I3 mended in corner, some letters in pen facsimile. Halliwell's note: "The title & some portions of the text are in FS. but still it will be interesting & valuable to the student. Daniel's copy, the finest known, fetched £267 but this large price does not afford any indication of the inferior value of a made-up copy." The Capell, Kinsman (sold, 1870), Halliwell (presented, 1872) copy. Bound in half morocco, by Bedford. [565

ELIZABETHAN CLUB. 6 15/16 x 5 3/16". Title soiled and mended in margins; cropped at top, injuring headlines on A4, Bi-C4, I3. The Huth (November, 1911, No. 1210), Cochran (presented, December, 1911) copy. Bound in brown levant morocco, by Bedford. [566

FOLGER. The Griswold (probably sold, August, 1889) copy. [567

HUNTINGTON. 7 11/16 x 5 3/8". Lewis, Locker and Church book-plates, and note by Locker on fly-leaf. The Heber (June, 1834, No. 5445), Daniel (July, 1864, No. 1433), Lewis (May, 1868, No. 235), Locker (sold, January, 1905), Church (sold, April, 1911) copy. Bound in green straight-grained morocco, with George Daniel's monogram on front cover. [568

HUNTINGTON. 6 3/4 x 4 1/8". Corner off C4, several words lacking; with scribbling on several pages written before Lady day, 1602. "Collated & Perfect. J. P. K. 1798." The Kemble (sold, 1821), Devonshire (sold, January, 1914) copy. Inlaid and bound with other plays in Vol. 120. [569

PERRY. 6 15/16 x 4 11/16". Extended on upper margins throughout. The Perkins (July, 1889, No. 1692), Sotheby (December 6, 1905, No. 926) copy. Bound in red levant morocco, gilt tooling, green levant doublure gilt tooled, green silk fly-leaves, by Lortic Frères. [570

TRINITY COLLEGE, CAMBRIDGE. 7 x 5". The Capell (presented, June, 1779) copy. Bound in brown calf, with other old plays. Pressmark, S. 34. 3. [571

WHITE. 7 x 5 1/8". Bi-B4, Gi-I4, in facsimile; E3 has upper outer portion in facsimile; Fi extended on upper margin; F4 extended on two upper corners. The Utterson (April, 1852, No. 1686), Halliwell (sold, March, 1866), Tite (June, 1874, No. 2761), Halliwell (July, 1889, No. 907) copy. Bound in red levant morocco, by Bedford. [572

OTHELLO.

OTHELLO, 1622.

The | Tragœdy of Othello, | The Moore of Venice. | As it hath beene diuerse times acted at the | Globe, and at the Black-Friers, by | his Maiesties Seruants. | Written by William Shakespeare. | [Okes's device] | London, | Printed by N. O. for Thomas Walkley, and are to be sold at his | shop, at the Eagle and Child, in Brittans Bursse. | 1622.

First edition. A^2; $B-M^4$; N^2; total, 48 leaves. Type-page, 6 7/16 x 3 1/2".

Catchwords: Bi, More; Ci, In; Di, And; Ei, *Enter;* Fi, For; Gi, *Cas.;* Hi, Your; Ii, *Des.;* Ki, *Iag.;* Li, And; Mi, *Des.;* Ni, *Oth*.

COPIES.

BODLEIAN. 6 3/4 x 4 5/8". Small wormhole in top margin throughout; title badly stained. Note by Malone: "In Pope's list he gives the title of this play (of which he had only one copy) exactly as it stands here, except that he has given no date, from which it has been supposed that there is another edition published by Thos. Walkley without a date, and not long after Shakespeare's death. Perhaps the date was cut off from his copy. In 70 years no undated copy of this play has been discovered, which makes me doubt whether it ever existed. The Quarto copies which had belonged to Pope, afterwards fell into the hands of Warburton, who put them into Mallet's Sale in 1766; but I know not to whom they were sold. If they could be recovered, this point might be ascertained. That Pope's copy had no date appears from his *inferring* from Walkley's preface that the play was published soon after Shakespeare's death: which he need not have done if his copy had had the date; but I have no doubt that the date was wanting merely by being cut off which frequently happens in old plays. The gentleman who possesses the two 4to vols above mentioned could ascertain the point". The Malone (presented, 1821) copy. Inlaid and bound with other plays in Vol. V. Pressmark, Malone, 36. [573

BOSTON PUBLIC. 6 3/4 x 4 13/16". Somewhat foxed. The Rodd (sold, February, 1838), Barton (sold, May, 1873) copy. Bound in green straight-grained morocco, by Lewis. [574

BRITISH MUSEUM. 6 13/16 x 4 5/8". Title cut close; cropped at top, injuring several headlines; very tender throughout. Purchased, July 10, 1857. Bound in red morocco. Pressmark, C. 34. k. 32. [575

A CENSUS OF SHAKESPEARE QUARTOS

BRITISH MUSEUM. 6 13/16 x 4 3/4". N1 and N2 lacking; about 1/3 of lower portion of title and A2 torn away; C1 mended at top corner. Pages 9-16 wrongly bound as follows: C1, C4, C3, C2. Three leaves of early manuscript supplied in place of two leaves lacking, with "Marmaduke ffarrells" on back of last leaf. The Garrick (bequeathed, January, 1779) copy. Bound in red straight-grained morocco, Garrick's arms on back. Pressmark, C. 34. k. 33. [576

DYCE COLLECTION. 7 7/16 x 5 3/8". Title, A2, N1, N2, in facsimile; M4 mended; most leaves tender and stained. The Dyce (bequeathed, 1869) copy. Bound in green morocco. [577

EDINBURGH UNIVERSITY. 7 x 4 3/4". Title, A2, B1-D4, I2, I3, K1-N2 in facsimile. Halliwell's note: "18 leaves in this volume are original. All the rest are in FS. but 18 leaves of so very rare an edition should not be dispised." The Halliwell (presented, 1872) copy. Bound in half levant morocco, by Bedford. [578

ELIZABETHAN CLUB. 7 x 5 1/8". Cropped at top, injuring some headlines. The Bindley (February, 1819, No. 2043), Heber (June, 1834, No. 5472), Daniel (July, 1864, No. 1446), Huth (November, 1911, No. 1200), Cochran (presented, December, 1911) copy. Bound in purple straight-grained morocco, elaborate gilt tooling, with George Daniel's monogram in gilt on front cover, purple morocco doublure with gilt tooling. [579

FOLGER. C2 mended in margin; writing on title. The Jennens (collected, c. 1740, bequeathed, 1773, to W. P. A. Curzon, ancestor of Lord Howe), Howe (sold, December, 1907) copy. Bound in half blue morocco. [580

FOLGER. Lacking D1-D4, N1, N2. The Sotheby (July 28, 1903, No. 497) copy. Unbound. [581

HUNTINGTON. 6 7/8 x 5 1/2". Few headlines cut into; scribbling on several pages. "George Steevens"; "Collated & Perfect. J. P. K. 1804"; note on verso title: "This copy has been collated with another printed in 1630. I have likewise an edition published by William Leake in 1655, but it is no more than a republication of that in 1630." The collation is in red ink. The Steevens (May, 1800, No. 1287), Kemble (sold, 1821), Devonshire (sold, January, 1914) copy. Inlaid and bound with other plays in Vol. 375. [582

NEW YORK PUBLIC. 7 x 5 1/4". K2 and K3 extended on outer margin; M1-M3 mended on outer margins. Note on fly-leaf: "June 1834. From Heber's sale. See Cat. 5472"; this is however wrong as the Heber copy (No. 5472) is now in the Elizabethan Club. The H. Stevens (sold, December, 1855), Lenox (incorporated as Lenox Library, 1870; New York Public, May, 1895) copy. Bound in purple morocco, by Clarke. [583

TRINITY COLLEGE, CAMBRIDGE. 7 1/4 x 5 1/2". I1-N2 supplied from smaller copy. The Capell (presented, June, 1779) copy. Bound in brown calf, with other old plays. Pressmark, S. 27. 2. [584

WHITE. 7 1/8 x 5 1/4". Small hole in upper margin of some leaves. The Perkins (July, 1889, No. 1707) copy. Bound in red morocco, Perkins's arms in gilt on covers. [585

OTHELLO, 1630.

The | Tragœdy of Othello, | The Moore of Venice. | As it hath beene diuerse times acted at the | Globe, and at the Black-Friers, by | his Maiesties Seruants. | Written by VVilliam Shakespeare. | [White's device] | Lon-

OTHELLO

don, | Printed by A. M. for Richard Hawkins, and are to be sold at | his shoppe in Chancery-Lane, neere Sergeants-Inne. | 1630.

Second edition. A-M⁴; total, 48 leaves. Type-page, 6 ½ x 4″.

Catchwords: A2, He; Bi, To; Ci, But; Di, You'd; Ei, *Cas.;* Fi, Boy; Gi, Then; Hi, To; Ii, To; Ki, I; Li, *Enter;* Mi, I.

COPIES.

BODLEIAN. 7 ¼ x 5 5/16″. Wormhole in lower margin throughout, injuring some last lines of text. "2-6" in pencil on title. The Malone (presented, 1821) copy. Inlaid and bound with other plays in Vol. II. Pressmark, Malone, 33. [586

BOSTON PUBLIC. 7 ⅛ x 5 ¼″. Probably the Jolley (June, 1844, No. 616) copy. The Barton (sold, May, 1873) copy. Bound in maroon straight-grained morocco, by Lewis. [587

BRITISH MUSEUM. 7 ⅛ x 5 ¼″. Small stain on title and A2. "9466" pasted on inner margin of title at foot. The King George III (presented, 1823) copy. Bound in half morocco. Pressmark, C. 21. g. 28. [588

BRITISH MUSEUM. 7 ⅞ x 5 ½″. C4 lacking; title mutilated at foot and made up; A2, A3, lower corner made up; G4, M3, M4 stained; H2, H3 and I4 soiled; I3, soiled and mended. Probably the Pearson (April, 1788, No. 3954) copy. Bound in red morocco. Pressmark, C. 34. k. 34. [589

CLEMENS. 8 x 5 ⅞″. Every leaf mended; title backed. The Quaritch (sold, 1889), White (sold, 1895) copy. Inlaid and bound in red levant morocco, by Zaehnsdorf. [590

CRICHTON STUART. [591

DYCE COLLECTION. 7 1/16 x 5 ⅛″. Outer margin of title extended and piece cut out, below which is "1656", written lengthwise; cropped at top, injuring many headlines. Probably the Sotheby (1856, No. 257) copy. The Dyce (bequeathed, 1869) copy. Bound in calf, with Hamlet, 1637. [592

EDINBURGH UNIVERSITY. 7 3/16 x 5 9/16″. Title extended on all margins but foot, "THE" shaved at top; duplicate sheet Bi inserted. Halliwell's note: "A leaf, sig. Bi in duplicate, on account of the second l in Holla, p. 8, 1. 17, being nearly dropped. It was no doubt quite dropped in the copy used by the reprinters of ed. 1655, which reads Ho la, a curious example of the way in which some printers errors arise." The Halliwell (presented, 1872) copy. Bound in red levant morocco, by Bedford. [593

ELIZABETHAN CLUB. 7 ¼ x 5 ⅜″. Title mended; A2, A3, strengthened on upper margins; B3 has ink stain. Huth book-plate. The Huth (November, 1911, No. 1201), Cochran (presented, December, 1911) copy. Bound in green straight-grained morocco. [594

FOLGER. The Warwick copy. [595

FOLGER. C2, C3, Mi-M4, in facsimile. The Sotheby (May 25, 1905, No. 645) copy. Bound in half russia. [596

HUNTINGTON. 6 ⅞ x 5 5/16″. Leaves stabbed on inner margin throughout. Locker and Church book-plates. Probably the Tite (May, 1874, No. 2763) copy. The Locker (sold, January, 1905), Church (sold, April, 1911) copy. Bound in green morocco, by Bedford. [597

HUNTINGTON. 7 x 4 ¾". Title, A₂-D₄, Fi-F₄, Hi, H₄, Ki-K₃, L₃-Mi, badly cropped at top; scribbling on several pages. The Devonshire (sold, January, 1914) copy. Bound in crimson morocco, by Birdsall. [598

JOHN CARTER BROWN LIBRARY. 7 3/16 x 5 ¼". Acquired prior to 1871. Bound in red levant morocco. [599

MINER. 7 13/16 x 5 11/16". Title extended on inner margin and mended; A₂, A₃, extended on upper inner margin; M₄ extended on margin. Bound in dark blue levant morocco, gilt tooling, white satin doublures, by Pratt. [600

MORGAN. 7 1/16 x 5 ⅜". The Asay (sold, December, 1881), Irwin (sold, March, 1900) copy. Bound in boards, roan back, arms of Kinnear on cover. [601

MURRAY. 7 1/16 x 5 ¼". C₄ lacking; title stained; stabbed throughout; cropped at top, injuring some headlines; M₄ mended. "S. W. H. Ireland" on title; "J. Mitford, 1819. May 1819" and one line note on fly-leaf. The S. Ireland (May, 1801), Mitford (April, 1860, No. 3497) copy. Bound in half roan. [602

NEW YORK PUBLIC. 6 ⅞ x 5". Title mended; fore edge of A₂ shaved; cropped at top, injuring some headlines. Roxburghe arms on verso title. The Roxburghe (May, 1812, No. 3867), H. Stevens (sold, December, 1855), Lenox (incorporated as Lenox Library, 1870; New York Public, 1895) copy. Bound in red morocco, by Bedford. [603

RICHARDSON. 6 11/16 x 5". Cropped at top, injuring some headlines. Bookplates of E. V. Utterson and Sir Robert Comyn. The Utterson (April, 1852, No. 1700), Hart (April, 1890, No. 2206), Comyn (March 13, 1893) copy. Bound in dark blue calf. [604

SHAKSPERE SOCIETY OF PHILADELPHIA. 6 ⅞ x 5". Title, A₄, Bi, E₂, and portions of A₂ and A₃ lacking. Cropped at top, injuring some headlines. The Halliwell (presented, March, 1870) copy. Bound in half morocco. [605

TRINITY COLLEGE, CAMBRIDGE. 7 ⅛ x 5". Outer margins cut close occasionally injuring page numbers. The Capell (presented, June, 1779) copy. Bound in brown calf, with other old plays. Pressmark, S. 34. 5. [606

TROWBRIDGE. 6 15/16 x 4 ⅞". Title mended in center and bottom margin. Bound in red levant morocco, by Bedford. [607

VALENTINE. [608

WHITE. 6 15/16 x 4 ⅞". Title mended and extended on inner margin; A₃ extended on lower inner corner, a few letters in facsimile; Hi, K₄, M₄ mended in margins; K₃ mended, some letters in facsimile. The Pope (sold, June, 1895), Dodd, Mead & Co. (sold, October, 1895) copy. Bound in green levant morocco, by Bedford. [609

OTHELLO, 1655.

The | Tragœdy of Othello, | The Moore of Venice |As it hath beene divers times Acted at the | Globe, and at the Black-Friers, by | his Majesties Servants. | Written by William Shakespeare. | The fourth Edition. | [Ornament] | London, | Printed for William Leak at the Crown in Fleet-| street, between the two Temple Gates, 1655.

Third edition. A-M⁴; total, 48 leaves. Type-page, 6 ⅜ x 3 15/16".

OTHELLO

Catchwords: A2, He; Bi, To; Ci, Put; Di, You'd; Ei, *Cas.;* Fi, *Boy.;* Gi, Then; Hi, To; Ii, To; Ki, I; Li, *Enter;* Mi, I.

* With a list of books, "Printed or sold by William Leake," on the last page.

COPIES.

BODLEIAN. 7 x 5 ¼". Cropped at top, injuring a few headlines. "John Baker, Devon Sidmouth; Ex Libris Johis. Webber," on title. Dr. Philip Bliss's copy with his initial "P" before the "B" signature mark on Bi and "34" after it. Purchased, 1834. Bound in calf. Pressmark, Malone 874. [610

BODLEIAN. 8 x 6". M4 lacking; title torn in lower portion; E4 and H4 torn on lower outer corner, injuring a few words; side and foot totally uncut. Manuscript list of Dramatis Personae on verso title. The Anthony a Wood (bequeathed, 1695), Ashmolean Museum (transferred, 1861) copy. Bound with Dryden's "Religio Laici" and others, in boards. Pressmark, Wood, 320. [611

BODLEIAN. 7 5⁄16 x 5 ⅜". G4 cropped at top. Purchased, 1834. Bound in half calf; some leaves uncut at foot. Pressmark, Malone, 911. [612

BOSTON PUBLIC. 7 ¼ x 5 ¼". Ci mended in lower corner; cropped at top, injuring some headlines. The Barton (sold, May, 1873) copy. Bound in green morocco, gilt tooling, some lower edges uncut, by Lewis. [613

BRITISH MUSEUM. 7 1⁄16 x 5 ⅛". C3 mended at foot. "H. Go .pret. -o-9d." on title. The Garrick (bequeathed, January, 1779) copy. Bound in red morocco, Garrick's arms on back. Pressmark, C. 34. k. 35. [614

BRITISH MUSEUM. 7 ⅝ x 5 ⅝". Lower corner torn off Ei and E4; M4 outer margin strengthened; soiled and stained. The King George III (presented, 1823) copy. Bound in half morocco. Pressmark, C. 12. h. 13. [615

CRICHTON STUART. [616

EDINBURGH UNIVERSITY. 7 ⅛ x 5 1⁄16". Title mended in margin; cropped at top, injuring some headlines; many leaves uncut at foot. Halliwell's note: "Collated with the Cambridge edition, 19 March, 1870. This edition is distinguished by many hideous misprints. J. O. H." The Halliwell (presented, 1872) copy. Bound in green levant morocco, by Bedford. [617

ETON COLLEGE. 7 1⁄16 x 5". Cropped at top, injuring some headlines; stained. "5651" on title. The Storer (bequeathed, 1799) copy. Bound with other plays in Vol. IV. [618

FOLGER. The Warwick copy. [619

FOLGER. Few headlines shaved. The Sotheby (July 18, 1900, No. 1209), Jonas (sold, May, 1903) copy. Unbound. [620

FURNESS. 7 ¾ x 5 ⅝". With "Frances Wolfreston her book" on A2; book-plate of J. Kershaw. The Anderson (Sotheby, November, 1870, No. 411), Corser (February, 1871, No. 411), Kershaw (July, 1877, No. 1235) copy. Bound in red levant morocco, gilt tooling, many leaves uncut. [621

HUNTINGTON. 7 1⁄16 x 5". Cropped at top, injuring some headlines. Church book-plate. The Sewall (January, 1897, No. 3436), Church (sold, April, 1911) copy. Bound in blue levant morocco, by Riviere. [622

MORGAN. 7 ¼ x 5 ¼". Cropped at top, injuring some headlines; H1 and H2 extended on outer margins, a few letters injured. The Halliwell (sold, 1867), Tite (May, 1874, No. 2764), Asay (sold, December, 1881), Irwin (sold, March, 1900) copy. Bound in red levant morocco, some lower edges uncut, by Bedford. [623

NEW YORK PUBLIC. 7 ⅜ x 5 3/16". The H. Stevens (sold, December, 1855), Lenox (incorporated as Lenox Library, 1870; New York Public, May, 1895) copy. Bound in purple straight-grained morocco, some lower edges uncut, by Clarke. [624

PERRY. 8 x 5 ¾". M4 extended on upper margin. Book-plates of F. A. Marshall and Sir Henry Irving; inscription signed and dated, July 26, 1879, F. A. Marshall to Henry Irving. The Sotheby (May 24, 1856, No. 357), Marshall (presented, July, 1879), Irving (December, 1905, No. 373) copy. Bound in green levant morocco, uncut, by De Coverly. [625

TRINITY COLLEGE, CAMBRIDGE. 7 ⅛ x 5". Capell book-plate on verso title; stamp on verso M4. The Capell (presented, June, 1779) copy. Bound in brown calf, with other old plays. Pressmark, R. 22. 1. [626

WHITE. 7 ¼ x 5 ⅜". M4 lacking; title mended in margins and stained; M2 and M3 extended in outer margins. "L. T[heobald]" on title; signed note by Halliwell on fly-leaf; book-plate of W. Harrison, Samlesbury Hall. The Theobald (sold, 1767), Harrison (January, 1881, No. 936), Lamb (February, 1898, No. 1099), Libbie (December, 1898, No. 474) copy. Bound in half morocco. [627

OTHELLO, 1681.

Othello, | The | Moor of Venice. | A | Tragedy, | As it hath been divers times acted at the Globe, | and at the Black-Friers: | And now at the | Theater Royal, | By | His Majesties Servants. | Written by William Shakespear. | [Ornament] | London, | Printed for W. Weak, and are to be sold by Richard Bent-|ley and M. Magnes in Russel Street near Covent-| Garden, 1681.

Fourth edition. A^2; $B-K^4$; L^2; total, 40 leaves. Type-page, 8 x 4 11/16".

Catchwords: A2, Dram-; B1, *Rad.*; C1, You; D1, Lieutenant; E1, *King*; F1, *Enter*; G1, *Oth.*; H1, *Actus*; I1, Patience; K1, *Cas.*; L1, So.

COPIES.

ADLER. 8 ½ x 6 ⅜". A1-D3 lacking. L2 mended. Bound in boards. [628

BIRMINGHAM. 8 9/16 x 6 7/16". Title extended on inner margin. Book-plate of William Staunton of Longbridge in Warwickshire. Purchased, 1879. Bound in half calf. [629

BOSTON PUBLIC. 8 ¼ x 6 ⅜". The Barton (sold, May, 1873) copy. Bound in half brown morocco. [630

BRITWELL LIBRARY. 8 ½ x 6 ⅝". Unbound. [631

FOLGER. The Warwick copy. [632

FURNESS. 8 9/16 x 6 ½". Acquired prior to 1880. Bound in half leather. [633

KINGSLEY. 8 ⅜ x 6 ¼". G1 lacking. Bound in half red straight-grained morocco, original paper covers bound in. [634

OTHELLO

LINCOLN COLLEGE, OXFORD. 8 ½ x 6 ⅜". Last leaf torn. Bound with "Hamlet," 1676, in brown leather. Pressmark, Q. v. l. (2). [635

PERRY. 8 ¼ x 6 ¼". Book-plate of Sir William Horton, Chaderton. Bound in old half calf, with other plays. [636

UNIVERSITY OF MICHIGAN. 8 7/16 x 6 ⅜". Foxed. The Anderson (October 27, 1911, No. 135) copy. Unbound. [637

WHITE. 8 ⅝ x 6 ½". Purchased, March, 1892. Bound in half red levant morocco. [638

OTHELLO, 1687.

Othello, | The | Moor of Venice. | A | Tragedy. | As it hath been divers times Acted at the | Globe, and at the Black-Friers: | And now at the | Theatre Royal, | by | His Majesties Servants. | Written by William Shakespear. | London, | Printed for Richard Bentley and S. Magnes in Russel-Street near | Covent-Garden, 1687.

Fifth edition. 2 leaves without signatures; B-K^4; L^2; total, 40 leaves. Type-page, 7 ⅞ x 4 15/16".

Catchwords: A2, Dram-; Bi, *Rod.;* Ci, You; Di, Lieutenant; Ei, *King;* Fi, *Enter;* Gi, *Oth.;* Hi, (*Exeunt.* | *Actus;* Ii, Patience; Ki, *Cas.;* Li, So.

COPIES.

BIRMINGHAM. 8 ½ x 6 9/16". The R. Smith (sold, 1881) copy. Bound in half morocco, by Hawkins, Birmingham. [639

BOSTON PUBLIC. 8 5/16 x 6 7/16". Cropped at foot, injuring some catchwords. The Barton (sold, May, 1873) copy. Bound in half calf. [640

BRITISH MUSEUM. 8 ¾ x 6 ¼". Title backed and mended; F3 torn; L1 and L2 mended; some leaves uncut at foot. Probably the Marsh (May, 1882, No. 2421) copy. Bound with other plays in half calf. Pressmark, 841. c. 22. [641

FOLGER. The Halliwell Rarities (sold, January, 1897, No. 120), Perry (sold, March, 1907) copy. Bound in half brown morocco. [642

NEW YORK PUBLIC. 8 7/16 x 6 ½". The Duyckinck (presented, 1878) copy. Bound with collection of plays. [643

UNIVERSITY OF MICHIGAN. 8 5/16 x 6 ⅛". The Sotheran (sold, 1893) copy. Bound in half green calf. [644

WHITE. 8 ⅝ x 6 ¼". Purchased, April, 1903. Bound in calf. [645

OTHELLO, 1695.

Othello, | The | Moor of Venice. | A | Tragedy. | As it hath been divers times Acted at the | Globe, and at the Black-Friers: | and now at the | Theatre Royal, | by | His Majesties Servants. | Written by William Shakespear. | London, | Printed for Richard Bentley, in Russel-Street near | Covent-Garden, 1695.

A CENSUS OF SHAKESPEARE QUARTOS

Sixth edition. 2 leaves without signatures; B-K^4; L^2; total, 40 leaves. Type-page, 7 7/8 x 4 7/8".

Catchwords: Bi, *Rod.;* Ci, You; Di, Lieutenant; Ei, *King;* Fi, *Enter;* Gi, *Oth.;* Hi, *Actus;* Ii, Patience; Ki, *Cas.;* Li, So.

COPIES.

BIRMINGHAM. 8 3/8 x 6 5/16". Some headlines cropped. Purchased in 1871. Bound in half calf. [646

BODLEIAN. 8 11/16 x 6 3/16". Cropped at top, injuring "OTHELLO" on title and headline of B4. Purchased, 1866. Bound with Othello, 1705, in half calf, some lower edges uncut. Pressmark, Malone, 961. [647

BOSTON ATHENAEUM. 8 7/16 x 6 1/2". Purchased, 1896. Bound with other plays. [648

BOSTON PUBLIC. 8 3/8 x 6 1/8". Badly foxed; cropped at top, injuring some headlines. Probably the Jolley (June, 1844, No. 615) copy. The Barton (sold, May, 1873) copy. Bound in half calf. [649

BRITISH MUSEUM. 8 9/16 x 6 3/8". K3 mended in lower margin; foxed. "1703. The 21 of May Fryday" on title; notes on fly-leaves by previous owner dated July 1, 1703. Bound in cloth, with other plays. Pressmark, 841. c. 8. [650

CLAWSON. 8 3/4 x 6 3/4". With manuscript notes said to be by Alexander Pope. Purchased by G. D. Smith in London, 1914, and resold in 1915. Unbound and uncut. [650*

CRICHTON STUART. [651

FURNESS. 8 5/8 x 6 1/2". Cropped at foot, injuring some leaves; K3 torn, a few words lacking. Acquired prior to 1880. Bound in half morocco, lower edges uncut. [652

HARVARD UNIVERSITY. 8 3/4 x 6 3/16". The Lamb (February, 1898, No. 1104) copy. Bound in half morocco, lower edges uncut, January, 1899. [653

HUNTINGTON. 8 5/8 x 6 9/16". The Griswold (sold, August, 1889), Hoe (January, 1912, No. 3039) copy. Bound in red levant morocco, with Griswold's arms on sides, by Bedford. [654

PERRY. 8 3/4 x 6 5/8". Book-plate of F. A. Marshall. The Marshall (June, 1890, No. 1171) copy. Interleaved and bound in boards, leather back. [655

UNIVERSITY OF MICHIGAN. 8 5/16 x 6 1/4". Somewhat stained. The Sotheran (sold, 1897) copy. Bound in boards. [656

WHITE. 8 9/16 x 6 1/4". The Genest (sold, 1815), Pickering (sold, March 26, 1898) copy. Bound in half morocco, by Walters, 1912, for Mr. White. [657

WHITE. 8 3/8 x 6 1/4". Somewhat foxed. Bound in half morocco. [658

OTHELLO, 1705.

Othello, | The | Moor of Venice. | A | Tragedy. | As it hath been divers times Acted at the | Globe, and at the Black-Friers: | And now at the | Theatre Royal, | By | Her Majesties Servants. | Written by W. Shake-

OTHELLO

spear. | London: | Printed for R. Wellington, at the Dolphin and Crown, at the West-End | of St. Paul's Church-Yard. 1705. [9 lines of advertisements].

Seventh edition. Title and list of plays with Dramatis Personae on verso, 2 leaves; B-K^4; L^2; total, 40 leaves. Type-page, 8 x 5 ¼".
Catchwords: Bi, 'Tis; Ci, Hath; Di, For; Ei, *Mon.;* Fi, Oth.; Gi, As; Hi, This; Ii, *Em.;* Ki, *Jag.;* Li, *Lod.*

COPIES.

BIRMINGHAM. 8 ¾ x 6 ⅝". The Grant (sold, 1898) copy. Bound in cloth, August, 1898. [659

BODLEIAN. 8 ⅝ x 6 $^9/_{16}$". Cropped at top, injuring headlines on E$_4$, Gi, G$_4$, H$_2$, Ii, I$_4$, Ki. Purchased, 1866. Bound with Othello, 1695, in half calf. Pressmark, Malone, 961. [660

BOSTON ATHENAEUM. 8 ½ x 6 ½". Purchased prior to 1870. Bound with collection of old plays. [661

BOSTON PUBLIC. 8 ⅜ x 6 ¼". Cropped at top, injuring some headlines. With "Geo. Bromley, Theatre Royal, Norwich, 1814" and "Jermyn Bond" on title. The Barton (sold, May, 1873) copy. Bound with collection of late Shakespeare plays. [662

BRITISH MUSEUM. 8 $^9/_{16}$ x 6 ⅜". Bound with Hamlet, 1703, and other plays, in old calf. Pressmark, 841. c. 3. [663

BROOKS. 8 ⅝ x 6 ⅜". Probably the [Jonas] Sotheby (March 17, 1911, No. 521) copy. Purchased, 1911. Bound in calf, gilt edges on the rough, by Ramage for Mr. Brooks. [664

FOLGER. The Warwick copy. [665

MORGAN. 8 ⅜ x 6 ⅜". The Irwin (sold, March, 1900) copy. Bound in half levant morocco. [666

NEW YORK PUBLIC. 8 ½ x 6 $^7/_{16}$". The Sotheby (August, 1857, No. 482), Lenox (incorporated as Lenox Library, 1870; New York Public, May, 1895) copy. Bound in olive levant morocco, by Bedford. [667

PERRY. 8 ½ x 6 ½". The Marshall (June, 1890, No. 1171) copy. Bound in half calf. [668

UNIVERSITY OF MICHIGAN. 8 $^7/_{16}$ x 6 $^5/_{16}$". Slightly foxed. The Harris (April, 1883, No. 1617) copy. Bound in half morocco. [669

WHEATLEY. 8 ⅝ x 6 ⅛". Bound in red levant morocco, with device of H. B. Wheatley on covers, by Riviere. [670

WRENN, Estate of J. H. 8 $^9/_{16}$ x 6 ½". Purchased, July 27, 1905. Bound in polished calf, by Riviere. [671

RICHARD II.

RICHARD II, 1597.

The | Tragedie of King Ri-|chard the se-|cond. | As it hath beene publikely acted | by the right Honourable the | Lorde Chamberlaine his Ser-|uants. | [Simmes's device] | London | Printed by Valentine Simmes for Andrew Wise, and | are to be sold at his shop in Paules church yard at | the signe of the Angel. | 1597.

First edition. A–I⁴; K²; total, 38 leaves. Type-page, 6 5/16 x 3 9/16″.

Catchwords: A2, *Mow;* B1, what; C1, *Exit.* | *Au-;* D1, The; E1, But; F1, To; G1, Till; H1, *Bull.;* I1, I; K1, Our.

COPIES.

BRITISH MUSEUM. 6 15/16 x 5″. B4 mended in outer margin; G2 torn across and carelessly mended. "25, By W. Shakespear, df", all on title in old hands; George Daniel's copy with long note written in 1847 for which see introduction; Huth book-plate and Huth Bequest stamp. The Daniel (July, 1864, No. 1425), Huth (bequeathed, April, 1911) copy. Bound in crimson morocco with "G. D." on covers, by Lewis. Pressmark, Huth, 46. [672

HUNTINGTON. 6 5/8 x 4 13/16″. A4 cropped at foot, one line replaced in manuscript. "Collated & Perfect. J. P. K. 1792". The Kemble (sold, 1821), Devonshire (sold, January, 1914) copy. Inlaid and bound with other plays in Vol. 120. [673

TRINITY COLLEGE, CAMBRIDGE. 6 7/8 x 4 3/4″. K1 cropped at top, injuring headline. The Capell (presented, June, 1779) copy. Bound in brown calf, with other old plays. Pressmark, S. 35. 4. [674

RICHARD II, 1598.

The | Tragedie of King Ri-|chard the second. | As it hath beene publikely acted by the Right Ho-|nourable the Lord Chamberlaine his | seruants. | By William Shake-speare. | [Simmes's device] | London | Printed by Valentine Simmes for Andrew Wise, and | are to be sold at his shop in Paules churchyard at | the signe of the Angel. | 1598.

Second edition. A–I⁴; total, 36 leaves. Type-page, 6 7/16 x 3 3/8″.

A CENSUS OF SHAKESPEARE QUARTOS

Catchwords: A2, *Mow,;* B1, An; C1, *Bul.;* D1, Oh; E1, What; F1, Then; G1, You; H1, *Abbot.;* I1, This.

∗ Of the two editions of 1598 this one which has no commas after "Simmes" and "Churchyard" and no "e" at the end of "sold" is the earlier.

COPIES.

BODLEIAN. 6 ⅞ x 4 ¾". Title stained, with three rows of printer's ornaments cut from some other book pasted on upper margin; A2-I3 also stained; F3 has small hole; G3 torn, injuring last 11 lines. The Malone (presented, 1821) copy. Inlaid and bound with other plays in Vol. VII. Pressmark, Malone, 38. [675

BOSTON PUBLIC. 7 ½ x 5 9/16". B1-B4, G4, H1, are extended on upper margins; a few lower margins uncut. The Bright (March, 1845, No. 5099), Barton (sold, May, 1873) copy. Bound in vellum. [676

BRIDGEWATER HOUSE. 7 5/16 x 5 ⅛". Acquired prior to 1649 when it was catalogued by John, Second Earl of Bridgewater. Bound in green morocco, with arms of the Marquis of Stafford on covers, by Murton. [677

BRITISH MUSEUM. 6 ¾ x 5". Title mended, cropped at top, injuring top of "THE"; H1, H2, I4, mended; writing on H1. The Garrick (bequeathed, January, 1779) copy. Bound in red morocco, Garrick's arms on sides. Pressmark, C. 34. k. 42. [678

FOLGER. 6 ⅞ x 4 ¾". Title, A2, A3, and I4 slightly mended; cropped on fore edge, injuring some side notes. The Jennens (collected, c. 1740, bequeathed, 1773, to W. P. A. Curzon, ancestor of Lord Howe), Howe (sold, December, 1907) copy. Bound in half blue morocco. [679

FOLGER. Lacking B2-B4, G4, H1. Book-plate of J. F. Marsh. The Heber (June, 1834, No. 5453), Rodd (sold, 1837, No. 4165), Marsh (May, 1882, No. 2415), Kalbfleisch (sold, c. 1900) copy. Bound in old red straight-grained morocco. [680

HUNTINGTON. 7 x 5". Part of first word of title in facsimile; H4, I3, and I4 are extended on outer margins and have some letters in facsimile; stabbed on inner margin throughout and mended. "Geo. Steevens" and Roxburghe arms on title; signed note by W. Tite on last fly-leaf. The Steevens (May, 1800, No. 1290), Roxburghe (May, 1812, No. 3829), Daniel (July, 1864, No. 1426), Tite (June, 1874, No. 2772), Locker (sold, January, 1905), Church (sold, April, 1911) copy. Bound in red levant morocco, by Bedford. [681

TRINITY COLLEGE, CAMBRIDGE. 7 ¼ x 5 ¼". The Capell (presented, June, 1779) copy. Bound in brown calf, with other old plays. Pressmark, R. 22. 5. [682

RICHARD II, 1598.

The | Tragedie of King Ri-|chard the second. | As it hath beene pub-|likely acted by the Right Ho-|nourable the Lord Chamberlaine his | ser-uants. | By William Shake-speare. | [Simmes's device] | London | Printed by Valentine Simmes, for Andrew Wise, and | are to be solde at his shop in Paules churchyard, at | the signe of the Angel. | 1598.

Third edition. A-I⁴; total, 36 leaves. Type-page, 6 7/16 x 3 ⅜".

[82]

RICHARD II

Catchwords: A2, *Mow,;* Bi, An; Ci, *Bul.;* Di, Oh; Ei, What; Fi, Then; Gi, You; Hi, *Abbot.;* Ii, This.

COPY.

WHITE. 7 1/16 x 5 1/8". Stamp of Williams Library, Cheltenham, on front fly-leaf. The Williams, Trye (sold, January 21, 1890), Quaritch (sold, February 9, 1890) copy. Bound in half calf. [683

RICHARD II, 1608.

The | Tragedie of King | Richard the second. | As it hath been publikely acted by the Right | Honourable the Lord Chamberlaine | his seruantes. | By William Shake-speare. | [Device] | London, | Printed by W. W. for Mathew Law, and are to be | sold at his shop in Paules Church-yard, at | the signe of the Foxe. | 1608.

Fourth edition, earlier title. A-K⁴; total, 40 leaves. K4 blank. Type-page, 6 3/8 x 3 5/8".

Catchwords: A2, *Mow.;* Bi, An; Ci, *Bul;* Di, Oh; Ei, What; Fi, Then; Gi, You; Hi, Oh; Ii, Where; Ki, And.

∗Copies of this edition differ only in title.

COPIES.

BRITISH MUSEUM. 6 15/16 x 5". K4 blank and genuine. Title, A2-A4, cut close to outer margin; rest of book cut close to sewing; lower corner of Bi restored; B3 stained. "Thos. Jolley, 1809" and his book-plate. The Jolley (June, 1844, No. 589) copy, purchased, January 16, 1845. Bound in red morocco. Pressmark, C. 34. k. 43. [684

ELIZABETHAN CLUB. 6 7/8 x 5 1/16". K4 blank and genuine. Somewhat stained. Huth book-plate. The Huth (November, 1911, No. 1194), Cochran (presented, December, 1911) copy. Bound in red levant morocco, by Bedford. [685

HUNTINGTON. 6 3/4 x 4 3/4". Cropped at top, injuring some headlines. Locker and Church book-plates. The [Halliwell] Sotheby (May, 1857, No. 876), Tite (June, 1874, No. 2773), Locker (sold, January, 1905), Church (sold, April, 1911) copy. Bound in brown straight-grained morocco. [686

HUNTINGTON. 6 3/4 x 4 1/8". Cropped at top and bottom, injuring a few headlines and catchwords. "George Steevens"; "Collated & Perfect. J. P. K. 1804"; scribbling at end. The Bowle (January 19, 1790), Steevens (May, 1800, No. 1291), Kemble (sold, 1821), Devonshire (sold, January, 1914) copy. Inlaid and bound with other plays in Vol. 375. [687

RICHARD II, 1608.

The | Tragedie of King | Richard the Second: | With new additions of the Parlia-|ment Sceane, and the deposing | of King Richard, | As it hath been lately acted by the Kinges | Maiesties seruantes, at the Globe. | By

William Shake-speare. | [Device] | At London, | Printed by W. W. for Mathew Law, and are to | be sold at his shop in Paules Church-yard, | at the signe of the Foxe, | 1608.

Fourth edition, later title.

*This differs from the preceding only in the title.

COPIES.

BODLEIAN. 7 x 4 3/8″. Cropped close to imprint on outer margin. Malone's note facing title: "This is the third edition; but the first in which the Scene of the deposition of King Richard was printed. The folio, 1623, was printed from this copy of 1608. The copy of King Richard II (collated with the first edition of 1597, and the variations are set down in the margins E. M. The title of the original edition is as follows (etc). Mr. Kemble has a copy of this play printed in 1608; on the titlepage of which no mention is made of the additional scene, though found there; and it is the same edition with merely that variation in the titlepage. The words were probably thought offensive by Mr. Tylney, the Master of the Revels, and ordered to be omitted." The Malone (presented, 1821) copy. Inlaid and bound with other plays in Vol. V. Pressmark, Malone, 36. [688

RICHARD II, 1608.

Issue Uncertain.

COPIES.

CRICHTON STUART. Lacking title and last leaf. [689

PERRY. 6 7/8 x 4 3/4″. Lacking title and A4. The [Carrington] Sotheby (July, 1905, No. 380) copy. Bound in boards. [690

WHITE. 7 3/16 x 5 1/4″. Lacking title; A2 mended on margin; A4 extended on inner margin; C3 and C4 on upper margins. Probably the Rhodes (April, 1825, No. 2078) copy. The Perkins (July, 1889, No. 1701) copy. Bound in red morocco, Perkins's arms in gilt on covers. [691

RICHARD II, 1615.

The | Tragedie of King | Richard the Se-|cond: | With new additions of the Parliament Sceane, | and the deposing of King | Richard. | As it hath been lately acted by the Kinges | Maiesties seruants, at the Globe. | By William Shake-speare. | [Ornament] | At London, | Printed for Mathew Law, and are to be sold | at his shop in Paules Church-yard, at the | signe of the Foxe. | 1615.

Fifth edition. A-I^4; K^3; total, 39 leaves. Type-page, 6 3/8 x 3 1/2″.

Catchwords: A2, *Mow.*; Bi, An; Ci, *Bul.*; Di, Oh; Ei, What; Fi, Then; Gi, You; Hi, Oh; Ii, Where; Ki, And.

RICHARD II

COPIES.

BODLEIAN. 7 x 4 ⅞″. Note by Malone: "D4. York. Should I do so, I should bely my thought. This line is wanting in the folio. *This* therefore was probably not the copy the editor printed from. M." Portrait of Richard II, by R. Elstrack "to be sold by Compton Holland" (probably from the Basiliologia), inserted facing title. The Malone (presented, 1821) copy. Inlaid and bound with other plays in Vol. I. Pressmark, Malone, 32. [692

BOSTON PUBLIC. 6 $^{11}/_{16}$ x 4 ⅞″. Title mended; cropped at top, injuring some headlines. The Jadis (March, 1828, No. 157), Rodd (sold, 1842), Barton (sold, May, 1873) copy. Bound in dark green straight-grained morocco, by Lewis. [693

BRITISH MUSEUM. 6 ¾ x 5″. Cropped at top, injuring most headlines; two large holes in B1 clumsily mended. "John Bancroft" on title; writing on H2-H4. The Garrick (bequeathed, January, 1779) copy. Bound in red morocco, Garrick's arms on back. Pressmark, C. 34. k. 44. [694

CLAWSON. 6 $^{9}/_{16}$ x 4 ⅞″. Cropped at foot, injuring some signatures. Hoe book-plate. The Pope (sold, June, 1895), Hoe (April, 1911, No. 2974), G. D. Smith (sold, 1915) copy. Bound in brown levant morocco, with brown levant doublure, brown silk fly-leaves, by Riviere. [695

CRICHTON STUART. The Steevens copy. [696

EDINBURGH UNIVERSITY. 6 $^{15}/_{16}$ x 5 $^{1}/_{16}$″. F3 in facsimile; K1 extended in lower corners. The Windus (March, 1868, No. 909), Halliwell (presented, 1872) copy. Bound in red morocco. [697

FOLGER. The Gott (sold through Sotheran, 1907) copy. Bound in red morocco, by Lewis. [698

FOLGER. Thick paper. The Halliwell (June, 1859, No. 339), Tite (May, 1874, No. 2774) copy. Bound in red morocco, by Bedford. [699

HUNTINGTON. 6 $^{11}/_{16}$ x 4 ⅝″. "George Steevens" on title and his manuscript notes in book; Roxburghe arms on verso title; signature of J. F. Marsh; Locker and Church book-plates. The Steevens (May, 1800, No. 1292), Roxburghe (May, 1812, No. 3830), Marsh (May, 1882, No. 2416), Locker (sold, January, 1905), Church (sold, April, 1911) copy. Bound in half red calf. [700

HUNTINGTON. 6 ⅝ x 4″. Badly cropped at top and foot, injuring some headlines, catchwords and signatures; title stained. "Collated & Perfect. J. P. K. 1802"; "An Bosvil"; Remains of a number "?077" at top of title. The Kemble (sold, 1821), Devonshire (sold, January, 1914) copy. Inlaid and bound in crimson levant morocco, by Birdsall. [701

NEW YORK PUBLIC. 7 x 4 ⅞″. Title mended. "Jo. Ffowle, 1675. Nulla dies linea J. ffow." on B2, in old handwriting. The H. Stevens (sold, December, 1855), Lenox (incorporated as Lenox Library, 1870; New York Public, 1895) copy. Bound in brown levant morocco, with Kinnear arms in gilt on sides. [702

TRINITY COLLEGE, CAMBRIDGE. 7 ¼ x 5 ¼″. Title and first page of text collated in red by Capell with the 1608 edition; other corrections throughout but probably not exhaustive. The Capell (presented, June, 1779) copy. Bound in brown calf, with other old plays. Pressmark, R. 19. 2. [703

WHITE. 6 ⅞ x 5 $^{3}/_{16}$″. K2 and K3 lacking and replaced in manuscript; title torn in margin. The Sotheby (July 13, 1908, No. 89) copy. Unbound. [704

A CENSUS OF SHAKESPEARE QUARTOS

RICHARD II, 1634.

The | Life and | Death of King | Richard the | Second. | With new Additions of the | Parliament Scene, and the | Deposing of King Richard. | As it hath beene acted by the Kings Majesties | Servants, at the Globe. | By William Shakespeare. | [Ornament] | London, | Printed by Iohn Norton. | 1634.

Sixth edition. A-K^4; total, 40 leaves. Type-page, 6 ½ x 3 9/16″.

Catchwords: A2, *Enter;* B1, Thou; C1, *Bul.;* D1, I; E1, *Percy;* F1, The; G1, Speake; H1, *Car.;* I1, And; K1, His.

COPIES.

BODLEIAN. 6 ¾ x 4 ¾″. C4, E2, E3, E4 torn, injuring some words; cropped at top, injuring some headlines; several stains. Purchased, 1830. Bound in calf. Pressmark, Malone, 877. [705

BOSTON PUBLIC. 7 9/16 x 5 1/16″. Slightly stained; title extended on inner and lower margins and mended; K4 mended and extended on all margins except foot. "Thos. Jolley, 1809" on fly-leaf and his book-plate. The Jolley (June, 1844, No. 591), Burton (October, 1860, No. 4615), Barton (sold, May, 1873) copy. Bound in half leather. [706

BRITISH MUSEUM. 6 ⅞ x 4 ¾″. Title mended; either headlines or catchwords cut into on many leaves; small holes in F3. A2 verso, beginnings of eight lines inked over by hand. The Garrick (bequeathed, January, 1779) copy. Bound in red morocco, Garrick's arms on back. Pressmark, C. 34. k. 45. [707

BRITISH MUSEUM. 6 ¾ x 4 ¾″. Title, A2-A4 lacking; cropped throughout, injuring headlines; B1 mended; C4, H2, K2, K3, mended in margins; text of sheet A supplied in six leaves. The King George III (presented, 1823) copy. Bound in half morocco. Pressmark, C. 12. g. 19. [708

BRITWELL LIBRARY. 8 ⅛ x 5 ⅞″. With five old signatures on title; "frances wolfreston her book" on A2; manuscript note by W. Tite: "This copy of Shakespeare's play, of Richd. the 2d. was bought by me at Messrs Sotheby & Wilkinsons at a sale 24 May 1856 of which I preserve the Catalogue (oddly enough misprinted 1586). The Play is in the state in which they were sold for 1/ at the time. I gave £13. 13. 0. & I chose it as being the best of several in the same plight, it was Lot 353 of this sale. W. Tite." The Sotheby (May 24, 1856, No. 353), Tite (May, 1874, No. 2775) copy. Uncut, unbound. [709

CRICHTON STUART. [710

DODD. 7 ⅛ x 5 ¼″. Some margins stained. Bound in wine colored levant morocco, by Riviere. [711

DYCE COLLECTION. 7 ⅜ x 5 ¼″. A3, A4, B3, C3, C4, D3, D4, E3, E4, F3, F4, G3, G4, H3, H4, extended on outer margin about 1 ⅛″; title browned. "C. P. A. Dyce". The Dyce (bequeathed, 1869) copy. Bound in calf. [712

ETON COLLEGE. 7 1/16 x 5 ⅛″. Cropped at top, injuring some headlines. "5652" on title. The Storer (bequeathed, 1799) copy. Bound with Taming of the Shrew, 1631, and other plays in Vol. IV. [713

FOLGER. The Halliwell Rarities (sold, January, 1897, No. 13), Perry (sold, March, 1907) copy. Bound in olive morocco. [714

[86]

RICHARD II

FOLGER. The Jonas (sold, May, 1903) copy. Bound in morocco, by Riviere.
[715

HUNTERIAN MUSEUM, GLASGOW. Size not given. Top slightly cropped, stained in parts. Bound with books by other authors. Pressmark, Co. 3. 31. [716

HUNTINGTON. 6 ¾ x 5″. Long note in faded ink signed "Jos. Edgerton" on verso title; Church book-plate. The Sewall (January, 1897, No. 3433), Church (sold, April, 1911) copy. Bound in brown levant morocco, by Hammond. [717

NEW YORK PUBLIC. 6 $\frac{15}{16}$ x 5 $\frac{1}{16}$″. Cropped at top, injuring one or two headlines. The H. Stevens (sold, December, 1855), Lenox (incorporated as Lenox Library, 1870; New York Public, 1895) copy. Bound in red morocco, by Bedford.
[718

QUARITCH. 7 ⅜ x 5 $\frac{1}{16}$″. Title mended in lower corner, date in facsimile; headlines shaved. Probably the Utterson (April, 1852, No. 1701), Corser (February, 1871, No. 413), Kershaw (July, 1877, No. 1238) copy. Bound in red levant morocco, by Riviere.
[719

TRINITY COLLEGE, CAMBRIDGE. 7 ⅛ x 5 ¼″. The Capell (presented, June, 1779) copy. Bound with other old plays. Pressmark, R. 20. 5. [720

WHITE. 6 $\frac{11}{16}$ x 4 ⅞″. Cropped top and foot, injuring some headlines and signatures; stained in first part; holes in margin of title. The Lamb (February, 1898, No. 1095) copy. Bound in calf.
[721

RICHARD III.

RICHARD III, 1597.

[Ornament] The Tragedy of | King Richard the third. | Containing, | His treacherous Plots against his brother Clarence: | the pittiefull murther of his iunocent nephewes: | his tyrannicall vsurpation: with the whole course | of his detested life, and most deserued death. | As it hath beene lately Acted by the | Right honourable the Lord Chambe-|laine his seruants. | [Ornament] | At London | ¶Printed by Valentine Sims, for Andrew Wise, | dwelling in Paules Chuch-yard, at the | Signe of the Angell. | 1597.

First edition. A-M^4; total, 48 leaves. M$_4$ blank. Type-page, 6 ⅜ x 3 ⅜".

Catchwords: A$_2$, I am; B$_i$, *La.;* C$_i$, *Glo.;* D$_i$, Ile; E$_i$, *Enter;* F$_i$, Then; G$_i$, Who; H$_i$, When; I$_i$, *King.;* K$_i$, bloudie; L$_i$, These; M$_i$, Me.

COPIES.

BODLEIAN. 6 ⅞ x 4 ¼". C$_i$, C$_2$, D$_4$, L$_4$, M$_i$, M$_2$, M$_3$, lacking and are supplied from the edition of 1598; cropped at top, injuring headlines on A$_3$, H$_i$-H$_3$, I$_i$; C$_4$, L$_i$-L$_3$, mended; B$_4$, K$_4$, L$_i$, stained; portrait of Lord Hunsdon inserted to face A$_2$. Malone's note: "This copy of the original edition of King Richard III was imperfect, when I purchased it, wanting Signat. C$_i$ and 2, D$_4$, L$_4$, M$_i$, 2 & 3. These seven leaves I have supplied from a later copy (that of 1598) and have collated with the edition of 1597. The variations are set down in the margins. It is remarkable that the name of the author does not appear on the title-page, a presumptive proof that he had not in 1597 arrived to so high reputation as he undoubtedly afterwards acquired. Mr. Penn Ashton Curzon and Mr. Kemble are possessed of copies of this original edition of this play. I know of no other except that in this volume." The Malone (presented, 1821) copy. Inlaid and bound in tree calf, "E. M." on covers, with other plays in Vol. VI of the collection. Pressmark, Malone, 37.   [722

BRITISH MUSEUM. 6 ⅞ x 5 ¹⁄₁₆". B$_i$, B$_4$, some places in inner margin made good; A$_3$ small rust hole mended; K$_2$, K$_3$ cropped at top, injuring headlines. Huth book-plate and Huth Bequest stamp. The Nixon (May, 1818, No. 649), Heber (June, 1834, No. 5463), Daniel (July, 1864, No. 1427), Huth (bequeathed, April, 1911) copy. Bound in purple morocco with "G. D." monogram on covers. Pressmark, Huth, 47.   [723

A CENSUS OF SHAKESPEARE QUARTOS

ELIZABETHAN CLUB. 7 3/4 x 5 9/16". Ci-C4, Di-D4, eight leaves in all, uncut and unsewed as originally printed; mounted on large quarto sheets. Stamp of British Museum duplicates. Exchanged with British Museum which took the perfect copy from the Huth collection and substituted this; Huth (November, 1911, No. 1192), Cochran (presented, December, 1911) copy. Bound in red levant morocco, elaborate gilt tooling. [724

FOLGER. 7 1/4 x 5". Title mended in margins; A4 mended in lower outside corner, four lines defective. The Jennens (collected, c. 1740, bequeathed, 1773, to W. P. A. Curzon, ancestor of Lord Howe), Howe (sold, December, 1907) copy. Bound in half blue morocco. [725

HUNTINGTON. 6 15/16 x 4 3/16". Cropped at top, injuring some headlines. "Collated & Perfect, J. P. K. 1798". The Kemble (sold, 1821), Devonshire (sold, January, 1914) copy. Inlaid and bound with other plays in Vol. 120. [726

RICHARD III, 1598.

The | Tragedie | of King Richard | the third. | Conteining his treacherous Plots against his | brother Clarence: the pitiful murther of his innocent | Nephewes: his tyrannicall vsurpation: with | the whole course of his detested life, and most | deserued death. | As it hath beene lately Acted by the Right honourable | the Lord Chamberlaine his seruants. | By William Shake-speare. | [Creede's device] | London | Printed by Thomas Creede, for Andrew Wise, | dwelling in Paules Church-yard, at the signe | of the Angell. 1598.

Second edition. A-M^4; total, 48 leaves. M4 blank. Type-page, 6 1/2 x 3 3/8".

Catchwords: A2, I am; Bi, *La.*; Ci, *Glo.*; Di, Ile; Ei, *Enter;* Fi, Then; Gi, Who; Hi, When; Ii, *King;* Ki, Bloudie; Li, These; Mi, Me.

COPIES.

BODLEIAN. 7 3/8 x 5 3/8". Title extended on lower margin and mended; A4 remargined front and foot: margins mended throughout, injuring some words on A3; wormhole mended in lower inner corner, Bi-Di; Heber stamp and note on fly-leaf: "July 1816, Bt. of Whites stock G. Saunders £ 5.7.6." The Heber (June, 1834, No. 5464) copy. Bound in red straight-grained morocco. Pressmark, Malone, 879. [727

BRIDGEWATER HOUSE. 7 3/8 x 5 1/8". Acquired prior to 1649 when it was catalogued by John, Second Earl of Bridgewater. Bound in green morocco, with arms of the Marquis of Stafford, by Murton. [728

BRITISH MUSEUM. 6 3/4 x 5 1/8". M2 and M3 lacking and replaced in facsimile. Cropped top and foot, injuring last line of text on verso of A2 and I2, and many headlines, signatures and catchwords. The Garrick (bequeathed, January, 1779) copy. Bound in red morocco, Garrick's arms on sides. Pressmark, C. 34. k. 47. [729

BRITISH MUSEUM. 7 3/4 x 5 1/2". Lacking title, replaced in facsimile. G2 has slight mend and small hole; I2 mended; scribble on B3. The Halliwell (sold, November 9, 1858) copy. Bound in red morocco. Pressmark, C. 34. k. 46. [730

RICHARD III

HUNTINGTON. 6 ⅞ x 4 3/16″. Badly cropped at top, injuring most of the headlines on sheets A-F. "Collated & Perfect. J. P. K. 1814". The Kemble (sold, 1821), Devonshire (sold, January, 1914) copy. Inlaid and bound in crimson levant morocco, by Birdsall. [731

HUNTINGTON. 7 7/16 x 5 1/16″. Title, A$_3$, Ci-C$_4$, D$_4$, L$_4$, M$_1$ and M$_2$ in Harris's facsimile; lower margins extended throughout, some signatures, catchwords, and last lines of text in facsimile. Locker and Church book-plates. The Jolley (June, 1844, No. 582), Halliwell (May, 1856, No. 339), Tite (June, 1874, No. 2776), Locker (sold, January, 1905), Church (sold, April, 1911) copy. Bound in red morocco, by Bedford. [732

TRINITY COLLEGE, CAMBRIDGE. 7 ¼ x 5 ¼″. M$_1$ mutilated; M$_2$ and M$_3$ from smaller copy (6 ⅞ x 3″) and mutilated. "George Lettin his book" on verso M$_1$; some collation with second folio. The Capell (presented, June, 1779) copy. Bound in brown calf, with other plays. Pressmark, R. 22. 4. [733

RICHARD III, 1602.

The | Tragedie | of King Richard | the third. | Conteining his treacherous Plots against his brother | Clarence: the pittifull murther of his innocent Ne-|phewes: his tyrannicall vsurpation: with the | whole course of his detested life, and | most deserued death. | As it hath bene lately Acted by the Right Honourable | the Lord Chamberlaine his seruants. | Newly augmented, | By William Shakespeare. | [Creede's device] | London | Printed by Thomas Creede, for Andrew Wise, dwelling | in Paules Church-yard, at the signe of the | Angell. 1602.

Third edition. A-L^4; M^2; total, 46 leaves. Type-page, 6 7/16 x 3 ⅜″.
Catchwords: A$_2$, By; B$_1$, La.; C$_1$, I can; D$_1$, 2 Ile; E$_1$, Enter; F$_1$, Ile; G$_1$, Hast.; H$_1$, Glo.; I$_1$, And; K$_1$, Qu.; L$_1$, By; M$_1$, And.

COPIES.

BRITISH MUSEUM. 6 13/16 x 5″. Small holes in K$_4$, L$_2$. The Garrick (bequeathed, January, 1779) copy. Bound in red morocco, Garrick's arms on sides. Pressmark, C. 34. k. 48. [734

HUNTINGTON. 6 ¾ x 4 ⅜″. "Collated & Perfect. D. 1827". The Bunbury (exchanged, 1823), Payne & Foss (sold, 1823), Devonshire (sold, January, 1914) copy. Inlaid and bound with other plays in Vol. 542. [735

TRINITY COLLEGE, CAMBRIDGE. 7 x 5″. Capell book-plate on verso title. The Capell (presented, June, 1779) copy. Bound in brown calf, with other plays. Pressmark, S. 30. 1. [736

RICHARD III, 1605.

The | Tragedie | of King Richard | the third. | Conteining his treacherous Plots against his brother | Clarence: the pittifull murthur of his innocent Ne-|phewes: his tyrannicall vsurpation: with the | whole course of his detested life, and | most deserued death. | As it hath bin lately Acted by the Right Honourable | the Lord Chamberlaine his seruants. | Newly augmented, | By William Shake-speare. | [Creede's device] | London, | Printed by Thomas Creede, and are to be sold by Mathew | Lawe, dwelling in Paules Church-yard, at the Signe | of the Foxe, neare S. Austins gate, 1605.

Fourth edition. A-L⁴; M², total, 46 leaves. Type-page, 6 7/16 x 3 7/16″.

Catchwords: A₂, By; Bi, La; Ci, I can; Di, 2 Ile; Ei, *Enter;* Fi, Ile; Gi, Haft.; Hi, *Glo.;* Ii, And; Ki, *Qu.;* Li, By; Mi, And.

COPIES.

BODLEIAN. 7 ¼ x 5 ¼″. A₄, D₄ extended in lower outer corner; B₃ mended and strengthened in upper margin; Bi-C₃ extended in upper outer corner; Ei, E₂, Fi, I₄-M₂ extended and strengthened in upper inner corner; wormhole mended in B₄-Di. Purchased, 1840. Bound in half calf, marbled paper sides. Pressmark, Malone, 880. [737

BRITISH MUSEUM. 7 x 5″. A few slight stains. Manuscript notes by Halliwell: "Cost me £84" and "A perfect copy of this most rare edition, which is not even noted in any bibliographical list, was unknown to all the older commentators, & first mentioned in Collier's recent edition. The only other known copy is in the Bodleian." The Halliwell (sold, November 9, 1858) copy. Bound in red morocco. Pressmark, C. 34. k. 49. [738

HUNTINGTON. 7 ½ x 5 5/16″. Title, Mi and M₂ in facsimile. Locker and Church book-plates. The Tite (June, 1874, No. 2777), Locker (sold, January, 1905), Church (sold, April, 1911) copy. Bound in red levant morocco, by Bedford. [739

PERRY. 6 ⅞ x 4 13/16″. Cropped at top, injuring some headlines; lower outer corners worn off. With signature of Admiral William Penn in five places. The Penn (c. 1670), Carrington, Sotheby (July 10, 1905, No. 1004) copy. Bound in boards, in silk case. [740

RICHARD III, 1612.

The | Tragedie | of King Richard | the third. | Containing his treacherous Plots against his brother | Clarence: the pittifull murther of his innocent Ne-|phewes: his tyrannicall vsurpation: with the | whole course of his detested life, and | most deserued death. | As it hath beene lately Acted by the Kings Maiesties | seruants. | Newly augmented, | By William Shake-speare. | [Creede's device] | London, | Printed by Thomas Creede, and are to be sold by Mathew | Lawe, dwelling in Pauls Church-yard, at the Signe | of the Foxe, neare S. Austins gate, 1612.

Fifth edition. A-L⁴; M²; total, 46 leaves. Type-page, 6 9/16 x 3 ¾″.

Catchwords: A₂, By; Bi, *La.;* Ci, I can; Di, 2. Ile; Ei, *Enter;* Fi, Ile; Gi, *Hast.;* Hi, *Glo.;* Ii, And; Ki, *Qu.;* Li, By; Mi, And.

RICHARD III

COPIES.

BODLEIAN. 7 x 4 ⅞". K3 verso, last two lines, part of text caught off by paste. Facing title is a portrait of Richard III from "Basiliologia," also an impression in red wax from a seal with note above: "This impression was taken from the seal of Richard the Third, which was dug up some years ago in Bosworth Field, and fell into the hands of the late Dr. Lort. A boar was Richard's cognizance. E. M." Note on verso title: "The title-page of the original edition of this play printed in 1597, corresponds with that at the other side to the word *death;* after which follows 'As it hath been lately acted . . . 1597'. The words *newly augmented* first appeared in the titlepage of the edition printed in 1602, which was, I believe, the copy principally followed in printing the folio. This copy has been collated with the edition of 1598, and the various readings are in the margin. From this collation it appears that the errors of *omission* in this copy (to say nothing of the other numerous faults) are no less that twenty six: a striking proof of the value of first editions, and of what I have so often stated in my edition, that omission of words (and sometimes of lines) is one of the most common errors of the press. E. M. Since the above collation was made, I have met with the edition of 1597, and collated it. The variations between the copy of 1597 and that of 1598 are set down, and are distinguished by being written in imitation of print. Since I wrote the above I have got a copy of this 1st edition. See it in Vol. vi." The Malone (presented, 1821) copy. Inlaid and bound with other plays in Vol. I. Pressmark, Malone, 32. [741

BRITISH MUSEUM. 6 ⅞ x 4 11/16". Title and some catchwords covered by inlay so that the date is gone from title. Indistinct names on title, some leaves stained. The King George III (presented, 1823) copy. Inlaid throughout and bound in half morocco. Pressmark, C. 12. h. 10. [742

CRICHTON STUART. L. Theobald's signature. The Theobald, Steevens, Bute copy. [743

EDINBURGH UNIVERSITY. 6 15/16 x 5". Cropped at foot, cutting off last line of title and some signatures, catchwords and last lines of text; with A2, A3, Bi, Ei, G2, H4, I4, Ki, K4, in duplicate at end. Halliwell's note on fly-leaf: "Perfect but some of the lower lines are cut into. The 9 leaves at the end are from an imperfect copy of the same edition, here inserted to show variations. Malone's copy is also cut into. There is no copy of it in the British Museum, the statements of Bohn & Hazlitt to the contrary being erroneous. It is in fact of great rarity." Halliwell is wrong in this note and Bohn and Hazlitt were right, the British Museum possessed at that time and still owns the King George III copy. The duplicate leaves at the end were taken from the copy now in the possession of Mr. Furness. The Halliwell (presented, 1872) copy. Bound in brown levant morocco, by Bedford. [744

FURNESS. 7 x 5 ⅛". Fragment only, lacking title, A2-A4, Bi, Ei, G2, H4, I2-M2. Presentation inscription from J. O. Halliwell to H. H. Furness. The Halliwell (presented, December, 1871) copy. Bound in half calf. [745

HUNTINGTON. 7 ⅛ x 4 13/16". Ai-A4, and M2 are supplied from a shorter copy. Locker and Church book-plates. The Locker (sold, January, 1905), Church (sold, April, 1911) copy. Bound in green levant morocco, by De Coverly. [746

NEW YORK PUBLIC. 6 ¾ x 4 13/16". Last line of title including date cut off; cropped at foot, injuring last line of M2 and signatures throughout. "George Steevens" on title; Roxburghe arms on verso title. The Steevens (May, 1800, No.

1295), Roxburghe (May, 1812, No. 3845), H. Stevens (sold, December, 1855), Lenox (incorporated as Lenox Library, 1870; New York Public, 1895) copy. Bound in red morocco, by Bedford. [747

NEW YORK PUBLIC. 7 1/16 x 5 1/8". M2 in facsimile. With note on front flyleaf: "Collated perfect. A. Dyce. (the last leaf reprinted). Boswell (Malone's Shakespeare) says it is uncertain whether the date of this edition is -12 or -13; in the present copy it is distinctly the former". Probably the Sotheby (April, 1826, No. 96) copy. The H. Stevens (sold, December, 1855), Lenox (incorporated as Lenox Library, 1870; New York Public, 1895) copy. Bound in red straight-grained morocco. [747*

TRINITY COLLEGE, CAMBRIDGE. 7 1/4 x 5 1/4". Ii-M4 supplied from shorter copy (7 1/8"). Old scribbling on title. The Capell (presented, June, 1779) copy. Bound in brown calf, with other plays. Pressmark, R. 19. 3. [748

WHITE. 6 3/4 x 4 7/8". Cropped top and foot, injuring some headlines and signatures; last line of title including date cut off. The Pope (sold, June, 1895), Hoe (sold through Dodd, Mead & Co., April, 1896) copy. Bound in red levant morocco. [749

RICHARD III, 1622.

The | Tragedie | of | King Richard | The Third. | Contayning his treacherous Plots against | his brother Clarence: The pittifull murder of his innocent | Nephewes: his tyrannicall Vsurpation: with the whole | course of his detested life, and most | deserued death. | As it hath been lately Acted by the Kings Maiesties | Seruants. | Newly augmented. | By William Shakespeare. | [Ornament] | London, | Printed by Thomas Purfoot, and are to be sold by Mathew Law, dwelling | in Pauls Church-yard, at the Signe of the Foxe, neere | S. Austines gate. 1622.

Sixth edition. A-L⁴; M²; total, 46 leaves. Type-page, 6 9/16 x 3 1/2".

Catchwords: A2, By; Bi, *La.;* Ci, I can; Di, 2. Ile; Ei, *Enter;* Fi, Ile; Gi, *Hast.;* Hi, Or; Ii, *King.;* Ki, *Qu.;* Li, But; Mi, In.

COPIES.

BODLEIAN. 7 3/16 x 5 5/16". Cropped at top, cutting off headlines on Mi and M2; ink stains on margins of I4 verso and Ki recto; wormhole in K2-L4. Probably the Jolley (June, 1844, No. 583) copy. Purchased, 1844. Bound in half calf. Pressmark, Malone, 922. [750

BRITISH MUSEUM. 6 15/16 x 4 5/8". Cropped at foot of title, last line cut off; some leaves a little soiled. The Garrick (bequeathed, January, 1779) copy. Bound in red morocco, Garrick's arms on back. Pressmark, C. 34. k. 51. [751

BRITISH MUSEUM. 7 x 4 3/4". Badly cropped, injuring headlines or signatures and catchwords on most leaves; last two lines of imprint cut off from title. The King George III (presented, 1823) copy. Bound in half morocco. Pressmark, C. 12. g. 14. [752

RICHARD III

BRITISH MUSEUM. 6 ¾ x 4 ¾". L1-M2 lacking; cropped at top, injuring "THE" on title and most headlines; some stains. Manuscript note by Halliwell pasted in fly-leaf facing title: "The only curiosity of this imperfect copy of the 1622 edition of Richard the third arises from the circumstance of the titlepage being perfect, the imprint being almost invariably cut off. Indeed so rare is it to meet with a copy with the date of 1622, (that) Mr. Collier, in his ed. of Shakespeare, declares that 'the existence of a copy of that date is more than doubtful.' There are, I believe, two copies in the British Museum, the imprints of both of which are imperfect." The Halliwell (sold, November 9, 1858) copy. Bound in red morocco. Pressmark, C. 34. k. 50. [753

HUNTINGTON. 7 5/16 x 5 3/16". Leaves stabbed on inner margins throughout. Ives and Church book-plates. The Perkins (July, 1889, No. 1708), Ives (March, 1891, No. 892), Church (sold, April, 1911) copy. Bound in maroon morocco, with Perkins's arms on covers. [754

TRINITY COLLEGE, CAMBRIDGE. 7 ⅛ x 5". Title a little cropped at top and worn. The Capell (presented, June, 1779) copy. Bound in brown calf, with other plays. Pressmark, S. 34. 2. [755

RICHARD III, 1629.

The | Tragedie | of | King Richard | the Third. | Contayning his trecherous Plots, against | his brother Clarence: The pittifull murther of his ino- | cent Nepthewes: his tiranous vsurpation: with the whole | course of his detested life, and most | deserued death. | As it hath beene lately Acted by the Kings Maiesties | Sernauts [sic]. | Newly agmented [sic] | By William Shake-speare. | [Ornament] | London. | Printed by Iohn Norton, and are to be sold by Mathew Law, | dwelling in Pauls Church-yard, at the Signe of the | Foxe, neere St. Austines gate, | 1629.

Seventh edition. A-L^4; M^2; total, 46 leaves. Type-page, 6 7/16 x 3 ⅜".
Catchwords: A2, By; Bi, *La.;* Ci, I can; Di, 2.Ile; Ei, *Enter;* Fi, Ile; Gi, *Hast.;* Hi, Or; Ii, *King.;* Ki, *Qu.;* Li, But; Mi, In.

COPIES.

BODLEIAN. 6 11/16 x 4 11/16". Cropped top and foot, injuring "THE" on title and some headlines, signatures and catchwords; stabbed on inner margins. "purchased 1827" on title. Purchased, 1827. Bound in boards, leather back. Pressmark, Malone, 767. [756

BRITISH MUSEUM. 7 ¼ x 5 ¼". Lower corners of sheet A and M2 extended; top corners throughout extended; margins of M2 mended. "Richard Warner, 1748" on title; scribbles on several leaves. The Garrick (bequeathed, 1779) copy. Bound in red morocco, Garrick's arms on back. Pressmark, C. 34. k. 52. [757

CRICHTON STUART. [758

DODD. 7 ⅛ x 5 ⅜". Stabbed throughout on inner margins. Signature K is on thick paper. Probably the Sotheby (May 31, 1907, No. 477) copy. Bound in green levant morocco, by Riviere. [759

DYCE COLLECTION. 7 3/8 x 5 1/4". Title mended in lower inner margins; many pages soiled. "C. P. A. Dyce". The Dyce (bequeathed, 1869) copy. Bound in calf. [760

EDINBURGH UNIVERSITY. 6 3/4 x 4 11/16". L3-M2 in facsimile; title extended in upper margin; cropped top and foot, injuring signatures, headlines and catchwords. With duplicate page, verso of I2, pasted in back. The Halliwell (presented, 1872) copy. Bound in green levant morocco, by Bedford. [761

FOLGER. 7 1/8 x 5". Two margins mended; slightly stained. The Jennens (collected, c. 1740, bequeathed, 1773, to W. P. A. Curzon, ancestor of Lord Howe), Howe (sold, December, 1907) copy. Bound in half blue morocco. [762

FOLGER. From the library of a German noble whose ancestor bought plays in England 150 years ago. The Sotheby (July 13, 1909, No. 323) copy. Bound with Henry IV, 1632, and other plays. [763

FOLGER. Title, B2 and B3 in facsimile. [764

HUNTERIAN MUSEUM, GLASGOW. Size not given. Closely cropped top and bottom. Bound with works by other authors. Pressmark, Co. 3. 32. [765

NEW YORK PUBLIC. 7 1/4 x 5 5/16". Dramatis Personnae in old handwriting on verso title. The H. Stevens (sold, December, 1855), Lenox (incorporated as Lenox Library, 1870; New York Public, May, 1895) copy. Bound in red morocco, by Mackenzie. [766

TRINITY COLLEGE, CAMBRIDGE. 6 3/4 x 5". Cropped at bottom, cutting off most of signatures; stains on top margins of many leaves. The Capell (presented, June, 1779) copy. Bound in brown calf, with other old plays. Pressmark, T. 8. 5. [767

WHITE. 6 15/16 x 5". Cropped top and foot, injuring some headlines, signatures, catchwords and last lines of text. The Sotheby (July 28, 1903, No. 491) copy. Bound in maroon levant morocco, by Club Bindery for Mr. White. [768

RICHARD III, 1634.

The | Tragedie | of | King Richard | the Third. | Contayning his treacherous Plots, a-|gainst his brother Clarence: The pitifull | murder of his innocent Nephewes: his | tyranous vsurpation: with the | whole course of his detested life, | and most deserued death. | As it hath beene Acted by the Kings | Maiesties Seruants. | VVritten by William Shake-speare. | [Ornament] | London, | Printed by Iohn Norton. 1634.

Eighth edition. A-L⁴; M²; total, 42 leaves. A2 and K3 are wrongly marked A3 and C2. Type-page, 6 9/16 x 3 5/8".

Catchwords: A3 (should be A2), By; Bi, *Lady;* Ci, I can; Di, 2 ile; Ei, *Enter;* Fi, Ile; Gi, Hast.; Hi, Or; Ii, *Kin;* Ki, *Qu.;* Li, But; Mi, In.

COPIES.

BIRMINGHAM. 6 3/4 x 5 1/16". Di-D4 extended on outer blank margins; some headlines cropped. Notes on margins throughout. The R. Smith (sold, March, 1884) copy. Bound in green levant morocco, by Hammond. [769

RICHARD III

BODLEIAN. 7 ¼ x 5 5⁄16″. Title mended in lower margin; A2 torn, injuring a few letters; many headlines cropped. Purchased, 1830. Bound in calf. Pressmark, Malone, 881. [770

BOSTON PUBLIC. 7 ¼ x 5 3⁄16″. The Barton (sold, May, 1873) copy. Bound in half red morocco. [771

BOSTON PUBLIC. 7 ⅛ x 5 ¼″. "Richard Exirey, Exon. Collegge" on title. The Barton (sold, May, 1873) copy. Bound in blue morocco, by Bedford. [772

BRITISH MUSEUM. 7 5⁄16 x 5 ⅜″. Headlines of K4 deeply cropped. The Halliwell (sold, November 9, 1858) copy. Bound in green morocco, by Bedford. Pressmark, C. 34. k. 53. [773

BRITISH MUSEUM. 7 1⁄16 x 5 1⁄16″. E2 lacking; cropped at top, injuring several headlines. "David (?) Mather, 1652" on C3 recto. The Garrick (bequeathed, 1779) copy. Bound in red morocco, Garrick's arms on back. Pressmark, C. 34. k. 54. [774

CRICHTON STUART. [775

DYCE COLLECTION. 7 ¼ x 5″. K4, lower corner mended; title brown. "C. P. A. Dyce". The Dyce (bequeathed, 1869) copy. Bound in calf. [776

EDINBURGH UNIVERSITY. 6 ⅞ x 4 ⅞″. Cropped at top, injuring some headlines; B1, B4 extended on upper margin, lacking headlines. The Halliwell (presented, 1872) copy. Bound in red levant morocco, by Pratt. [777

ETON COLLEGE. 7 1⁄16 x 5 1⁄16″. Cropped at top, injuring some headlines. The Storer (bequeathed, 1799) copy. Bound with Merchant of Venice, 1652, and other plays in Vol. III. [778

FOLGER. 7 x 5″. Title and some leaves stained; signature on L3 and headline on L4 cut into; K2 mended. The Jennens (collected, c. 1740, bequeathed, 1773, to W. P. A. Curzon, ancestor of Lord Howe), Howe (sold, December, 1907) copy. Bound in half blue morocco. [779

FOLGER. Fine copy. Bound in red morocco, by Bedford. [780

HUNTINGTON. 7 ¼ x 4 ⅞″. Some leaves resized. The Devonshire (sold, January, 1914) copy. Bound in orange morocco. [781

HUNTINGTON. 7 1⁄16 x 4 ⅞″. M2 has part of text in facsimile; stabbed throughout and mended on inner margins. Church book-plate. The Pope (sold, October, 1895), Church (sold, April, 1911) copy. Bound in red levant morocco, by Bedford. [782

NEW YORK PUBLIC. 6 ¾ x 4 ¾″. Cropped top and foot, injuring some headlines and signatures. The H. Stevens (sold, December, 1855), Lenox (incorporated as Lenox Library, 1870; New York Public, May, 1895) copy. Bound in green morocco, by Bedford. [783

TRINITY COLLEGE, CAMBRIDGE. 7 ¼ x 5 ¼″. Title lacking; M2 somewhat torn. Scribbles on B1, recto. The Capell (presented, June, 1779) copy. Bound in brown calf, with other old plays. Pressmark, R. 21. 4. [784

WHITE. 7 5⁄16 x 5 ½″. The Quaritch (sold, June, 1892) copy. Bound in brown levant morocco, by Hayday. [785

ROMEO AND JULIET.

ROMEO AND JULIET, 1597.

An | Excellent | conceited Tragedie | of | Romeo and Iuliet. | As it hath been often (with great applause) | plaid publiquely, by the right Ho-| nourable the L. of Hunsdon | his Seruants. | [Danter's device] | London, | Printed by Iohn Danter. | 1597.

First edition. A-K^4; total, 40 leaves. Title, A2. Type-page, 6 ⅜ x 3½″.

Catchwords: Bi, *Mount;* Ci, *Rom:*Nay; Di, That; Ei, fights; Fi, *Mer.;* Gi, *Rom.;* Hi, I; Ii, choose; Ki, Heape.

COPIES.

BODLEIAN. 7 ⅛ x 4 ⅜″. Corner of margin off Di, D2, H4, Mi; F3 and Gi stained. With autograph of George, Lord Hunsdon, inserted facing L2; and note by Malone saying that this is the Lord Hunsdon mentioned in the title-page; above Prologue "Edward Holbeck His booke" and other writing. The copy had originally certain leaves missing and supplied from Capell's edition of 1766, but these defects were subsequently made good, and a bill of C. Lewis to Mr. Bandinel for inlaying and inserting leaves is pasted in front of volume. A leaf marked "A" is bound between Romeo, 1597, and Romeo, 1599, in this volume with a note in Mr. Madan's handwriting: "This leaf was found loose in front of title of Richard III in this volume but it can hardly belong to that play, 1833". The Malone (presented, 1821) copy. Bound in tree calf, with "E. M." on covers. Pressmark, Malone, 37. [786

BRITISH MUSEUM. 6 ⅝ x 4 ¾″. Title mended in lower portion; cropped at foot, injuring some signatures and catchwords; B2 extended on outer margin; B3 extended, a few words in facsimile; Ci, mended and extended; C4, Di, F3, H4, I2, I3, mended, injuring some letters; I4 mended in margins; Ki-K4 mended in lower margins. The Garrick (bequeathed, January, 1779) copy. Bound in red morocco, Garrick's arms on sides. Pressmark, C. 34. k. 55. [787

HUNTINGTON. 6 ¾ x 4 5/16″. Cropped at top, injuring headlines on G4 verso to H4 verso; "Collated & Perfect, J. P. K. 1809". Scribbling on some leaves. The Stace (sold), Kemble (sold, 1821), Devonshire (sold, January, 1914) copy. Inlaid and bound in crimson levant morocco, by Birdsall. [788

A CENSUS OF SHAKESPEARE QUARTOS

TRINITY COLLEGE, CAMBRIDGE. 7 1/8 x 5 1/8". Very tender condition throughout, C_3-E_1 mutilated at foot; C_2-D_3 mended with transparent paper; E_3 mutilated at side; G_1-I_2 wormed at lower inner margin so that paper is eaten away. "J. Payne" on title. The Payne, Capell (presented, June, 1779) copy. Bound in brown calf, with other old plays. Pressmark, R. 20. 2. [789

ROMEO AND JULIET, 1599.

The | Most Ex-|cellent and lamentable | Tragedie, of Romeo | and Iuliet. | Newly corrected, augmented, and | amended: | As it hath bene sundry times publiquely acted, by the | right Honourable the Lord Chamberlaine | his Seruants. | [Creede's device] | London | Printed by Thomas Creede, for Cuthbert Burby, and are to | be sold at his shop neare the Exchange. | 1599.

Second edition. A-L^4; M^2; total, 46 leaves. Type-page, 6 1/4 x 3 5/8".

Catchwords: A_3, *Grego*.The; B_1, *Rom*. Not; C_1, Being; D_1, Young; E_1, Thats; F_1, My; G_1, Towards; H_1, Digressing; I_1, But; K_1, And; L_1, *Law*. Who; M_1, Came.

COPIES.

BODLEIAN. 6 11/16 x 4 3/16". E_2, line 14 from foot has hole; E_3 and E_4 mended; L_3 verso cropped, cutting off first letter of most of last 21 lines. The Malone (presented, 1821) copy. Inlaid and bound with other plays in Vol. VI. Pressmark, Malone, 37. [790

BRIDGEWATER HOUSE. 6 7/8 x 4 3/4". Acquired prior to 1649 when it was catalogued by John, Second Earl of Bridgewater. Bound in morocco, with arms of the Marquis of Stafford, by Murton. [791

BRITISH MUSEUM. 6 5/8 x 4 3/4". F_1-G_2, large wormhole mended; G_3-H_1, small wormhole; L_3 signature and catchword cropped; stained. "Agst 23, 1621" after "FINIS" on M_2 recto. The King George III (presented, 1823) copy. Bound in half morocco. Pressmark, C. 12. g. 18. [792

EDINBURGH UNIVERSITY. 7 1/16 x 4 13/16". M_2 mended in margin. With "Wil. Sha." on title probably in Drummond's hand; some numbers and initials in old hand on title. The Drummond (presented, 1627) copy. Bound in green morocco. [793

ELIZABETHAN CLUB. 6 5/8 x 4 13/16". C_2 mended in lower margin. "George Steevens" on title and "G. Steevens" on verso title; Roxburghe arms on title; "Elizabeth Rotton Her Lot is to b neat" on verso H_3; Huth book-plate; old manuscript notes on some leaves. The Steevens (May, 1800, No. 1299), Roxburghe (May, 1812, No. 3860), White Knights (June, 1819, No. 3957), Daniel (July, 1864, No. 1430), Huth (November, 1911, No. 1193), Cochran (presented, December, 1911) copy. Bound in red straight-grained morocco, with George Daniel's monogram on front cover. [794

FOLGER. F_1-F_4 lacking; title backed and mended; M_2 mended and backed, injuring headline and next two lines; stained. The Jennens (collected, c. 1740, bequeathed, 1773, to W. P. A. Curzon, ancestor of Lord Howe), Howe (sold, December, 1907) copy. Bound in half blue morocco. [795

ROMEO AND JULIET

FOLGER. The Gott (sold through Sotheran, 1907) copy. Bound in red morocco, by Lewis. [796

FOLGER. The Warwick copy. [797

HUNTINGTON. 6 $\frac{13}{16}$ x 4 $\frac{3}{8}$". "Collated & Perfect. J. P. K. 1798." The Kemble (sold, 1821), Devonshire (sold, January, 1914) copy. Inlaid and bound with other plays in Vol. 305. [798

HUNTINGTON. 7 $\frac{9}{16}$ x 5 $\frac{5}{8}$". Title, A2-B2 and part of E1 in facsimile. Locker and Church book-plates. The Tite (June, 1874, No. 2778), Locker (sold, January, 1905), Church (sold, April, 1911) copy. Bound in red levant morocco, by Bedford. [799

WHITE. 6 $\frac{3}{4}$ x 4 $\frac{5}{8}$". Title rebacked and mended; some headlines cropped. The Perkins (July, 1889, No. 1691) copy. Bound in red morocco, Perkins's arms on covers. [800

ROMEO AND JULIET, 1609.

The | Most Ex-|cellent and | Lamentable Tragedie, of | Romeo and Juliet. | As it hath beene sundrie times publiquely Acted, | by the Kings Maiesties Seruants | at the Globe. | Newly corrected, augmented, and | amended: | [Ornament] | London | Printed for Iohn Smethwick, and are to be sold | at his Shop in Saint Dunstanes Church-yard, | in Fleetestreete vnder the Dyall. | 1609.

Third edition. A-L^4; M^2; total, 46 leaves. Type-page, 6 $\frac{1}{8}$ x 3 $\frac{3}{4}$".

Catchwords: A3, *Grego*. The; B1, *Rom*. Not; C1, Being; D1, Young; E1, Thats; F1, My; G1, Towards; H1, Digressing; I1, I am; K1, And; L1, *Law*. Who; M1, Came.

COPIES.

BODLEIAN. 6 $\frac{7}{8}$ x 4 $\frac{11}{16}$". M2 lacking and replaced in manuscript facsimile; M1 extended in both corners; B4 extended in lower corner, injuring a few letters. Heber stamp and note on fly-leaf: "A copy of this 3rd ed. bd. in morocco (probably the same) sold at Ld. Thorlo's Auction by Christie, April 1804 for 4-18-0. It is very rare. See Steevens Cat." The [Thorlo] Christie (April, 1804, No. 94), Heber (June, 1834, No. 5468) copy. Bound in maroon straight-grained morocco, blind tooled, by Riley. Pressmark, Malone, 884. [801

BRITISH MUSEUM. 6 $\frac{15}{16}$ x 5". Small stains on several leaves; three small holes in outer margin A2; soiled. Notes by Halliwell: "For this most rare edition (most rare in perfect state) I gave Mr. Daniel in exchange The History of Tom Thumb, 1625 bought by me at Utterson's sale for £6.2.6, and a volume of curious Penny Romances, no. 1516 at Utterson's sale, which cost me (with commission) £33.10. The present volume cost me altogether therefore £ 39. 12.6.", "Another perfect copy of this edition has since been discovered & sold at Sotheby's for £ 86." The Daniel (exchanged), Halliwell (sold, November 9, 1858) copy. Bound in limp vellum. Pressmark, C. 34. k. 57. [802

FOLGER. 7 $\frac{3}{4}$ x 5 $\frac{1}{4}$". The Cope (March 4, 1913, No. 184) copy. Bound in blue morocco. [803

A CENSUS OF SHAKESPEARE QUARTOS

HUNTINGTON. 6 5/16 x 5". Locker and Church book-plates. The [Halliwell] Sotheby (June, 1858, No. 323), Tite (June, 1874, No. 2779), Locker (sold, January, 1905), Church (sold, April, 1911) copy. Bound in red morocco, by Bedford. [804

HUNTINGTON. 6 7/8 x 4 7/8". Cropped at top, injuring headlines on several pages; two holes in title-page. Signature and note of George Steevens: "This Play has been collated with the copies in 1599 & 1637, the few various readings from the former are on the white margins. This copy seems to have been printed from that in 1599 as there is little variation & that too merely accidental. G. S."; "Collated & Perfect. J. P. K. 1814"; Roxburghe arms on title. The 1637 variants are on the book's own margins. The Steevens (May, 1800, No. 1300), Roxburghe (May, 1812, No. 3861), Kemble (sold, 1821), Devonshire (sold, January, 1914) copy. Inlaid and bound in crimson levant morocco, by Birdsall. [805

TRINITY COLLEGE, CAMBRIDGE. 6 3/4 x 5". Li torn in outer margin; some leaves stained at top. The Capell (presented, June, 1779) copy. Bound in brown calf, with other old plays. Pressmark, T. 8. 2. [806

ROMEO AND JULIET, n. d.

The Most | Excellent | And Lamentable Tragedie, | of Romeo and | Iuliet. | As it hath beene sundrie times publikely Acted, | by the Kings Maiesties Seruants | at the Globe. | Newly Corrected, augmented, and amended. | [Smethwicke's device] | London, | Printed for Iohn Smethwicke, and are to bee sold at his Shop in | Saint Dunstanes Church-yard, in Fleetestreete | vnder the Dyall.

Fourth edition, earlier title. A-L^4; total, 44 leaves. Type-page, 6 1/4 x 3 3/4".
Catchwords: A2, *Samp;* Bi, *Enter;* Ci, *Ben;* Di, In; Ei, the; Fi, *Ti.;* Gi, There; Hi, *RO.;* Ii, And; Ki, O; Li, *Balt.*

*Copies of this play differ in title only, one form having the name inserted, the other being anonymous; it is probable that the anonymous one is earlier.

COPIES.

BRITISH MUSEUM. 6 3/4 x 4 3/4". Small hole in Fi; cropped at top, injuring many headlines; badly soiled throughout. "Richard Warner, 1752" on title; "Sarah Downes her book 1709" on verso title; ". . . Downes 1698 her book" at end. The Garrick (bequeathed, January, 1779) copy. Bound in red morocco, with Garrick's arms on sides, by Tuckett for the Museum. Pressmark, C. 34. k. 56. [807

EDINBURGH UNIVERSITY. 7 x 4 3/4". Title, C4, L2-L4 in facsimile. Halliwell's note on fly-leaf: "The Title & a few leaves are in Facsimile. A copy sold at Sotheby's, 31 March, 1856, for £23." The Halliwell (presented, 1872) copy. Bound in green levant morocco, by Bedford. [808

HUNTINGTON. 7 1/4 x 5 1/8". Locker and Church book-plates. The Tite (May, 1874, No. 2780), Locker (sold, January, 1905), Church (sold, April, 1911) copy. Bound in purple morocco, elaborately tooled sides, by Tuckett. [809

ROMEO AND JULIET

ROMEO AND JULIET, n. d.

The Most | Excellent | And Lamentable Tragedie, | of Romeo and | Iuliet. | As it hath beene sundrie times publikely Acted, | by the Kings Maiesties Seruants | at the Globe. | Written by W. Shake-speare | Newly Corrected, augmented, and amended. | [Smethwicke's device] | London, | Printed for Iohn Smethwicke, and are to bee sold at his Shop in | Saint Dunstanes Church-yard, in Fleetestreete | vnder the Dyall.

Fourth edition, later title.

∗ This differs from the preceding only in the title.

COPIES.

BODLEIAN. 7 ½ x 5″. Title mended in margins; stained throughout. "Collated & perfect A. Dyce" on fly-leaf; old sale number, 690, on cover. The Dyce (sold, 1836) copy. Purchased, 1836. Bound in old stamped calf. Pressmark, Malone, 883. [810

BOSTON PUBLIC. 6 ¾ x 4 ⅞″. Cropped at foot, injuring some signatures. The Barton (sold, May, 1895) copy. Bound in green straight-grained morocco, by Lewis. [811

ELIZABETHAN CLUB. 6 15/16 x 5 ⅛″. Soiled throughout. Huth book-plate. The Huth (November, 1911, No. 1215), Cochran (presented, December, 1911) copy. Bound in red levant morocco, by Bedford. [812

FOLGER. 7 ⅛ x 5″. Title inlaid, mended and slightly defective; last leaf mounted. The Jennens (collected, c. 1740, bequeathed, 1773, to W. P. A. Curzon, ancestor of Lord Howe), Howe (sold December, 1907) copy. Bound in half blue morocco. [813

HUNTINGTON. 7 1/16 x 5 3/16″. Stabbed throughout on inner margin. Utterson, Ives, Comyn and Church book-plates. The Utterson (April, 1852, No. 1692), Sotheby (March 31, 1856, No. 258), Ives (March, 1891, No. 889), Comyn (March, 1893), Church (sold, April, 1911) copy. Bound in half blue straight-grained morocco. [814

TRINITY COLLEGE, CAMBRIDGE. 7 x 5 ⅛″. Title mutilated, lacking top four lines and part of fifth line; outer margin of last leaf mutilated and backed; prologue pasted over. The Capell (presented, June, 1779) copy. Bound in brown calf, with other plays. Pressmark, S. 37. 5. [815

WHITE. 6 ⅞ x 5 ⅛″. The Quaritch (sold, June, 1892) copy. Bound in maroon morocco, by Hayday. [816

ROMEO AND JULIET, 1637.

The Most | Excellent | And Lamentable Tragedie | of Romeo and | Juliet. | As it hath been sundry times publikely Acted | by the Kings Majesties Servants | at the Globe. | Written by W. Shake-speare. | Newly corrected, augmented, and amended. | [Smethwicke's device] | London,

A CENSUS OF SHAKESPEARE QUARTOS

Printed by R. Young for John Smethwicke, and are to be sold at | his Shop in St. Dunstans Church-yard in Fleetstreet, | under the Dyall. 1637.

Fifth edition. A-L⁴; total, 44 leaves. Type-page, 6 3/16 x 3 11/16″.

Catchwords: A2, *Samp.*; B1, *Enter;* C1, *Ben.*; D1, *Jul.*; E1, the; F1, *Tib.*; G1, There; H1, *Rom.*; I1, And; K1, O; L1, *Balt.*

COPIES.

BIRMINGHAM. 7 1/16 x 5 3/16″. F2-L4 extended in upper outer corner; I4-L3 have each a few letters in facsimile. The Sotheby (July 28, 1903, No. 496) copy. Purchased, March, 1905. Bound in red levant morocco, by Riviere. [817

BODLEIAN. 7 x 5″. Slightly browned. The Malone (presented, 1821) copy. Inlaid and bound with Love's Labors Lost, 1631, and other plays in Vol. II. Pressmark, Malone, 33. [818

BOSTON PUBLIC. 7 x 5 1/4″. The Barton (sold, May, 1873) copy. Bound in red morocco, by Lewis. [819

BRITISH MUSEUM. 7 x 4 13/16″. Title mended on inner margin; B2 top corner mended; L4 has small piece out of top margin, inner margin mended. The Garrick (bequeathed, January, 1779) copy. Bound in red morocco, Garrick's arms on sides, by Tuckett for the Museum. Pressmark, C. 34. k. 58. [820

CAMBRIDGE UNIVERSITY. 7 x 5 1/8″. Title injured, part of imprint torn away. Signature of "John Fitchett Marsh". The Marsh (May, 1882, No. 2418), Sandars (bequeathed, 1894) copy. Bound in green morocco. Pressmark, SSS. 44. 24. [821

CRICHTON STUART. The Steevens (May, 1800, No. 1301) copy. [822

EDINBURGH UNIVERSITY. 7 x 5 1/16″. Title mended on lower margin; C1 extended on inner and upper margins; I2 mended; K2, L2, L3, remargined except at inner side. The Halliwell (presented, 1872) copy. Bound in red morocco, by Bedford. [823

ELIZABETHAN CLUB. 7 15/16 x 5 9/16″. Title and last leaf soiled. Huth bookplate. The [Halliwell] Sotheby (June, 1859, No. 343), Corser (February, 1871, No. 416), Huth (November, 1911, No. 1216), Cochran (presented, December, 1911) copy. Bound in red morocco, entirely uncut, by Bedford. [824

ETON COLLEGE. 7 1/16 x 5 1/4″. L4 torn in margin. The Storer (bequeathed, 1799) copy. Interleaved and bound with Henry IV, 1639, in Vol. I. [825

FOLGER. 7 x 5″. Title mended; F4 mended, injuring nine lines; last leaf mended in margin. The Jennens (collected, c. 1740, bequeathed, 1773, to W. P. A. Curzon, ancestor of Lord Howe), Howe (sold, December, 1907) copy. Bound in half blue morocco. [826

FOLGER. The Halliwell Rarities (sold, January, 1897, No. 45), Perry (sold, March, 1907) copy. Bound in red levant morocco, by Pratt. [827

FOLGER. Several leaves mended. Probably the Sotheby (May 24, 1856, No. 352), George Smith (July, 1867, No. 2584) copy. The Kalbfleisch (sold, c. 1900) copy. Bound in red levant morocco, uncut, by Bedford. [828

FOLGER. 7 3/8 x 5 1/4″. The Sotheby (June 20, 1904, No. 630) copy. Bound in modern vellum. [829

ROMEO AND JULIET

FOLGER. The Warwick copy. [830

HUNTINGTON. 7 ¼ x 5 ½". Jonas book-plate. The [Jonas] Sotheby (March 15, 1911, No. 516) copy. Bound in white levant morocco, gilt tooling, uncut, by Riviere. [830*

MURRAY. 6 $\frac{15}{16}$ x 5 $\frac{3}{16}$". Title torn in upper margin; foxed. "J. Mitford, 1819. May 1819" and seventeen lines of note on front fly-leaf; twelve line note also by Mitford on back fly-leaf. Book-plate of John Murray. The Mitford (April, 1860, No. 3499) copy. Bound in half brown calf, marbled paper sides. [831

NEW YORK PUBLIC. 6 $\frac{15}{16}$ x 5 $\frac{1}{16}$". Lower portion of title torn away, several words lacking in imprint. The H. Stevens (sold, December, 1855), Lenox (incorporated as Lenox Library, 1870; New York Public, May, 1895) copy. Bound in green morocco, by Bedford. [832

PICKERING & CHATTO. 6 $\frac{15}{16}$ x 4 $\frac{13}{16}$". L_3 in facsimile; L_1 has a few words in facsimile; C_2 shaved on front margin. The Fitzgerald (June, 1907, No. 235) copy. Bound in green levant morocco, by Larkins. [833

SHAKSPERE SOCIETY OF PHILADELPHIA. 6 ½ x 4 ⅜". C_1, C_3, L_2-L_4 and last two lines of title lacking; C_4 mended in margins, some words lacking; cropped at foot, injuring some signatures. The Halliwell (presented, March, 1870) copy. Bound in old sprinkled calf. [834

TRINITY COLLEGE, CAMBRIDGE. 7 ⅛ x 5". The Capell (presented, June, 1779) copy. Bound in brown calf, with other plays. Pressmark, S. 34. 1. [835

WHITE. 6 ¾ x 4 ¾". Small portion of margin of title mended; C_1, L_2, L_3 extended on outer and lower margins; cropped at top, injuring some headlines. The Ellis (sold, June, 1896) copy. Bound in red levant morocco. [836

WRENN, Estate of J. H. 7 ¾ x 4 ⅞". The Sotheby (May 25, 1905, No. 640), Van Antwerp (March, 1907, No. 204) copy. Bound in crimson levant morocco, uncut at foot, by Riviere. [837

TAMING OF THE SHREW.

TAMING OF THE SHREW, 1631.

A Wittie | and Pleasant | Comedie | Called | The Taming of the Shrew. | As it was acted by his Maiesties | Seruants at the Blacke Friers | and the Globe. | Written by VVill. Shakespeare. | [Smethwicke's device] | London. | Printed by W. S. for Iohn Smethwicke, and are to be | sold at his Shop in Saint Dunstones Church-|yard vnder the Diall. | 1631.

First edition. A-I^4; total, 36 leaves. Type-page, 6 ⅝ x 3 ⅞".

Catchwords: A2, I; Bi, *Lord;* Ci, *Gru.;* Di, Talke; Ei, 'Twill; Fi, So; Gi, And; Hi, Euen; Ii, *Gre.*

COPIES.

BODLEIAN. 7 ⅜ x 5 ⅜". Front edges uncut. Bound in half calf. Pressmark, Malone, 912.   [838

BODLEIAN. 7 x 5 ⅛". Cropped at foot, date cut from title, signatures and catchwords injured throughout; E3 torn at foot. "1631" on title; old number "945" on fly. The Farmer (May, 1798, No. 7872) copy, purchased, 1842. Bound in half calf. Pressmark, Malone, 885.   [839

BOSTON PUBLIC. 7 $^{15}/_{16}$ x 5 $^{7}/_{16}$". Title extended at upper margin and washed; a few blank margins mended. The Barton (sold, May, 1873) copy. Bound in blue levant morocco, gilt tooling, many leaves uncut.   [840

BOSTON PUBLIC. 6 $^{15}/_{16}$ x 4 ¾". Lower corner of title cut, injuring parts of two words; all margins cut close; badly torn and mended. Portrait of Shakespeare inserted. "John Crump" on title. Dramatis Personnae on verso title in old handwriting. The Barton (sold, May, 1873) copy. Bound in old sprinkled calf.   [841

BRITISH MUSEUM. 7 ¼ x 5¼". Title mounted on inner margin, 1 ½". The King George III (presented, 1823) copy. Bound in half morocco. Pressmark, C. 12. g. 25.   [842

BRITISH MUSEUM. 6 ¾ x 5". Title badly mutilated, top cut off, injuring "Witttie" and all below "Written by" gone; badly cropped, injuring many catchwords and signatures; headlines on sheet E slightly cut. The Garrick (bequeathed, January, 1779) copy. Bound in red morocco, Garrick's arms on back. Pressmark, C. 34. k. 59.   [843

A CENSUS OF SHAKESPEARE QUARTOS

CAMBRIDGE UNIVERSITY. 6 ¾ x 4 11/16″. Title, H1-H4, I1, I4, lacking; title replaced in facsimile; badly cropped and washed. On fly-leaf "Saml. Sandars A. M. Trin. Coll. Cant. London, 1888". Inscription partially cut away on A2. The Sandars (bequeathed, 1894) copy. Bound in red morocco, by Bedford. Press-mark, SSS. 32. 17. [844

CRICHTON STUART. [845

EDINBURGH UNIVERSITY. 7 ⅝ x 5 3/16″. Title mended and backed; A2 extended on outer margin; A4 extended on upper margin; I2-I4 mended in outer margin; the date on the title is supplied from another genuine copy of the same edition. Note on fly-leaf by Halliwell. The Halliwell (presented, 1872) copy. Bound in green morocco, by Bedford. [846

ELIZABETHAN CLUB. 7 ¼ x 4 15/16″. I4 mended in blank margin. The Cochran (presented, December, 1911) copy. Bound in red levant morocco, by Bedford. [847

ETON COLLEGE. 7 1/16 x 5 3/16″. Title shaved at top. The Storer (bequeathed, 1779) copy. Bound in sprinkled calf, with Richard II, 1634, and other plays in Vol. IV. [848

FOLGER. Title-page slightly mended. The Halliwell Rarities (sold, January, 1897, No. 11), Perry (sold, March, 1907) copy. Bound in olive green morocco, by Bedford. [849

FOLGER. The Dodd, Mead & Co. (sold, June, 1901) copy. [850

FOLGER. The Warwick copy. [851

FOLGER. Very imperfect. The Jonas (sold, May, 1903) copy. [852

FURNESS. 7 x 4 15/16″. Title washed and has the date cut out and skillfully mended to look like an undated edition; H1-H4 remargined. The Bright (March, 1845, No. 5108), Halliwell (presented, April, 1871) copy. Bound in red levant morocco, by Bedford. [853

HUNTINGTON. 8 x 5 7/16″. Title extended and mended in margins. Church book-plate. The Pope (sold, December, 1895), Church (sold, April, 1911) copy. Bound in red levant morocco, blue levant doublures, gilt borders, some edges uncut, by Motte. [854

MORGAN. 7 ⅜ x 5 ¼″. I4 mended in outer margin. "W. Tite, 1851, Sotheby" inside cover. The Sotheby (1851), Tite (June, 1874, No. 2782), Asay (sold, December, 1881), Irwin (sold, March, 1900) copy. Bound in purple straight-grained morocco, by Clarke. [855

NEW YORK PUBLIC. 7 ⅜ x 5 3/16″. Wormhole in upper blank margin. The H. Stevens (sold, December, 1855), Lenox (incorporated as Lenox Library, 1870; New York Public, May, 1895) copy. Bound in red morocco, by Mackenzie. [856

TRINITY COLLEGE, CAMBRIDGE. 7 ⅝ x 5 ⅜″. The Capell (presented, June, 1779) copy. Bound in brown calf, with Spenser's Colin Clout, etc. Press-mark, Q. 10. 5. [857

WHITE. 6 ¾ x 4″. Cropped at top, injuring some headlines. The Perkins (July, 1889, No. 1716) copy. Inlaid and bound in red morocco, with Perkins's arms on covers. [858

TITUS ANDRONICUS.

TITUS ANDRONICUS, 1594.

The | Most La-|mentable Romaine | Tragedie of Titus Andronicus: | As it was Plaide by the Right Ho-|nourable the Earle of Darbie, Earle of Pembrooke | and Earle of Sussex their Seruants. | [Danter's device] | London, | Printed by Iohn Danter, and are | to be sold by Edward White & Thomas Millington, | at the little North doore of Paules at the | signe of the Gunne. | 1594.

First edition. A-K^4; total, 40 leaves. Ai blank; title, A2. Type-page, Catchwords: A2, ; Bi, ; Ci, ; Ei, ; Fi, ; Gi, ; Hi, ; Ii, ; Ki, .

COPIES.

FOLGER. B2 torn at foot, two letters lacking on recto and seven on verso. Belonged to Charles Robson of Stockholm, Sweden, who lived 1735-1794; acquired during the 19th century by Herr Krafft, whose son sold it through Sotheran to Mr. Folger in January, 1905. [859

TITUS ANDRONICUS, 1600.

The most lamenta-|ble Romaine Tragedie of Titus | Andronicus. | As it hath sundry times beene playde by the | Right Honourable the Earle of Pembrooke, the | Earle of Darbie, the Earle of Sussex, and the | Lorde Chamberlaine theyr | Seruants | [Ornament] | At London, | Printed by I. R. for Edward White | and are to bee solde at his shoppe, at the little | North doore of Paules, at the signe of | the Gun. 1600.

Second edition. A-K^4; total, 40 leaves. Size of type-page, 5 $13/16$ x 3 $1/2$″.
Catchwords: A2, *Marcus;* Bi, Vpright; Ci, And; Di, *Moore;* Ei, *Demet.;* Fi, *Titus;* Gi, I; Hi, But; Ii, When; Ki, And.

COPIES.

BRIDGEWATER HOUSE. 6 $15/16$ x 4 $7/8$″. Acquired prior to 1649, when it was catalogued by John, Second Earl of Bridgewater. Bound in green morocco, with arms of the Marquis of Stafford, many leaves uncut at foot, by Murton. [860

A CENSUS OF SHAKESPEARE QUARTOS

EDINBURGH UNIVERSITY. 6 7/16 x 4 1/2". C3 and C4 mended; some numbers in ink on title; few leaves stained at bottom. The Drummond (presented, 1627) copy. Bound in blue levant morocco, with arms of Edinburgh University on covers.   [861

TITUS ANDRONICUS, 1611.

The | Most Lamen-|table Tragedie | of Titus Andronicus. | As it hath sundry | times beene plaide by the Kings | Maiesties Seruants. | [Device] | London, | Printed for Eedward [sic] White, and are to be solde | at his shoppe, nere the little North dore of | Pauls, at the signe of the | Gun. 1611.

Third edition. A-K^4; total, 40 leaves. Type-page, 5 13/16 x 3 5/8".

Catchwords: A2, *Marcus;* Bi, Vpright; Ci, And; Di, *Moore;* Ei, *Demet;* Fi, *Titus;* Gi, I; Hi, But; Ii, when; Ki, And.

COPIES.

BODLEIAN. 6 1/2 x 4 9/16". Long note by Malone facing title and on back of title: "Langbaine appears to have possessed an edition of this play printed in 1594. 'This play' says he 'was first printed at London 1594 and acted by the Earls of Darby Pembroke and Essex their servants'. Doubtless he had it before him. The description of the companies by whom it was plaid is different both from the enumeration of the edition of 1600 and that at the head of A2 1611. In the year 1800 a copy of this play printed in 1600 was discovered in the Duke of Bridgewater's Library at Ashridge which has since been removed to London. I have collated the present copy with it, and the variations are set down. No other copy of the edition of 1600, except this of the D of Bs is known to exist; nor was it ever seen by any of the editors of Shakespeare before 1800. The title of the edition of 1600, which is in 4to is as follows (etc.)." The Malone (presented, 1821) copy. Inlaid and bound with other plays in Vol. V. Pressmark, Malone, 37.   [862

BOSTON PUBLIC. 6 11/16 x 4 7/8". Title in Harris's facsimile; K4 mended on inner margin. The Rodd (sold, 1842), Barton (sold, May, 1873) copy. Bound in red morocco, by Lewis.   [863

BRITISH MUSEUM. 6 7/8 x 4 7/8". Hi lacking; margins of E3, I2 mended. The King George III (presented, January, 1823) copy. Bound in half morocco. Pressmark, C. 12. g. 16.   [864

BRITISH MUSEUM. 6 13/16 x 4 13/16". Title lacking; slightly soiled throughout. The Garrick (bequeathed, January, 1779) copy. Bound in red morocco, with Garrick's arms on sides, by Tuckett, for the Museum. Pressmark, C. 34. k. 60.   [865

CRICHTON STUART.   [866

ELIZABETHAN CLUB. 6 11/16 x 4 7/8". A2 and A3 mended in blank corners. Huth book-plate. The Daniel (July, 1864, No. 1444), Huth (November, 1911, No. 1207), Cochran (presented, December, 1911) copy. Bound in green levant morocco, by Lewis.   [867

[110]

TITUS ANDRONICUS

FOLGER. 7 ½ x 5 ¼". Wormholes in a few top margins, a few letters injured. The Jennens (collected, c. 1740, bequeathed, 1773, to W. P. A. Curzon, ancestor of Lord Howe), Howe (sold, December, 1907) copy. Bound in half blue morocco. [868

FOLGER. Title in facsimile. Purchased from Dodd, Mead & Co. [869

HUNTINGTON. 6 x 3 ⅝". Cropped on all margins so that some letters are injured. "Collated & Perfect. J. P. K. 1798." "The Ms. variations in the margins of this play are from the Revd. Mr. Todd's collation with the Duke of Bridgewater's copy, 4to. 1600, which was lately found in his Grace's Library at Ashridge. J. P. K. 1803". The Kemble (sold, 1821), Devonshire (sold, January, 1914) copy. Inlaid and bound with other plays in Vol. 305. [870

HUNTINGTON. 7 ⅛ x 5 3/16". Church book-plate. The Sotheby (February 26, 1901, No. 1506), Church (sold, April, 1911) copy. Bound in red levant morocco, red levant doublures elaborately tooled, red silk end papers, by Club Bindery, 1901, for Mr. Church. [871

PERRY. 7 x 4 ¾". Manuscript notes by Mr. Locker and book-plate. The Locker (sold, January, 1905), Dodd, Mead & Co. (sold, April, 1905) copy. Bound in red levant morocco, by Bedford. [872

QUARITCH. 7 3/16 x 5 ⅛". The Cope (March, 1913, No. 186) copy. Bound in red levant morocco, by Riviere. [873

TRINITY COLLEGE, CAMBRIDGE. 7 ¼ x 5 ¼". Additional stage directions in old hand on K2, verso. The Capell (presented, June, 1779) copy. Bound in brown calf, many fore edges uncut, with other old plays. Pressmark, R. 19. 4. [874

WHITE. 7 x 5". Title much washed. The Perkins (July, 1889, No. 1704) copy. Bound in red morocco, Perkins's arms on covers. [875

TROILUS AND CRESSIDA.

TROILUS AND CRESSIDA, 1609.

The | Historie of Troylus | and Cresseida. | As it was acted by the Kings Maiesties | seruants at the Globe. | Written by William Shakespeare. | [Ornament] | London | Imprinted by G. Eld for R. Bonian and H. Walley, and | are to be sold at the spred Eagle in Paules | Church-yeard, ouer against the | great North doore. | 1609.

First edition, first issue. A-L⁴; M²; total, 46 leaves. M² blank. Type-page, 6 9/16 x 3 3/8".

Catchwords: A2, As; Bi, heires; Ci, Successe; Di, Will; Ei, melan-; Fi, *Hell.* Com-; Gi, At; Hi, *Cres.;* Ii, *Vliss.;* Ki, *Tat.;* Li, Ile; Mi, Ile.

∗ There are two issues of this year; this one has no Prologue.

COPIES.

BRITISH MUSEUM. 6 7/8 x 4 13/16". Small hole in Mi; stained. With "George Steevens" on title and Roxburghe arms. The Steevens (May, 1800, No. 1305), Roxburghe (May, 1812, No. 3846), King George III (presented, 1823) copy. Inlaid and bound in half red morocco. Pressmark, 163. i. 12. [876

ELIZABETHAN CLUB. 7 1/8 x 5". Huth book-plate. With title and prologue of second issue (2 leaves, the second marked "¶2") inserted before first title. Ai, the first title, has watermark like rest of book, ¶ and ¶2 have no watermark. The Daniel (July, 1864, No. 1439), Huth (November, 1911, No. 1199), Cochran (presented, December, 1911) copy. Bound in light brown straight-grained morocco, with George Daniel's monogram on front cover, by Lewis. [877

HUNTINGTON. 6 3/4 x 4 5/16". Cropped, injuring title and many headlines. Signature and note of Humphrey Dyson: "Written by William Shakespeare & printed amongst his workes". "Collated & Perfect. J. P. K. 1798." The Dyson, Kemble (sold, 1821), Devonshire (sold, January, 1914) copy. Inlaid and bound with other plays in Vol. 305. [878

TROILUS AND CRESSIDA, 1609.

The | Famous Historie of | Troylus and Cresseid. | Excellently expressing the beginning | of their loues, with the conceited wooing | of Pandarus

A CENSUS OF SHAKESPEARE QUARTOS

Prince of Licia. | Written by William Shakespeare. | [Ornament] | London | Imprinted by G. Eld for R. Bonian and H. Walley, and | are to be sold at the spred Eagle in Paules | Church-yeard, ouer against the | great North doore. | 1609.

First edition, second issue. ¶²; A²-A⁴; B-L⁴; M¹; total, 46 leaves. Type-page, 6 9/16 x 3 5/8″.

Catchwords: ¶2, *much;* A2, As; B1, heires; C1, Successe; D1, Will; E1, melan-; F1, *Hell.* Com-; G1, At; H1, *Cres.;* I1, *Vliss.;* K1, *Tat.;* L1, Ile; M1, Ile.

✱ The second issue with the Prologue.

COPIES.

BODLEIAN. 6 ¾ x 4 ¼″. C1-L4 slightly stained; title brown; ¶2 stained. Note by Malone facing title: "There is another copy of this play, for it appears to be the same edition, running to sig. M, of which Pope was possessed. In the title-page are the words 'As it was acted by the King's Majesty's servants at the Globe' and the word famous is omitted. For Cresseid, it has Cresseida. It was printed for the same booksellers in *the year 1609;* and so says the titlepage. Mr. Pope having thought it unnecessary to repeat the year, it has been erroneously supposed that the copy in which the play is said to have been acted at the Globe was *undated,* but that is not the fact. I have now seen the copy, which is in Mr. Kemble's possession. I do not find that there is any other authority than the misapprehension of Pope's words for supposing that there was any edition of this play printed without a date. The only difference between the copy that mentions the play's being acted & the other is in the titlepage, and in the omission of the preface in that copy which would have been inconsistent with that titlepage: for in this preface is asserted that the play had never been performed on the stage; as soon as that was found to be a false assertion the booksellers cancelled the preface and inserted the words As it was acted, etc." The Malone (presented, 1821) copy. Inlaid and bound with other plays in Vol. V. Pressmark, Malone, 36. **[879**

BRITISH MUSEUM. 6 ⅞ x 4 13/16″. Small rust holes in A2, A3, B4; G1 mended in two places. Manuscript note by Halliwell: "This beautifully clean perfect copy of the first edition of Troilus & Cressida, with the preface has never been in any sale and is perfectly genuine throughout, having been cut out by myself from a volume of tracts collected and bound at the period". The Halliwell (sold, November 9, 1858) copy. Bound in brown morocco. Pressmark, C. 34. k. 61. **[880**

DYCE COLLECTION. 7 3/16 x 5″. Title mended; D1-D3 and M1 apparently from much smaller copy and inlaid on modern paper; many leaves stained. "C. P. A. Dyce"; "Wm. Wavell (?)" on title. The Dyce (bequeathed, 1869) copy. Bound in olive morocco. **[881**

ETON COLLEGE. 7 ⅛ x 5 3/16″. M1 torn, some words in facsimile; title mended; D3 torn; stained. The Storer (bequeathed, 1799) copy. Bound with other plays in Vol. IV. **[882**

HUNTINGTON. 6 ⅝ x 4 ⅝″. Cropped at top, injuring first line of title and headlines throughout. Locker and Church book-plates. Probably the Ives (March, 1891, No. 890) copy. The Locker (sold, January, 1905), Church (sold, April, 1911) copy. Bound in red levant morocco, by Bedford. **[883**

[114]

TROILUS AND CRESSIDA

HUNTINGTON. 6⅞ x 4 13/16″. Small hole in A4 and L3. Book-plate of R. Hoe. The Pope (sold, June, 1895), Hoe (November, 1912, No. 2892) copy. Bound in red levant morocco, by Bedford. [883*

TRINITY COLLEGE, CAMBRIDGE. 6⅞ x 5″. Cropped at top, injuring many headlines; Prologue, line six, "your" corrected to "that"; five lines from end, "them" corrected to "it." The Capell (presented, June, 1779) copy. Bound in brown calf, with other plays. Pressmark, T. 7. 1. [884

WHITE. 6 11/16 x 4 ½″. Cropped at top, injuring some headlines, top line of title and some top lines of text. The Perkins (July, 1889, No. 1702) copy. Bound in red morocco, Perkins's arms on covers. [885

TROILUS AND CRESSIDA, 1609.
ISSUE UNCERTAIN.
COPY.

CRICHTON STUART. [886

UNIDENTIFIED COPIES.

The following copies have been listed in sales but without sufficient description to enable us to identify them in the hands of the present owners. It is probable that by far the greater part are included in the Census but this list is given in case copies turn up hereafter which may be traced from these records. When the name of an owner is given in brackets, that sale was anonymous and the auctioneer's name is given; where the books were sold under the owner's name, the auctioneer is omitted. Where a copy has been listed in several sales but has not been traced to its present owner, the earlier records are given under the latest known date.

HAMLET, 1611.

	No.
Christie, Apr. 25, 1804. To Street.	95
Rhodes, Apr. 1825.	2098
Jadis, Mar. 1828. To Nichol.	168
[Halliwell], Sotheby, June, 1858. Morocco, by Bedford. To Thomson.	315
[Cope, Sir Anthony], Sotheby, Mar. 4, 1913. Morocco. Holes in D4 and M3. To Sabin.	185

HAMLET, n. d.

Pearson, Apr. 1788. To Tonson.	3950
Bindley, Feb. 1819. To Lepard.	2046
Sotheby, May 24, 1856. N1 lacking; uncut. To Lilly.	351
[Halliwell], Sotheby, June, 1858. Morocco, uncut, by Bedford. To Thomson.	314
Perkins, July, 1889. Few headlines cut into. Red morocco.	1697
Sotheby, July 13, 1909. Bound with other pamphlets, old calf; 3 leaves shaved. From library of German nobleman whose ancestor bought plays in England 150 years ago. To Tregaskis.	322
Sotheby, Dec. 1, 1910. Unbound, few headlines cut into. To Desborough.	134

HAMLET, 1637.

Farmer, May, 1798. To Egerton.	7871
Brand, May, 1807.	6449
Malone, Nov. 1818.	2532

A CENSUS OF SHAKESPEARE QUARTOS

Rhodes, Apr. 1825.	2099
[Inglis], Sotheby, Apr. 12, 1826. To Harding.	108
Heber, June, 1834.	5471
Jolley, June, 1844. To Thorpe.	607
[Halliwell], Sotheby, May, 1856. Morocco. To Lilly.	335
[Halliwell], Sotheby, June, 1859. Lacking title.	345
Marsh, May, 1882. Half calf.	2405
[Simes], Sotheby, July, 1886. Morocco, several leaves uncut.	1534
Sotheby, June 16, 1910. Some leaves defective, title and some margins mended. Morocco. To Pickering.	108

HAMLET, 1676.

Reid, Nov. 2, 1807. To Thomas.	8417
Bindley, Feb. 1819. To Triphook.	2049
Pickering, Aug. 7, 1854. (With others.)	3131
Harrison of Samlesbury, Jan. 1881.	919
Harrison of Samlesbury, Jan. 1881. Half morocco, with manuscript notes.	920
Marsh, May, 1882. Half calf. With other plays.	2421
Cosens, Nov. 1890. Half morocco, with other title added.	4074
Sotheby, June, 1892. Half bound. To Pickering.	802
Lamb, Edinburgh, Feb. 1898. Boards. To Grant.	1102
[Constable], Sotheby, Nov. 1899. With other plays. To Pickering.	593
Hodgson, Nov. 29, 1906. Calf, with other plays. To Tregaskis.	97
Sotheby, Dec. 14, 1906. Half morocco. To Hozier.	396
Humphries, May 27, 1913. Morocco, by Broca. To Young.	127

HAMLET, 1683.

Rhodes, Apr. 1825.	2101
Cosens, Nov. 1890. With manuscript notes. Half morocco.	4073
Young, Dec. 1895. To Sotheran.	828
[Mann], Anderson, Apr. 1907. Margins of last 4 leaves strengthened. Morocco.	1219
[Jonas], Sotheby, Mar. 15, 1911. Half calf. To Warren.	523
[Adler], Sotheby, June 20, 1912. Margin of last leaf mended. Half morocco. (Sotheby, Mar. 21, 1905, No. 261.) To Goss.	315

HAMLET, 1695.

Jolley, June, 1844. To Vaughan.	628
Jolley, June, 1844. To Vaughan.	629
Sotheby, Apr. 12, 1864. Red morocco. To Smith.	658
Cosens, Nov. 1890. End leaves slightly defective. Half morocco.	4073
Cosens, Nov. 1890. Margin of title and few leaves mended.	4073
[Jonas], Sotheby, Mar. 15, 1911. Half morocco. (Sotheby, July, 1889, No. 898.) To Warren.	524

HAMLET, 1703.

Burton, Oct. 8, 1860.	4660
Daniel, July, 1864. To Lilly.	1442
Sotheby, Mar. 14, 1870. To Trimmins.	568*

UNIDENTIFIED COPIES

Harrison of Samlesbury, Jan. 1881. Half morocco.	921
Marshall, July, 1890. Title backed. Half morocco.	1174
Cosens, Nov. 1890. Half morocco.	4073
Bangs, Jan. 15, 1900. Half leather, uncut.	443
Hodgson, Nov. 6, 1901. Some pages mended. Old calf. To Quaritch.	177
Sotheby, June 20, 1904. Unbound. To J. Paul.	435
Sotheby, Feb. 23, 1905. "Barnardo." To Denby.	154
Sotheby, June 27, 1906. "Barnardo." To Parr.	362
Sotheby, Dec. 19, 1910. "Barnardo." To Ripley.	144
[Jonas], Sotheby, Mar. 17, 1911. Half morocco. (Halliwell, July, 1889, No. 898.)	525
[Jonas], Sotheby, Mar. 17, 1911. Lacking title and next leaf.	525

HENRY IV, 1599.

White Knights, June, 1819. To Jervis.	3955
White Knights, June, 1819.	3956
Bright, Mar. 1845. Lacks last 4 leaves. To Pickering.	5101
Utterson, Apr. 1852. Title mended, some leaves cut close. Green morocco. To Walker.	1685
Sotheby, 1856. Title mended, a few headlines cropped. Green morocco. Probably Utterson copy.	254
Daniel, July, 1864. Half morocco. To Stevens. (Sold to Griswold.)	1429
McKee, Apr. 1901. Lacks title, corners of 5 leaves mended. Red morocco, by J. B. Brechin.	2608

HENRY IV, 1608.

Tyssen, Dec. 1801.	2284
Rhodes, Apr. 1825.	2086

HENRY IV, 1613.

[Inglis], Sotheby, Apr. 12, 1826. To Rodd.	98
Jadis, Mar. 1828. Olive morocco. To Thorpe.	164
Heber, June, 1834.	5457

HENRY IV, 1622.

Rhodes, Apr. 1825.	2087

HENRY IV, 1632.

Farmer, May, 1798. To Forster.	7876
[Halliwell], Sotheby, May, 1856. Morocco. To Stevens.	341
[Halliwell], Sotheby, May, 1857. Morocco, by Bedford. To Morrison.	865

HENRY IV, 1639.

Pearson, Apr. 1788.	3955
Farmer, May, 1798. To Forster.	7878
Christie, Apr. 25, 1804. To Street.	88
Bindley, Feb. 1819. To Triphook.	2048

A CENSUS OF SHAKESPEARE QUARTOS

White Knights, June, 1819. To Rodd.	3956
Rhodes, Apr. 1825.	2088
Jolley, June, 1844. To Thorpe.	593
[Alvanley, Lord], Sotheby, Feb. 15, 1858. (With others not Shakespeare, one lot.) To Burrestead.	1543
Mitford, Apr. 1860.	3500
Sotheby, 1865. Morocco, by Bedford. To Burrestead.	956
Marsh, 1882. Citron morocco, few headlines cut. Steevens copy, with autograph. To Pearson.	2406
Mackenzie, Mar. 1889. Lacks portion of last leaf. Half morocco.	1876
Sotheby, July 18, 1900. Lacks E2. Old MS. notes, unbound. To Pickering.	1208
Anderson, May 28, 1906. Lacks title. Morocco, margins of 5 leaves mended.	750

HENRY IV, 1700.

Jolley, June, 1844. To Rodd.	594
[Halliwell], Sotheby, June, 1859.	270
Burton, Oct. 8, 1860. Half morocco.	4618
Sotheby, Apr. 12, 1864. To Thompson.	661
[Smith], Sotheby, July, 1867. To Pickering.	2585
Harrison of Samlesbury, Jan. 1881. Half morocco.	922
[Halliwell], Sotheby, July, 1889. Half morocco, by Bedford.	901
Sotheby, Feb. 1906. Unbound. To Maggs.	966

HENRY IV, PART 2, 1600.

Tyssen, Dec. 1801. With "11 December 1610. price v d." in contemporary hand.	2285
Roxburghe, May, 1812.	3835
Utterson, Apr. 1852. 2 leaves in facsimile. Green morocco, gilt edges. To Halliwell.	1687
Sotheby, 1871. Green morocco. 2 leaves in facsimile. (Probably Utterson copy.) To Ellis.	258

HENRY V, 1608 [1619].

Beauclerk, Apr. 1781.	4404
Farmer, May, 1798. To Barker.	7859
Ireland, May, 1801. To Barker.	474
Tyssen, Dec. 1801.	2279
[Grafton], Evans, June, 1815.	705
Bindley, Feb. 1819. To Triphook.	2047
Rhodes, Apr. 1825.	2091
[Inglis], Sotheby, Apr. 12, 1826. To Rodd.	93
Dent, Apr. 1827. To Thorpe.	1031
Heber, June, 1834.	5462
Heber, Dec. 1834. Morocco.	2020
Jolley, June, 1844. To Pickering.	603
Holgate, June, 1846. Red morocco.	825
Puttick, Apr. 16, 1849. Calf, gilt edges.	323
Knight, Aug. 1850.	627

UNIDENTIFIED COPIES

Utterson, Apr. 1852. Green morocco, gilt edges. To Walker.	1694
Loscombe, June, 1854. Half red morocco. To Halliwell.	1042
Gardner, J. D., July, 1854. Old calf. To Skeffington.	2197
Gancia, June, 1856. Large copy. To Boone.	551
[Halliwell], Sotheby, June, 1858. Morocco, by Bedford. To Lilly.	325
[Halliwell], Sotheby, June, 1859. Morocco, by Bedford.	335
Sotheby, Mar. 21, 1864. Olive morocco, by Bedford.	109
Sotheby, Nov. 21, 1864. Red morocco, by Lewis. To Quaritch.	281
Sotheby, 1864. Red morocco, by Lewis. Margins of last leaf mended. To Ellis.	76
Sotheby, Aug. 11, 1865. C3 defective. To Halliwell.	143
[Smith], Sotheby, July, 1867. Green morocco, by Lewis. To Lilly.	2577
Corser, Feb. 1871. Headlines cropped on some pages.	405
Tite, May, 1874. Half morocco. To Ellis.	2740
Craufurd, July, 1876. Red morocco, by Bedford.	1035
Gardner, C. D., June, 1880. Purple morocco, by Hayday. To Quaritch.	1423
Marsh, May, 1882. (Steevens, May, 1800, No. 1272.)	2407
Puttick, 1883. Morocco, lower corner of title mended.	608
Perkins, July, 1889. Red morocco.	1699
[Thorold], Sotheby, July, 1889. Unbound. To Quaritch.	1631
Sewall, Jan. 1897. Morocco, by Hammond. Title in facsimile.	3428
Hussey, May 25, 1906. 7 x 5 ¼". Unbound. To Pickering.	379
Van Antwerp, Mar. 1907. Purple morocco, by Bedford. Some corners mended. (Crawford, Mar. 1891, No. 2891.)	197

JULIUS CAESAR, 1684.

Beauclerk, Apr. 1781. (With others.)	4380
Pickering, Aug. 7, 1854. (With others.)	3131
[Halliwell], Sotheby, June, 1859.	290
Harrison of Samlesbury, Jan. 1881. Half morocco.	925
Cosens, Nov. 1890. Half morocco.	4084
Sewall, Jan. 1897. Half morocco.	3441
Lamb, Edinburgh, Feb. 1898. Half morocco. To Grant.	1106
McKee, Apr. 1901. Brown levant morocco, by Bradstreet. One margin mended.	2616
Mathews & Neilthorp, Jan. 1902. Morocco, 2 or 3 headlines cropped. To Crockford.	620
Bangs, June 5, 1902. Morocco.	550
Poor, Nov. 1908. Calf, by Club Bindery. (Lefferts, Apr. 1902, No. 1207.)	960

JULIUS CAESAR, n. d.

Jolley, June, 1844. To Vaughan.	630
[Halliwell], Sotheby, June, 1859.	89
Harrison of Samlesbury, Jan. 1881. Red morocco.	923
Harrison of Samlesbury, Jan. 1881. With manuscript notes. Uncut.	924
[Halliwell], Sotheby, July, 1889.	902
Cosens, Nov. 1890. Half morocco.	4085
Sewall, Jan. 1897. 2 leaves stained. Half calf, by R. W. Smith.	3440
Hodgson, Dec. 10, 1902. Sewed, one headline cropped. To Robson.	253

A CENSUS OF SHAKESPEARE QUARTOS

Sotheby, Oct. 20, 1904. With others, one volume, old calf. To Hayley.	594
Hodgson, Mar. 1906. Morocco.	148
Sotheby, May 1, 1911. Morocco. To Goss.	292

JULIUS CAESAR, 1691.

Ireland, May, 1801. (With Othello.)	462
[Halliwell], Sotheby, June, 1859.	88
Burton, Oct. 1860. Paper.	4645
Sotheby, Mar. 14, 1870. Red morocco, by Bedford. To Kershaw.	570
Harrison of Samlesbury, Jan. 1881. Half morocco.	926
Marsh, May, 1882. Half calf, with others.	2421
Harris, Apr. 1883. Half morocco.	2048
Cosens, Nov. 1890. Half morocco.	4085
Sewall, Jan. 1897. Spotted. Paper.	3443
Bangs, Mar. 19, 1900. Unbound.	550
Bangs, Nov. 26, 1900. Half morocco.	650
Sotheby, June 18, 1903. Unbound. To Barry.	202
Sotheby, Dec. 6, 1905. Last line of F_2 cropped. Morocco. To Taine.	808
Sotheby, Dec. 14, 1906. Half morocco.	397

KING LEAR, 1608.

Heber, Dec. 1834. Red morocco.	2020
Loscombe, June, 1854. To Halliwell.	1046

KING LEAR, 1608 [1619].

Crofts, Apr. 1783.	5132
Ireland, May, 1801. To Barker.	467
Christie, Apr. 25, 1804. To Foster.	96
[Inglis], Sotheby, Apr. 12, 1826. To Rodd.	95
Heber, Dec. 1834.	2017
Jolley, June, 1844. To Thorpe.	609
Holgate, June, 1846. Red morocco.	824
Gardner, J. D., July, 1854. Russia.	2198
[Halliwell], Sotheby, May, 1856. Morocco. To Lilly. Bought by Halliwell "Many years ago" from Thorpe.	344
Gancia, June, 1856. Large copy. To Boone.	550
Sotheby, 1864. Red morocco, by Bedford. Autograph of Hon. Francis North on title. To Stevens.	110
Corser, Feb. 1871.	403
Tite, May, 1874. Green morocco, by Lewis. (Steevens, May, 1800, No. 1278; Roxburghe, May, 1812, No. 3856; Grafton, June, 1815, No. 704; Halliwell, May, 1857, No. 866.) To Ellis.	2745
Russell, June, 1885. Fine copy.	1071
Perkins, July, 1889. Red morocco.	1700
Cosens, Nov. 1890. Red morocco, by Lewis.	4063
Drake, July 29, 1901. Lacking title and L1; 2 leaves imperfect at top, a few words lacking.	

[122]

UNIDENTIFIED COPIES

KING LEAR, 1608.

Edition Uncertain.

Farmer, May, 1798. A little stained in center. To Nicol.	7860
Rhodes, Apr. 1825. Lacks 4 leaves.	2102
Dent, Apr. 1827. To Rodd.	1030
Jadis, Mar. 1828. Green morocco.	173

KING LEAR, 1655.

Bowle, Jan. 1790.	4260
Farmer, May, 1798.	7861
Brand, May, 1807.	7203
Rhodes, Apr. 1825.	2103
Heber, June, 1834.	5452
Thorpe, 1836. Half morocco.	1282
[Halliwell], Sotheby, May 24, 1856. To Stevens.	356

LOVE'S LABOR LOST, 1598.

Rhodes, Apr. 1825.	2084
Dent, Apr. 1827.	1025
Jadis, Mar. 1828.	156
Thorpe, 1828. Lacks title.	1205
Gaisford, Apr. 1890. Headlines cropped. Blue morocco, by Bedford. To Quaritch.	1737

LOVE'S LABOR LOST, 1631.

Farmer, May, 1798. To Barker.	7875
Farmer, May, 1798. To Forster.	7876
Reid, Nov. 2, 1807. Title lacking. To Thomas.	8418
White Knights, June, 1819. To Triphook.	3953
[Inglis], Sotheby, Apr. 12, 1826. To Harding.	105
Heber, June, 1834.	5449
Jolley, June, 1844. To Thorpe.	592
Burton, Oct. 1860. Half calf.	4577
Kinsman, 1870. Lower margin cropped, date cut from title. Capell's copy.	
Kershaw, July, 1877. Half morocco. (Tite, May, 1874, No. 2749, bought from Halliwell, May, 1856.)	333
Marsh, May, 1882. Some headlines cropped.	2419
Sotheby, July 18, 1900. A4 defective. Unbound. To Pickering.	1205
Howe, Dec. 1907. 7 1/8 x 5". Writing on two pages. Half blue morocco. To Quaritch.	16

MACBETH, 1673.

Jolley, June, 1844. To Rodd.	619
Burton, Oct. 1860. Lacks all after p. 64.	4600

A CENSUS OF SHAKESPEARE QUARTOS

MERCHANT OF VENICE, 1600.

Bindley, Feb. 1819. To Triphook.	2044
Thorpe, 1827.	9935
Jolley, June, 1844. (Rhodes, Apr. 1825, No. 2093.) To Thorpe.	597
[Halliwell], Sotheby, May, 1856. To Lilly. (Cost Halliwell, £44 5s.)	345
Mitford, Apr. 1860. Lacking title. (May be Roberts edition.)	3495

MERCHANT OF VENICE, 1608 [1619].

Crofts, Apr. 1783.	5128
Steevens, May, 1800. Inlaid.	1280
Ireland, May, 1801. Russia. To Barker.	466
Tyssen, Dec. 1801.	2277
[Grafton], Evans, June, 1815.	702
[Grafton], Evans, June, 1815.	703
Rhodes, Apr. 1825.	2094
[Inglis], Sotheby, Apr. 1826. To Rodd.	91
Dent, Apr. 1827.	1027
Dent, Apr. 1827.	1028
Heber, June, 1834. Morocco.	5447
Jolley, June, 1844. To Thorpe.	598
Bright, Mar. 1845. Half bound. To Wilson.	5103
Holgate, June, 1846. Blue morocco.	820
Gancia, June, 1856. Fine copy. Bumstead.	548
[Halliwell], Sotheby, June, 1858. To Lilly. Morocco, by Bedford.	316
[Halliwell], Sotheby, June, 1859. Morocco, by Bedford.	340
Holland, July, 1860. (Roxburghe, May, 1812, No. 3814; Sykes, May, 1824; Jadis, Mar. 1828, No. 163.) To Lilly.	1620
Sotheby, Aug. 11, 1865. Small hole in Sig. H.	137
[Smith], Sotheby, July, 1867. Red morocco, by Bedford. To Halliwell.	2575
[Windus], Sotheby, Mar. 1868. Red morocco, by Lewis. To Lilly.	906
Kinsman, 1870. Unbound.	
Corser, Feb. 1871. Half morocco. To Pickering.	398
Tite, May, 1874. Red morocco, by Hayday. (Utterson, Apr. 1852, No. 1689; Sotheby, Nov. 21, 1864, No. 279.) To Walford.	2753
Perkins, July, 1889. Red morocco.	1693
Cosens, Nov. 1890. Red morocco, by Bedford.	4059
Crawford, Mar. 1891. Morocco, by Bedford. To Pearson.	2897
[Hazlitt], Sotheby, Nov. 1893. Morocco. Last leaf in facsimile. To Ridge.	474
Burra, May, 1897. 7 1/8 x 5 1/2". Morocco. To Pickering.	608
Gott, Mar. 20, 1908. 7 1/8 x 5 3/16". Bottom corner of title in facsimile, small hole in Bi. Morocco, by Lewis.	238
Hoe, Jan. 1912. Blue morocco, by Mansell. (N. Q. Pope, sold, 1895.)	3032

MERCHANT OF VENICE, 1637.

Pearson, Apr. 1788. To Reed.	3952
Farmer, May, 1798.	7856
White Knights, June, 1819. To Jervis.	3952
Rhodes, Apr. 1825.	2095

UNIDENTIFIED COPIES

Heber, Dec. 1834.	2015
[Halliwell], Sotheby, May 24, 1856. To Smith.	352
Kershaw, July, 1877. Red morocco, by Lewis. To Quaritch.	1239
Lamb, Edinburgh, Feb. 1898. Morocco. To Pickering.	1097
Hodgson, Nov. 29, 1906. 6 15/16 x 5 3/16″. Unbound. Imprint in manuscript. (Sotheran, Bib. Pret, 1907, No. 390.)	95
[Mostyn], Sotheby, May 31, 1907. Unbound.	479
Sotheby, July, 1907. Small corner of title and B3 cut off. Old calf, rebacked. To B. F. Stevens.	352

MERCHANT OF VENICE, 1652.

Pearson, Apr. 1788.	3953
Farmer, May, 1798. To Forster.	7858
Christie, Apr. 1804.	91
Rhodes, Apr. 1825.	2096

MERRY WIVES OF WINDSOR, 1602.

Steevens, May, 1800.	1281

MERRY WIVES OF WINDSOR, 1619.

Pearson, Apr. 1788.	3951
Farmer, May, 1798. To Nicol.	7865
Ireland, May, 1801.	465
Ireland, May, 1801. To Barker.	471
Tyssen, Dec. 1801.	2288
Reid, Nov. 1807. To Barker.	8421
Rhodes, Apr. 1825.	2097
[Inglis], Sotheby, Apr. 12, 1826. To Thorpe.	102
Dent, Apr. 1827. To Rodd.	1033
Jadis, Mar. 1828. To Nicol.	167
Heber, June, 1834. Morocco.	5444
Jolley, June, 1844. To Thorpe.	600
[Halliwell], Sotheby, May, 1856. Morocco. To Stevens.	338
Gancia, June, 1856. Large copy.	553
Utterson, Mar. 1857. Title in manuscript. To Lilly.	1752
[Halliwell], Sotheby, June, 1858. Morocco, by Bedford. To Lilly.	317
[Halliwell], Sotheby, June, 1859. Imperfect.	345
Sotheby, 1863. Red morocco. (Utterson, Apr. 1852, No. 1696.)	573
Sotheby, Aug. 11, 1865. Fine copy. To Toovey.	147
[Smith], Sotheby, July, 1867. Red morocco, by Bedford. To Pickering.	2580
Kinsman, 1870. Unbound. Capell copy.	
Tite, June, 1874. Red morocco, by Bedford.	2757
Craufurd, July, 1876. Red morocco, by Bedford.	1036
Marsh, May, 1882. Blue morocco. Dyce copy.	2411
Russell, June, 1885. Brown morocco, by Lewis.	1072
Crawford, Mar. 1891. Morocco. To Pearson.	2894
[Mostyn], Sotheby, May 31, 1907. Unbound. To Quaritch.	480

A CENSUS OF SHAKESPEARE QUARTOS

MERRY WIVES OF WINDSOR, 1630.

Ireland, May, 1801.	453
Christie, Apr. 25, 1804. To Street.	89
Reid, Nov. 1807. To Barker.	8422
Loscombe, June, 1854. Half morocco. To Halliwell.	1047
Kershaw, July, 1877. Purple morocco. (Tite, May, 1874, No. 2758.) To Smith.	1233
Lamb, Edinburgh, Feb. 1898. Morocco. To Pickering.	1093

MIDSUMMER NIGHT'S DREAM, 1600 [1619].

Farmer, May, 1798. To Forster.	7853
[Grafton], Evans, June, 1815.	701
Rhodes, Apr. 1825. (Edition uncertain.)	2092
[Inglis], Sotheby, Apr. 12, 1826. To Rodd.	89
Dent, Apr. 1827. (Edition uncertain.) To Thorpe.	1029
Jadis, Mar. 3, 1828. To Thorpe.	161
Heber, Dec. 1834.	2013
Jolley, June, 1844. To Thorpe.	595
Puttick, Apr. 1849. Half morocco.	321
Gardner, J. D., July, 1854. Red morocco. To Boone.	2196
Sotheby, 1856. Red morocco. (Utterson, Apr. 1852, No. 1688.) To Toovey.	252
[Halliwell], Sotheby, May, 1856. Fine copy. To Lilly.	340
Gancia, June, 1856. Large copy. To Elkins.	549
Berry, Jan. 1857. Probably by Hayday.	805
Daniel, July, 1864. To Lilly.	1435
Sotheby, Nov. 21, 1864. Red morocco, with facsimile of Fisher title added. To Halliwell.	280
Sotheby, Aug. 11, 1865. Fine copy. To Pickering.	138
[Smith], Sotheby, July, 1867. Green morocco, by Lewis. To Halliwell.	2574
Corser, Feb. 1871. To Pickering.	401
Russell, June, 1885. Half russia.	1070
Sotheby, 1886. Red morocco, by Bedford. To Mollini.	574
Cosens, Nov. 1890. Blue morocco, by Lewis.	4060
Puttick, Dec. 1898. Calf. Lacking 3 leaves, in sheet E. To Robson.	878
Hussey, May 25, 1906. 7 x 5 ¼". Top margin of title and A2 defective. Unbound. To Pickering.	376
Sotheby, Dec. 14, 1906. Boards, morocco case. (Foster, June, 1894, No. 23.)	388
Amherst, Mar. 1909. 7 ¼ x 5 ½". D4 mended in margins, last 4 leaves remargined. Vellum. (J. F. Marsh, May, 1882, No. 2412.) To Austen.	849
Hoe, Apr. 1911. Olive levant morocco, doublure of red morocco, elaborate tooling, by Lortic. (N. Q. Pope, sold, 1895.) To Hill.	2975

MUCH ADOE ABOUT NOTHING, 1600.

Roxburghe, May, 1812.	3809
Bindley, Feb. 1819. To Triphook.	2042
Jolley, June, 1844. To Thorpe.	140
Loscombe, June, 1854. Old russia. To Halliwell.	1049
[Halliwell], Sotheby, May, 1857. Morocco, by Bedford. To Lilly.	868

UNIDENTIFIED COPIES

OTHELLO, 1622.

Rhodes, Apr. 1825.	2104
Dent, Apr., 1827. Red morocco.	1026
Jadis, Mar. 1828. Red morocco. To Evans.	169
Burton, Oct. 1860. Half calf.	4669

OTHELLO, 1630.

Steevens, May, 1800.	1288
Christie, Apr. 25, 1804.	92
Brand, May, 1807.	6447
White Knights, June, 1819. To Jervis.	3959
Rhodes, Apr., 1825.	2105
[Inglis], Sotheby, Apr. 12, 1826. To Valentine.	104
Hanrott, Feb. 1834. Red morocco.	2696
Heber, June, 1834.	5473
Puttick, Apr. 1849.	328
[Halliwell], Sotheby, May, 1856. Morocco, by Bedford. Good copy. To Hoskins.	334
[Halliwell], Sotheby, May, 1857. Fine copy. To Morrison.	871
Mitford, Apr. 1860.	3498
[Anderson], Sotheby, 1870. Red morocco. To Ellis.	410
Corser, Feb. 1871. Red morocco.	410
Gardner, C. D., June, 1880. Red morocco, by Bedford. Short copy. To Quaritch.	1427
[Simes], Sotheby, July, 1886. Title mended. Morocco, by Hayday.	1532
Daly, Mar. 19, 1900. Morocco, inlaid by Zaehnsdorf.	548
[Mostyn], Sotheby, May 31, 1907. Title defective, lacking part of last leaf, some fore-edges cut. Unbound. To Stevens.	484
Sotheby, Dec. 20, 1912. 8 x 5 1/8". Title and corners of 5 leaves mended. Paper, in case. To Gratton.	39

OTHELLO, 1655.

Steevens, May, 1800.	1289
Nixon, May, 1818. To Oakley.	653
Rhodes, April, 1825. To Lilly.	2106
[Halliwell], Sotheby, May, 1856. To Stevens.	329
[Stevens], Sotheby, 1857. Olive morocco, by Bedford. To Nicon.	482
[Halliwell], Sotheby, May, 1857. Morocco, by Bedford. To Lilly.	870
[Halliwell], Sotheby, June, 1859. Morocco, by Bedford.	342
Marsh, May, 1882. Morocco. Portions of 2 leaves lacking, few headlines cut.	2413

OTHELLO, 1681.

Ireland, May 7, 1801. (With Julius Caesar, 1691.)	462
Rhodes, Apr. 1825. (With Othello, 1687.)	2107
Pickering, Aug. 7, 1854. (With others.)	3131
Cosens, Nov. 1890. Headlines cut into. Half morocco.	4081
Sotheby, May 25, 1905. Corner of one leaf cut.	646
[Jonas], Sotheby, Mar. 17, 1911. Lower margins wormed, unbound. To Horne.	519

OTHELLO, 1687.

Farmer, May, 1798. To Money.	7879
Rhodes, Apr. 1825. (With Othello, 1681.)	2107
Harrison of Samlesbury, Jan. 1881. Half morocco.	933
Harrison of Samlesbury, Jan. 1881. Half morocco.	934
Cosens, Nov. 1890. Headlines cut. Half morocco.	4082
Lamb, Edinburgh, Feb. 1898. Half morocco. To Sotheran.	1103
McKee, April, 1901. Claret morocco, by Bradstreet.	2617
Hodgson, Nov. 29, 1906. Lacking 2 leaves at end. (With others.) Calf. To Tregaskis.	97

OTHELLO, 1695.

Burton, Oct. 1860.	4670
Harrison of Samlesbury, Jan. 1881.	935
Cosens, November, 1890. Half morocco.	4083
Sewall, Jan. 1897. Half calf. To R. W. Smith.	3446
McKee, Apr. 1901. Blue levant morocco, by Bradstreet. Some headlines cut, few corners mended.	2620
Sotheby, June 18, 1903. Half calf. To Richards.	445
Sotheby, March 21, 1905. Half morocco. To Leighten.	262
[Jonas], Sotheby, Mar. 17, 1911. Stained. Unbound. Uncut.	520

OTHELLO, 1705.

[Halliwell], Sotheby, June, 1858. To Smith.	317
[Halliwell], Sotheby, July, 1889.	902
Cosens, Nov. 1890. Headlines cut into. Half morocco.	4081
Wait, Dec. 21, 1910. Half morocco.	270

RICHARD II, 1598.

White Knights, June, 1819. To Jervis.	3954
Heber, Dec. 1834. Red morocco, with joints.	2018

RICHARD II, 1608.

Tyssen, Dec. 1801.	2283
Loscombe, June, 1854. Olive morocco. To Halliwell.	1052

RICHARD II, 1615.

Crofts, Apr. 1783.	5134
Rhodes, Apr. 1825. Lacking Ki.	2079
[Inglis], Sotheby, Apr. 12, 1826. To Rodd.	99
Heber, June, 1834.	5454
Jolley, June, 1844. To Pickering.	590
Bright, Mar. 1845. To Pickering.	5100
[Halliwell], Sotheby, June, 1858. Morocco. To Thompson.	324
Sotheby, 1871. Red morocco, by Lewis. To Bumstead.	2266

UNIDENTIFIED COPIES

RICHARD II, 1634.

Farmer, May, 1798. To Forster.	7874
Steevens, May, 1800.	1293
Ireland, May 7, 1801. One leaf manuscript, collated by Theobald.	469
Tyrrell, Dec. 1891. To Pearson.	211
Sotheby, May 6, 1901. Title backed, date erased. To Pickering.	882
[Mostyn], Sotheby, May 31, 1907. Unbound. To Pickering.	476

RICHARD III, 1602.

Steevens, May, 1800. Defective at end.	1294
Drake, July 29, 1901. Title, B2, B3, lacking; M2 imperfect, few signature marks shaved. (With Henry IV, 1632, and Lear, Butter, 1608.) Calf. To Pickering.	500

RICHARD III, 1612.

Pearson, Apr. 1788. Imperfect. To Thomson.	3956
Sotheby, Aug. 11, 1865. Inlaid, few catchwords cut off. To Toovey.	146

Quaritch owned in 1892 the Marsh (May, 1882, No. 2417) copy. Portrait by Hollar inserted. Several headlines cut into.

RICHARD III, 1622.

[Inglis], Sotheby, Apr. 12, 1826. To Rodd.	103

RICHARD III, 1629.

Farmer, May, 1798. To Money.	7873
Steevens, May, 1800.	1296
Ireland, May 7, 1801. To Barker.	476
Rhodes, Apr. 1825.	2081
Jolley, June, 1844. To Lilly.	584
Utterson, Apr. 1852. Half morocco. To Halliwell.	1698
Utterson, Mar. 1857. Headline cut into. Half morocco.	1754
Hermann, Mar. 1909. Morocco, by Riviere.	514

RICHARD III, 1634.

Steevens, May, 1800.	1297
Christie, Apr. 25, 1804.	90
Bindley, Feb. 1819. To Triphook.	2048
Rhodes, Apr. 1825.	2082
[Simes], Sotheby, July, 1886. Some headlines cropped. Morocco, by Hayday.	1533
Tyrrell, Dec. 1891. To Ellis.	212

ROMEO AND JULIET, 1597.

Heber, June, 1834. Lacking title, several leaves have text cut at bottom.	5466
Bright, Mar. 1845. Lacking title, H2, H3. To Thorpe.	5098

[129]

ROMEO AND JULIET, 1599.

Steevens, May, 1800. Fragment.	1298
Heber, June, 1834. (Nixon, May, 1818, No. 667.)	5467

ROMEO AND JULIET, 1609.

Jadis, Mar. 1828. To Rodd.	159
Heber, June, 1834. Morocco.	5468

ROMEO AND JULIET, n. d.

Christie, Apr. 25, 1804. Morocco.	
Jadis, Mar. 3, 1828. Russia. To Rodd.	160
Jolley, June, 1844. To Rodd.	588

ROMEO AND JULIET, 1637.

Pearson, Apr. 1788. To Reed.	3957
Christie, Apr. 25, 1804.	93
[Grafton], Evans, June, 1815.	707
Malone, Nov. 1818.	2536
Bindley, Feb. 1819. To Triphook.	2049
White Knights, June, 1819. To Hay.	3958
Rhodes, Apr. 1825.	2083
[Inglis], Sotheby, Apr. 12, 1826. To Davis.	106
[Inglis], Sotheby, Apr. 12, 1826. To Davis.	107
[Halliwell], Sotheby, May, 1856. Morocco, uncut. To Boone.	337
[Halliwell], Sotheby, May, 1857. Morocco, uncut, by Bedford. To Lilly.	864
Singer, May, 1860. Date cut off. Manuscript notes by Pickering inserted.	1420
Sotheby, Aug. 11, 1865. Lacking small part of C3. To Halliwell.	150
[Smith], Sotheby, 1878. (Tite, May, 1874, No. 2781.) Purple morocco, by Clarke.	232
[Craig], Sotheby, June, 1887. Wrong imprint attached. To Martin.	2381
Cosens, Nov. 1890. Date cut off title. Green morocco.	4070
Crawford, Mar. 1891. Morocco, by Bedford. To Ellis.	2896
Lamb, Edinburgh, Feb. 1898. Morocco. To Pickering.	1098

TAMING OF THE SHREW, 1631.

Steevens, May, 1800.	1303
Rhodes, Apr. 1825.	2108
Jolley, June, 1844. To Thorpe.	586
[Halliwell], Sotheby, May 24, 1856. Uncut. To Smith.	352
[Halliwell], Sotheby, May, 1857. Morocco, by Bedford. To Smith.	874
[Halliwell], Sotheby, June, 1859. Fine copy. To Boone.	334
Corser, Feb. 1871. Red morocco, by Bedford. To Quaritch.	412
Gardner, C. D., June, 1880. Red morocco, by Bedford. To Quaritch.	1428
Craig, Mar. 1888. Imperfect at end. To Bowden.	4542
Quaritch owned in 1892 the Marsh (May, 1882, No. 2420) copy. Vellum, uncut.	

UNIDENTIFIED COPIES

Van Antwerp, Mar. 1907. Red morocco, by Bedford. Several corners mended. (Rowfant sold, April, 1905.) To Pickering. 202
Sotheby, May 11, 1908. Lacking title, next leaf damaged. Unbound. To Sotheran. 539

TITUS ANDRONICUS, 1611.

Crofts, Apr. 1783. 5133
Steevens, May, 1800. Inlaid. 1304
Roxburghe, May, 1812. 3854
Nixon, May, 1818. To Triphook. 669
Jadis, Mar. 3, 1828. Red morocco. 171
Jolley, June, 1844. To Rodd. 587
Sotheby, Aug. 11, 1865. Fine copy. To Halliwell. 145
[Smith], Sotheby, July, 1867. Red morocco. To Halliwell. 2583
Tite, May, 1874. Fine copy. Red morocco, by Bedford. To Pearson. 2783
Sotheby, Mar. 27, 1906. Lacking title, corners mended. Morocco. To Maggs. 860

TROILUS AND CRESSIDA, 1609.

Jadis, Mar. 3, 1828. 172
Heber, June, 1834. (2nd issue.) (Nixon, May, 1818, No. 668.) 5465
Bright, Mar. 1845. Lacking title. To Rodd. 5105
Corser, Feb. 1871. (2nd issue.) Headlines partly cut off a few leaves. Red morocco, rich borders. 406

INDEX OF OWNERS AND BINDERS

This Index includes all known owners and binders of identified Quartos. In some cases we have been unable to trace the name and can only give the information found in the book itself.

ADLER, E. N., 20 Portchester Square, London. Fine Hebrew collection; some English books.
Nos. 81, 104, 196, 275, 286, 304, 628.

ALINGTON, REV. C. A., Headmaster of Shrewsbury School, Shrewsbury, England.
No. 177.

ALLIS, WILLIAM W., Milwaukee, Wisconsin. Books sold at auction, March 25, 1912.
No. 292.

ANDERSON, MATTHEW, Newcastle-on-Tyne, England. Books sold at Sotheby's, November 14, 1870.
No. 621.

ANDERSON GALLERIES, INC., 284 Madison Avenue, New York City. John Anderson, Jr., founded this auction firm in 1900 under his own name; it has subsequently done business as Bangs & Co., The Anderson Auction Co., Metropolitan Art Association and the Anderson Galleries, Inc.
Nos. 273, 637.

ASAY, E. G., Chicago, Illinois. Books sold to Theodore Irwin, December, 1881.
Nos. 192, 259, 550, 601, 623, 855.

ASHMOLEAN MUSEUM, Oxford, England. Founded by Elias Ashmole; books transferred to the Bodleian in 1860.
No. 611.

BAKER, JOHN.
No. 610.

BALLIOL COLLEGE, Oxford, England.
Nos. 8, 487.

BANCROFT, JOHN.
No. 694.

BANDINEL, BULKELEY, 1781-1861. Librarian of Bodleian Library, Oxford, 1813-1860. Collection sold: Part 1, 1861; Part 2, 1862.
No. 14.

BANGS & COMPANY, New York City. See Anderson Galleries, Inc.

BARTON, THOMAS P., 1803-1869. American Shakespeare collector, from 1834-1866. Bequeathed library to his widow who sold it to the Boston Public Library, May, 1873, for a small price, to be kept intact as the Barton Collection. Catalogued by J. M. Hubbard, 1878.
Nos. 10, 24, 39, 70, 94, 106, 117, 156, 167, 179, 200, 238, 266, 288, 308, 332, 360, 384, 412, 429, 452, 453, 489, 516, 526, 534, 559, 574, 587, 613, 630, 640, 649, 662, 676, 693, 706, 771, 772, 811, 819, 840, 841, 863.

INDEX

BEDFORD, FRANCIS, 1799-1883. English bookbinder. Started in Lewis' shop; partner of John Clarke, 1841-1850; afterwards carried on business alone.
Nos. 13, 20, 27, 28, 37, 46, 52, 130, 152, 156, 160, 169, 182, 184, 185, 193, 215, 222, 224, 226, 232, 236, 247, 259, 279, 291, 314, 318, 337, 347, 350, 356, 364, 368, 370, 377, 388, 396, 398, 420, 432, 433, 439, 440, 462, 463, 464, 467, 471, 479, 484, 503, 507, 509, 510, 540, 554, 563, 565, 566, 572, 578, 593, 597, 603, 607, 609, 617, 623, 654, 667, 681, 685, 699, 718, 732, 739, 744, 747, 761, 772, 773, 780, 782, 783, 799, 804, 808, 812, 823, 824, 828, 832, 844, 846, 847, 849, 853, 872, 883, 883*.

BERET, RICHARD.
No. 74.

BIGGE, ARTHUR, High Wickham, England. Books sold at auction, March 9, 1714.
No. 74.

BINDLEY, JAMES, 1765-1818. English Commissioner of stamp duties. Collector of Early English and Miscellany. Books sold at auction: Part 1, December, 1818; Part 2, January, 1819; Part 3, February, 1819; Part 4, August, 1820; Part 5, January, 1821.
Nos. 375, 483, 529, 579.

BIRDSALL, Northampton, England. English bookbinder.
Nos. 18, 142, 599, 701, 731, 788, 805.

BIRMINGHAM PUBLIC LIBRARY, Birmingham, England.
Nos. 62, 82, 93, 105, 197, 236, 287, 296, 305, 359, 404, 629, 639, 646, 659, 769, 817.

BLANDFORD, MARQUIS OF. See White Knights.

BLISS, DR. PHILIP, 1787-1857. Librarian of Bodleian Library, Oxford. Collected books printed in Oxford; Character books; Psalms. Books sold at Sotheby's: Part 1, June, 1858; Parts 2 and 3, August, 1858.
No. 610.

BOADEN, JAMES, 1762-1839. English biographer, dramatist; interested in Ireland's forgeries which he helped detect; wrote account of Shakespeare's portraits.
No. 43.

BODLEIAN LIBRARY, Oxford, England. Acquired the Malone collection of Shakesperiana in 1821.
Nos. 9, 23, 38, 63, 125, 136, 138, 145, 155, 178, 198, 199, 211, 218, 228, 237, 306, 321, 322, 331, 373, 383, 405, 411, 428, 451, 482, 488, 515, 525, 533, 558, 573, 586, 610, 611, 612, 647, 660, 675, 688, 692, 705, 722, 727, 737, 741, 750, 756, 770, 786, 790, 801, 810, 818, 838, 839, 862, 879.

BOND, JERMYN.
No. 662.

BOONE. English bookseller.
Nos. 1, 265.

BOSTON ATHENÆUM, Boston, Massachusetts.
Nos. 307, 648, 661.

BOSTON PUBLIC LIBRARY, Boston, Massachusetts. Shakespeare collection bought intact from Mrs. Thomas P. Barton, May, 1873, at a price below its value to comply with the desire of her husband, who died some months previous and left it to her; catalogue compiled in 1878 by J. M. Hubbard.
Nos. 10, 24, 39, 70, 83, 94, 106, 117, 156, 167, 179, 200, 238, 266, 288, 308, 332, 360, 384, 412, 429, 452, 453, 489, 516, 526, 534, 559, 574, 587, 613, 630, 640, 649, 662, 676, 693, 706, 771, 772, 811, 819, 840, 841, 863.

INDEX

BOSVIL, ANN.
No. 701.

BOWLE, REV. JOHN, Idmiston, near Salisbury, England. Books sold at auction, January 19, 1790.
Nos. 138, 687.

BRADSTREET & CO., 346 Broadway, New York City. American bookbinders.
Nos. 66, 289.

BRAND, JOHN, 1744-1806, London. Rector of a London church; secretary of Society of Antiquaries, 1784-1806. Collector of Early English. Sold at auction: Part 1, May, 1807; Part 2, February, 1808.
No. 74.

BREWER, JOHANNIS, fl. 1659.
No. 45.

BRIDGEWATER, JOHN, SECOND EARL OF. See Bridgewater House.

BRIDGEWATER HOUSE, St. James Park, London. Town house of the Earls of Ellesmere. The library was begun by Sir Thomas Egerton, Lord Chancellor under King James I, and was catalogued in 1649 by John, Second Earl of Bridgewater. The library has always been in the possession of the Egerton family but the head of the house has borne at different times the various titles of: Baron Ellesmere, 1603; Earl of Bridgewater, 1633; Duke of Bridgewater, 1720; Duke of Sutherland, 1803; Earl of Ellesmere, 1833. The present owner is John Francis Scrope Egerton, Fourth Earl of Ellesmere.
Nos. 126, 219, 361, 374, 413, 517, 527, 560, 677, 728, 791, 860.

BRIGHT, BENJAMIN HEYWOOD, fl. 1809-1845. English collector. Books sold at auction March, 1845.
Nos. 534, 559, 676, 853.

BRITISH MUSEUM, London. Acquired the Garrick collection, 1779; King George III's library in 1823; Huth bequest, 1911.
Nos. 1, 6, 11, 11*, 25, 26, 40, 64, 71, 84, 98, 99, 107, 122, 127, 128, 139, 146, 147, 157, 168, 180, 201, 202, 203, 212, 220, 221, 229, 239, 240, 267, 276, 309, 323, 324, 333, 334, 335, 362, 375, 385, 386, 406, 414, 415, 416, 430, 431, 454, 468, 469, 483, 490, 491, 518, 528, 535, 536, 561, 562, 575, 576, 588, 589, 614, 615, 641, 650, 663, 672, 678, 684, 694, 707, 708, 723, 724, 729, 730, 734, 738, 742, 751, 752, 753, 757, 773, 774, 787, 792, 802, 807, 820, 842, 843, 864, 865, 876, 880.

BRITWELL LIBRARY, Britwell Court, Burnham, Buckinghamshire, England. Begun by William H. Miller, 1789-1848, who bequeathed the library to Miss Marsh, who left it to Samuel Christie Miller, from whom it descended to the present owner, Sydney R. Christie Miller. It includes large parts of the Heber and Corser collections.
Nos. 65, 241, 268, 277, 310, 537, 563, 631, 709.

BROMLEY, GEORGE, fl. 1814, Theatre Royal, Norwich, England.
No. 662.

BROOKS, E. D., South 10th Street, Minneapolis, Minnesota. American bookseller.
Nos. 283, 311, 476, 664.

BRUCE, J. W.
No. 41.

BUNBURY, SIR HENRY EDWARD, d. 1860, Barton, England. Grandson of Sir William Bunbury of Barton, England, who owned the Hamlet, 1603, and other plays which were sold to Payne & Foss in 1823, and are now in possession of H. E. Huntington.
Nos. 2, 123, 223, 234, 485, 531, 735.

INDEX

BURTON, WILLIAM E., 1804-1860. American actor. Books catalogued by Joseph Sabin and sold in New York City, October 8, 1860.
Nos. 59, 179, 706.

BUTE, JOHN PATRICK CRICHTON STUART, THIRD MARQUIS OF, 1847-1900, Falklands, Fife, Scotland.
Nos. 227, 417, 743.

CAMBRIDGE UNIVERSITY LIBRARY, Cambridge, England. Sandars collection, bequeathed, 1894.
Nos. 41, 821, 844.

CAPELL, EDWARD, 1713-1781. English Shakespearian scholar. Presented his collection of early editions of Shakespeare to Trinity College, Cambridge, June, 1779. A few other quartos sold or exchanged by Capell or his heirs.
Nos. 7, 21, 36, 41, 60, 124, 135, 137, 154, 166, 175, 194, 217, 233, 235, 246, 254, 264, 329, 344, 355, 371, 381, 401, 426, 438, 447, 466, 480, 486, 511, 524, 532, 555, 565, 571, 584, 606, 626, 674, 682, 703, 720, 733, 736, 748, 755, 767, 784, 789, 806, 815, 835, 857, 874, 884.

CARRINGTON, GEORGE, Missenden Abbey, Great Missenden, England. Books sold at Sotheby's, July, 1905.
Nos. 143, 216, 336, 478, 690, 740.

CHAMBOLLE-DURU, R. S., Paris. French bookbinder. Chambolle succeeded to Duru's business and took his name.
No. 459.

CHENEY, FRANCES REDHEAD YORKE.
No. 388.

CHRISTIE, JAMES, 1730-1803, London. English auctioneer, founded auction room in 1766.
No. 481.

CHURCH, E. DWIGHT, died 1909, Brooklyn, New York. American collector of Americana and English books. Catalogued by G. W. Cole, Americana, 5 vols., English, 2 vols., 1905-1909. Library sold *en bloc,* April, 1911, to H. E. Huntington.
Nos. 20, 53, 134, 152, 164, 191, 215, 224, 232, 256, 282, 347, 369, 379, 396, 424, 440, 463, 484, 503, 548, 568, 597, 622, 681, 686, 700, 717, 732, 739, 746, 754, 782, 799, 804, 809, 814, 854, 871, 883.

CLAPCOTT, CATHERINE.
No. 268.

CLARKE, JOHN, London. English bookbinder, was a partner of Francis Bedford, 1841-1850.
Nos. 34, 57, 328, 477, 552, 583, 624, 855.

CLARKE AND BEDFORD, London. English bookbinders, 1841-1850; succeeded by Francis Bedford.
Nos. 24, 39.

CLAWSON, J. L., Buffalo, New York. American collector.
Nos. 492, 650*, 695.

CLEAVELAND, H.
No. 536.

CLEMENS, DR. JAMES B., 10 East 71st Street, New York City. American physician and collector.
No. 590.

INDEX

CLUB BINDERY, 1895-1909, New York City. Founded, 1895, by Robert Hoe and other members of the Grolier Club but distinct from that organization; discontinued, 1909.
   Nos. 330, 427, 494, 768, 871.

COBDEN-SANDERSON, T. J., Hammersmith, London. English bookbinder.
   No. 19.

COCHRAN, ALEXANDER S., Yonkers, New York. Bought the Huth collection of Shakespeare, November, 1911. In December, 1911, he presented the Huth copies with some other books to the Elizabethan Club which he had founded in June of the same year.
   Nos. 3, 14, 27, 130, 148, 222, 230, 247, 279, 338, 419, 433, 496, 529, 541, 566, 579, 594, 685, 724, 794, 812, 824, 847, 867, 877.

COCK, DR. MORRIS F., Glendale, Ashford, Middlesex, England. Physician and collector.
   No. 108.

COMYN, SIR ROBERT, London. Books sold, March 13, 1893.
   Nos. 604, 814.

COOPER, JOHN, fl. 1688.
   Nos. 141, 324.

COPE, SIR ANTHONY, Bramshill Park, Winchfield, Hampshire. Books sold at Sotheby's, March 4, 1913.
   Nos. 803, 873.

COPINGER, ELIZABETH.
   No. 137.

CORBIN, THOMAS.
   No. 207.

CORNEY, BOLTON, 1784-1870. Clerk at Greenwich Hospital, England. Books sold at Sotheby's, 1871.
   No. 465.

CORSER, REV. THOMAS, 1793-1876, Stand, Lancashire, England. Collected English poetry described in "Collectanea Anglo-Poetica"; books sold at auction: Part 1, July, 1868; Part 2, March, 1869; Part 3, August, 1869; Part 4, February, 1870; Part 5, July, 1870; Part 6, February, 1871; Part 7, July, 1871; Part 8, June, 1873.
   Nos. 184, 241, 458, 621, 719, 824.

COSENS, FREDERICK W. English collector of Shakespeare, Manuscripts, Spanish books, etc. Books sold at auction, November, 1890.
   Nos. 265, 403.

CRAUFURD. Books sold at auction, July, 1876.
   Nos. 458, 537.

CRAWFORD, W. H., "Lakelands," Cork, Ireland. Irish collector. Books sold at auction, March, 1891.
   Nos. 37, 226, 356, 467, 545.

CRICHTON STUART, LORD NINIAN, 1883-1915, Falklands, Fife, Scotland. Second son of the Third Marquis of Bute, from whom he probably inherited part of his collection. Killed in battle in France, October, 1915.
   Nos. 42, 76, 102, 129, 140, 158, 181, 227, 242, 299, 300, 358, 363, 387, 417, 455, 470, 493, 519, 538, 591, 616, 651, 689, 696, 710, 743, 758, 775, 822, 845, 866, 886.

CROUSMAKER, ELIZABETH MARY, fl. 1746.
   No. 180.

INDEX

CRUMP, JOHN.
No. 841.

CUMMING, JAMES. Keeper of the Lyon Records and first secretary to the Scottish Antiquarian Society. Books sold in 1793.
No. 3.

CURZON, WILLIAM PENN ASSHETON, Gopsal, Atherstone, Leicestershire. Inherited library of Charles Jennens of Gopsal, which afterwards descended to Lord Howe.
Nos. 4, 15, 48, 150, 171, 249, 340, 435, 473, 497, 521, 543, 580, 679, 725, 762, 779, 795, 813, 826, 868.

DALY, AUGUSTIN, 1838-1899, New York City. American theatrical manager and collector. Books sold at auction, March, 1900.
No. 403.

DANIEL, GEORGE, 1789-1864. Collector of Ballads, Shakesperiana, Early English. Books sold at auction, July, 1864.
Nos. 17, 93, 230, 345, 375, 422, 483, 529, 568, 579, 672, 681, 723, 794, 802, 867, 877.

DAVID, Paris, France. French bookbinder.
Nos. 50, 354.

DE COVERLEY, ROGER, London. English bookbinder. Set up business in 1863; bound for F. S. Ellis and William Morris.
Nos. 258, 625, 746.

DENT, JOHN, 1750-1826. English Member of Parliament, F.R.S.; F.S.A. Collected Incunabula, Early English, etc. Books sold at auction: Part 1, March, 1827; Part 2, April, 1827.
No. 153.

DEVONSHIRE, VICTOR C. W. CAVENDISH, NINTH DUKE OF, Chatsworth, England. General library, collected chiefly by William George Spencer Cavendish, Sixth Duke, 1790-1858, who purchased Thomas Dampier's library in 1812, J. P. Kemble's collection of plays in 1821, and many other books at Roxburghe and other sales. Part of the Devonshire collection sold to H. E. Huntington, New York City, January, 1914.
Nos. 2, 5, 18, 33, 54, 123, 133, 142, 151, 190, 205*, 214, 223, 231, 234, 257, 327, 346, 380, 423, 441, 485, 502, 531, 547, 569, 582, 599, 673, 687, 701, 726, 731, 735, 781, 788, 798, 805, 870, 878.

DODD, MEAD & CO., Fourth Avenue and 30th Street, New York City. American booksellers with a large, rare book department, which became a separate firm in 1910 under the name Dodd & Livingston; in 1913, the partnership was dissolved and business continued under Robert H. Dodd.
Nos. 51, 61, 243, 282, 388, 439, 494, 539, 554, 609, 711, 759, 850, 869, 872.

DOLBEN, ELIZA, fl. 1691.
No. 107.

DOWNES, SARAH, fl. 1698-1709.
No. 807.

DREW, JOHN, Easthampton, Long Island, New York. American actor.
No. 205.

DRUMMOND, WILLIAM, 1585-1649, Hawthornden, Scotland. Poet. Presented his library to Edinburgh University in 1627.
Nos. 376, 793, 861.

INDEX

DUYCKINCK, EVERT A., 1816-1878, New York City. Author of literary and biographical works. Collection presented to Astor Library in 1878.
No. 643.

DYCE, REV. ALEXANDER, 1798-1869. English Shakespearean scholar. See Dyce collection.

DYCE COLLECTION, Victoria and Albert Museum, London. Alexander Dyce bequeathed his books and prints to the Victoria and Albert Museum in 1869.
Nos. 12, 43, 44, 45, 153, 159, 244, 389, 407, 418, 495, 564, 574, 592, 712, 747*, 760, 776, 810, 881.

DYSON, HUMPHREY, fl. 1633. Collector of English literature.
No. 878.

EARLE, GEORGE H., Philadelphia, Pennsylvania. General collection.
No. 245.

EDGERTON, JOSEPH.
No. 717.

EDINBURGH UNIVERSITY, Edinburgh, Scotland. Acquired the Drummond collection in 1627; the Halliwell collection in 1872.
Nos. 13, 46, 72, 160, 169, 170, 182, 246, 269, 278, 337, 364, 376, 390, 432, 456, 471, 520, 540, 565, 578, 593, 617, 697, 744, 761, 777, 793, 808, 823, 846, 861.

ELIZABETHAN CLUB, Yale University, New Haven, Connecticut. Founded by A. S. Cochran, June, 1911.
Nos. 3, 14, 27, 130, 148, 222, 230, 247, 279, 338, 419, 433, 496, 529, 541, 566, 579, 594, 685, 724, 794, 812, 824, 847, 867, 877.

ELLESMERE, JOHN FRANCIS GRANVILLE SCROPE EGERTON, FOURTH EARL OF. See Bridgewater House.

ELLIS & ELVEY, London. English booksellers.
Nos. 52, 836.

ETON COLLEGE, Eton, England. Shakespeare collection and other rarities bequeathed, 1799, by Anthony Storer.
Nos. 47, 183, 248, 339, 365, 391, 434, 457, 472, 542, 618, 713, 778, 825, 848, 882.

EXIREY, RICHARD, Eton College, England.
No. 772.

FALCONBRIDGE, W. G., fl. 1885, Toronto, Canada.
No. 22.

FARMER, DR. RICHARD, 1735-1797. Canon of St. Paul, London; wrote Essay on the learning of Shakespeare; collector of Early English books which were sold at auction, May, 1798.
Nos. 420, 839.

FARRELLS, MARMADUKE.
No. 576.

FFOWLE, JO., fl. 1675.
No. 702.

FITZGERALD, PERCY. Books sold at auction, June, 1907.
Nos. 352, 833.

FLEMING, J., fl. 1695.
No. 251.

INDEX

FOLGER, H. C., 26 Broadway, New York City. Has fine collection of Shakesperiana.
Nos. 4, 15, 16, 28, 29, 30, 48, 49, 50, 51, 52, 66, 77, 78, 79, 85, 103, 120, 121, 131, 141, 149, 150, 161, 162, 163, 171, 172, 173, 174, 184, 185, 186, 204, 249, 250, 251, 252, 253, 270, 297, 301, 302, 303, 312, 313, 325, 326, 340, 341, 342, 343, 366, 367, 377, 378, 392, 393, 394, 395, 408, 420, 421, 422, 435, 436, 437, 458, 459, 460, 461, 473, 474, 475, 497, 498, 499, 500, 501, 521, 530, 543, 544, 545, 557, 567, 580, 581, 595, 596, 619, 620, 632, 642, 565, 679, 680, 698, 699, 714, 715, 725, 762, 763, 764, 779, 780, 795, 796, 797, 803, 813, 826, 827, 828, 829, 830, 849, 850, 851, 852, 859, 868, 869.

FORBES, JAMES.
No. 403.

FOSTER, BIRKET. English collector. Books sold at auction, June, 1894.
Nos. 253, 345, 442.

FREELING, SIR FRANCIS, 1764-1836. English collector. Books sold at auction, November 25, 1836.
No. 338.

FURNESS, HORACE HOWARD, Philadelphia, Pennsylvania. Editor of the late volumes of the Variorum Shakespeare. Inherited collection of Shakesperiana from his father, H. H. Furness, the original editor of the Variorum, who died in 1913.
Nos. 17, 31, 32, 86, 95, 96, 109, 110, 187, 188, 254, 255, 314, 344, 368, 409, 438, 462, 621, 633, 652, 745, 853.

GAISFORD, THOMAS, died 1889. English collector of early English poetry and drama. Books sold at auction, April, 1890.
Nos. 163, 484, 537, 563.

GARDNER, CECIL DUNN. English collector. Catalogue printed 1864. Books sold at auction, June, 1880.
Nos. 41, 366, 402.

GARDNER, JOHN DUNN. English collector. Books sold at auction, July, 1854.
No. 424.

GARRICK, DAVID, 1717-1779. English actor. Bequeathed English plays in January, 1779, to British Museum. Other books, with additions by Mrs. Garrick, sold at Saunders', 1823.
Nos. 6, 11, 25, 40, 98, 122, 128, 168, 180, 202, 221, 239, 334, 386, 416, 430, 454, 468, 469, 491, 518, 535, 562, 576, 614, 678, 694, 707, 729, 734, 751, 757, 774, 787, 807, 820, 843, 865.

GENEST, JOHN, 1764-1839. Private chaplain of Duke of Ancaster and author of "Some Account of the English Stage," 1832.
Nos. 115, 294, 657.

GEORGE III, KING OF ENGLAND, 1738-1820. Collection acquired by the British Museum authorities after the death of George III, in 1823.
Nos. 26, 127, 157, 201, 220, 229, 240, 333, 385, 414, 415, 431, 490, 536, 561, 588, 615, 708, 742, 752, 792, 842, 864, 876.

GOERTZ-WRISBERG, COUNT, Wrisbergholzen, Hanover. Sold one volume containing six genuine and three spurious plays to Quaritch, August, 1902; now in possession of Mr. M. J. Perry of Providence, Rhode Island.
Nos. 262, 351, 444, 506, 553.

GOSSE, EDMUND. Librarian of the House of Lords, London.
No. 295.

GOTT, BISHOP JOHN, of Truro, Wales. Shakespeare collection sold through Sotheran, 1907.
Nos. 16, 161, 250, 325, 378, 498, 530, 544, 698, 796.

INDEX

GOWER, fl. 1704.
No. 231.

GRANT.
No. 659.

GRIFFITH, MARY.
No. 71.

GRISWOLD, ALMON W., died 1890, New York City. American collector. His best books were sold privately through Dodd & Mead, August, 1889; but he had auctions March 6, 1876; January, 1878; and December 6, 1880.
Nos. 164, 191, 252, 343, 369, 396, 437, 567, 654.

GUILDHALL LIBRARY, London.
No. 189.

GWYNNE, EDWARD. English collector of 17th century.
Nos. 262, 351, 444, 506, 553.

HAGGARD, WILLIAM HENRY. Books sold at Sotheby's, 1867.
No. 446.

HALLIWELL-PHILLIPPS, J. O., 1820-1889. English editor and collector of Shakespeare. Sale catalogues in various years, 1856-1889. Presented some quartos to Edinburgh University, 1872; sold "Halliwell Rarities" to M. J. Perry, 1897.
Nos. 1, 13, 28, 46, 77, 121, 130, 134, 139, 146, 147, 148, 156, 160, 169, 182, 184, 185, 212, 215, 222, 236, 246, 254, 255, 269, 278, 297, 312, 318, 324, 326, 337, 341, 360, 364, 366, 368, 377, 384, 390, 392, 420, 432, 456, 458, 462, 471, 474, 479, 510, 520, 540, 565, 572, 578, 593, 605, 617, 623, 627, 642, 686, 697, 699, 714, 730, 732, 738, 744, 745, 753, 761, 773, 777, 802, 804, 808, 823, 824, 827, 834, 846, 849, 853, 880.

HALSEY, FREDERICK R., 22 West 53d Street, New York City. American collector of first editions of English, American and French books, and of prints. Sold his library to H. E. Huntington, December, 1915.
Nos. 345, 439, 546.

HAMMOND. Bookbinder.
Nos. 195, 359, 717, 769.

HANROTT, PHILIP AUGUSTUS. English collector of Incunabula, Classics, Early English, Manuscripts, etc., which were sold at Evans's: Part 1, July, 1833; Part 2, August, 1833; Part 3, February, 1834; Part 4, March, 1834; Part 5, March, 1835; Part 6, January, 1857.
No. 550.

HARFORD, HENRY CHARLES. Books sold at Sotheby's, May 6, 1907.
No. 30.

HARRIS, C. FISKE, Providence, Rhode Island. Books sold at auction, after his death, April, 1883.
No. 669.

HARRISON, WILLIAM, Samlesbury Hall, Lancashire, England. Books sold at Sotheby's, January, 1881.
Nos. 148, 305, 627.

HART, GERALD E., Montreal, Canada. Books sold at Libbie's, Boston, April, 1890.
No. 604.

HARVARD UNIVERSITY, Cambridge, Massachusetts.
Nos. 205, 653.

INDEX

HATCHARD, MESSRS, 187 Piccadilly, London. English booksellers.
No. 3.

HAWKINS, RICHARD.
No. 180.

HAWKINS, Birmingham, England. English bookbinder.
No. 639.

HAYDAY, JAMES, 1796-1872. English bookbinder, succeeded by William Mansell.
Nos. 148, 189, 349, 372, 390, 424, 548, 785, 816.

HEBER, RICHARD, 1773-1833, Hodnet, Salop, England. Collector of general literature. Sale catalogue in thirteen parts, 1834-1837.
Nos. 9, 10, 31, 134, 138, 155, 190, 215, 225, 226, 230, 328, 375, 412, 425, 483, 526, 529, 568, 579, 680, 723, 727, 801.

HELLMAN, GEORGE S., 366 Fifth Avenue, New York City. American bookseller.
No. 283.

HENNELL, EDWARD WHITTAKER.
No. 481.

HERING, CHARLES, London. English bookbinder.
No. 153.

HERMAN, HENRY, 1832-1894, London. English dramatist. Books sold at Sotheby's, January 23, 1885.
No. 297.

HODGSON & COMPANY, London. English auctioneers.
No. 58.

HOE, ROBERT, 1839-1910, New York City. American collector of Incunabula, Classics, French and English literature, Americana, Horæ, etc. Catalogue in sixteen volumes. Books sold at auction: Part 1, April, 1911; Part 2, January, 1912; Part 3, April, 1912; Part 4, November, 1912.
Nos. 19, 55, 149, 263, 354, 388, 459, 492, 654, 695, 749, 883*.

HOLBECK, EDWARD.
No. 786.

HOLGATE, WILLIAM. Books sold at auction, June, 1846.
Nos. 390, 548.

HOLLAND. Bookbinder.
No. 208.

HORTON, SIR WILLIAM, died 1774, Chaderton, Lancashire. English collector.
Nos. 89, 271, 636.

HOWE, RICHARD GEORGE PENN CURZON, EARL, Gopsal, Atherstone, Leicestershire. Inherited books from W. P. A. Curzon. Library sold at auction, December, 1907.
Nos. 4, 15, 48, 150, 171, 249, 340, 435, 473, 497, 521, 543, 580, 679, 725, 762, 779, 795, 813, 826, 868.

HULME, ELIZA, fl. 1813.
No. 288.

HUNTERIAN MUSEUM, The University, Glasgow, Scotland.
Nos. 73, 132, 213, 716, 765.

INDEX

HUNTINGTON, HENRY E., 2 East 57th Street, New York City. Collector. Purchased Church collection of Americana and Early English, April, 1911; Chew collection of Early English, October, 1912; Kane collection of Washingtoniana; Devonshire collection, January, 1914; many books from Hoe collection, 1911-1912; Halsey collection, December, 1915.

Nos. 2, 5, 18, 19, 20, 33, 53, 54, 123, 133, 134, 142, 151, 152, 164, 190, 191, 205*, 214, 215, 223, 224, 231, 232, 234, 256, 257, 282, 327, 345, 346, 347, 369, 379, 380, 396, 423, 424, 439, 440, 441, 463, 484, 485, 502, 503, 531, 546, 547, 548, 568, 569, 582, 597, 598, 622, 654, 673, 681, 686, 687, 700, 701, 717, 726, 731, 732, 735, 739, 746, 754, 781, 782, 788, 798, 799, 804, 805, 809, 814, 830*, 854, 870, 871, 878, 883, 883*.

HUSSEY, E. W. Books sold at Sotheby's, May 25, 1906.
Nos. 353, 445, 494.

HUTH, HENRY, 1815-1878. Collection of Early English and Americana; continued by his son, Alfred, and catalogued in five volumes by F. S. Ellis. Bequeathed fifty books to British Museum and the remainder is being sold at auction: Part 1, 1911; Part 2, 1912; Part 3, 1913; Part 4, 1914. A. S. Cochran bought the entire Shakespeare collection *en bloc* before the sale of Part 1 and presented it to the Elizabethan Club of Yale.
Nos. 3, 14, 27, 130, 148, 222, 230, 247, 279, 338, 419, 433, 483, 496, 529, 566, 579, 594, 672, 685, 723, 724, 794, 812, 824, 867, 877.

IRELAND, SAMUEL, died 1800. English commentator and collector. Books sold at auction, May, 1801, including many genuine quartos and copies of his son's forgeries.
Nos. 31, 431, 602.

IRELAND, W. H., 1777-1835. English literary forger. Forged Shakespeare's name and notes on many genuine and some spurious works, deceived many authorities including his father; finally exposed and wrote "Confessions."
Nos. 31, 602.

IRVING, SIR HENRY, 1838-1905. English actor. Books sold at auction, December, 1905.
No. 625.

IRWIN, THEODORE, 1825-1902, Oswego, New York. Collection of Americana, Incunabula, Early English; sold March, 1900, to Mr. Morgan. Catalogue privately printed in 1887.
Nos. 56, 192, 206, 259, 397, 504, 550, 601, 623, 666, 855.

IVES, GEN. BRAYTON, 1836-1914, New York City. American collector of English and French books and prints. Portion of his library sold at auction, March, 1891; remainder sold in 1915.
Nos. 348, 512, 548, 754, 814, 883.

JADIS, HENRY. English collector. Early English literature, voyages and travels. Privately printed catalogue appeared 1826. Books sold at Evans's, March 3, 1828.
Nos. 241, 422, 693.

JENNENS, CHARLES, 1700-1773, Gopsal, Atherstone, Leicestershire. Built the present house and bequeathed his library to William Penn Assheton Curzon from whom it descended to Lord Howe.
Nos. 4, 15, 48, 150, 171, 249, 340, 435, 473, 497, 521, 543, 580, 679, 725, 762, 779, 795, 813, 826, 868.

JERVIS. English bookseller.
No. 284.

JOHN CARTER BROWN LIBRARY, Providence, Rhode Island. Begun by the Brown family in the 18th century; greatly enlarged by John Carter Brown, 1797-1874, and his son, John Nicholas Brown, who left it to Brown University in 1904.
Nos. 258, 599.

INDEX

JOLLEY, SIR THOMAS. Collector of English literature and history, Americana, Voyages, etc. Sold at auction: Part 1, February, 1843; Part 2, June, 1843; Part 3, March, 1844; Part 4, June, 1844; Part 5, June, 1851; Part 6, June, 1852; Part 7, May, 1853.
Nos. 71, 200, 360, 467, 520, 587, 649, 684, 706, 732, 750.

JONAS, MAURICE, 4 Wildwood Road, Golders Green, London. Sold part of his Shakespeare collection to H. C. Folger, May, 1903: issued a catalogue of the remainder as part of "Notes of an Art Collector," 1907; sold some at Sotheby's, March 17, 1911.
Nos. 79, 253, 394, 410, 475, 501, 545, 620, 664, 715, 830*, 852.

KALBFLEISCH, CHARLES H., Brooklyn, New York. American collector. Books sold privately after his death.
Nos. 50, 680, 828.

KEAN, CHARLES, London. Descendant of Edmund Kean, the actor. Books sold at auction, June, 1898.
No. 394.

KELLEY, B., fl. 1774.
No. 492.

KEMBLE, JOHN PHILIP, 1757-1823. English actor. Sold his collection of old plays to the Sixth Duke of Devonshire for £2,000 in 1821.
Nos. 5, 18, 133, 205*, 214, 231, 257, 327, 346, 380, 423, 441, 502, 547, 569, 582, 673, 687, 701, 726, 731, 788, 798, 805, 870, 878.

KERSHAW, JOHN, Park House, Willesden Lane, London. Books sold at auction, July 9, 1877.
Nos. 163, 184, 314, 368, 392, 458, 621, 719.

KING GEORGE III. See George III, King of England.

KINGSLEY, DARWIN P., New York Life Insurance Co., New York City. American collector.
Nos. 55, 87, 88, 118, 289, 315, 634.

KINNEAR.
Nos. 241, 379, 450, 550, 601, 702.

KINSMAN, JOHN, Penzance, Cornwall. English bookseller.
Nos. 254, 344, 438, 565.

KRAFFT, Lund, Sweden. Owned the unique Titus Andronicus, 1594, during latter part of 19th century and sold it, through Sotheran, to H. C. Folger, in January, 1905.
No. 859.

LAMB, A. C., Dundee, Scotland. Books sold in Edinburgh, February, 1898.
Nos. 627, 653, 721.

LARKINS. English bookbinder.
Nos. 352, 833.

LENOX, JAMES, 1800-1880, New York City. Collector. Incorporated his library as Lenox Library, 1870, and left it to New York City; it was incorporated with the New York Public Library, 1895. Incunabula, Bibles, Americana, Early English.
Nos. 34, 57, 153, 193, 261, 291, 328, 350, 370, 398, 425, 443, 464, 477, 505, 523, 552, 583, 603, 624, 667, 702, 718, 747, 747*, 766, 783, 832, 856.

LETTIN, GEORGE.
No. 733.

[144]

INDEX

LETTSOM, W. NASON, 1796-1865. Assisted A. Dyce in his edition of Shakespeare and was editor of Walker's notes on Shakespeare. Books sold at Sotheby's, November 27, 1865.
Nos. 134, 192.

LEWIS, CHARLES, 1753-1836, London. English bookbinder.
Nos. 10, 16, 22, 93, 161, 167, 241, 250, 325, 332, 338, 341, 345, 348, 378, 412, 422, 429, 458, 489, 498, 526, 530, 544, 574, 587, 613, 672, 693, 698, 796, 811, 819, 863, 867, 877.

LEWIS, JOHN DELAWARE, 1828-1884, London. Books sold at Sotheby's, May 26, 1868.
No. 568.

LIBBIE, C. F. & CO., Boston, Mass. American auctioneers.
Nos. 176, 627.

LIBRARY OF CONGRESS, Washington, D. C.
Nos. 290, 549.

LILLY, JOHN. English bookseller.
No. 148.

LINCOLN COLLEGE, Oxford, England.
Nos. 80, 635.

LOCKER-LAMPSON, FREDERICK, 1821-1895, Rowfant, England. Author and collector. Left library to son who, after collecting for some time, sold the library to E. D. Church, January, 1905. A few books went to the Church library, the rest sold by Dodd, Mead & Co., April, 1905, to date. Catalogue in two vols., 1886, 1900.
Nos. 20, 134, 152, 215, 224, 232, 243, 347, 379, 424, 439, 440, 484, 503, 554, 568, 597, 681, 686, 700, 732, 739, 746, 799, 804, 809, 872, 883.

LORTIC FRERES, Paris, France. French bookbinders. Marcelin Lortic established the business in 1846.
Nos. 512, 570.

LOSCOMBE, REV. C. W., Clifton, England. Incunabula, Early English, Manuscripts, etc. Sold at auction, June 19, 1854.
Nos. 31, 153, 323, 551.

McKEE, THOMAS JEFFERSON, 1840-1899, New York City. American collector. Books sold at auction in eight parts, 1900-1902.
Nos. 66, 186.

MACKENZIE. American bookbinder.
Nos. 505, 534, 537, 766, 856.

McMILLAN, JAMES, 1838-1902. United States Senator and benefactor of the library of the University of Michigan, 1882-1902.
No. 114.

MAJOR, J. B.
No. 97.

MAJOR, J. W.
No. 316.

MALBONE, THOMAS, fl. 1639.
No. 456.

INDEX

MALONE, EDMUND, 1741-1812. Shakespeare critic. Best books presented to Bodleian Library in 1821. Remainder dispersed in 1803, 1818 and 1825.
Nos. 23, 38, 125, 136, 145, 178, 198, 199, 211, 218, 228, 237, 321, 322, 331, 373, 383, 411, 420, 428, 482, 488, 515, 525, 533, 558, 573, 586, 675, 688, 692, 722, 741, 786, 790, 818, 838, 862, 879.

MARSH, JOHN FICHETT, 1818-1880. English collector and author of work on portraits of Milton. Books sold at auction, May 12, 1882.
Nos. 176, 357, 450, 641, 680, 700, 821.

MARSHALL, FRANK A., 1840-1889, London. English dramatist and collector of Drama, Elizabethan literature, etc. Books sold at auction June-July, 1890.
Nos. 100, 197, 625, 655, 668.

MATHER, DAVID, fl. 1652.
No. 774.

MICHEL, MARIUS, Paris, France. French bookbinder.
Nos. 53, 263.

MIDDLETON, THOMAS, of Silkworth.
Nos. 141, 324.

MILLER, SYDNEY R. CHRISTIE. See Britwell Library.

MINER, WILLIAM H., Cedar Rapids, Iowa. Journalist.
No. 600.

MITFORD, REV. JOHN, 1781-1859, Benhall, Suffolk. Collector of Classics, English and Continental books and manuscripts, which were sold at auction: Part 1, December, 1859; Part 2, April, 1860; Part 3, July, 1860.
Nos. 522, 602, 831.

MONCKTON, HORACE W., 3 Harcourt Buildings, Temple, London.
No. 111.

MOORE, SAMUEL.
No. 564.

MORGAN, JOHN PIERPONT, New York City. American collector. Inherited collections of Manuscripts ancient and modern, Incunabula, and general literature from his father, J. P. Morgan, who died in 1913. Library in East 36th Street, New York City.
Nos. 56, 192, 206, 259, 348, 397, 442, 476, 504, 550, 601, 623, 666, 855.

MOSTYN, SIR LLEWELYN N. V. LLOYD-MOSTYN, BARON, Mostyn Hall, Holywell, Flintshire. Books sold anonymously at Sotheby's, May, 1907.
Nos. 35, 330, 427.

MOTTE, A. French bookbinder.
Nos. 504, 854.

MURRAY, JOHN, 50 Albemarle Street, Piccadilly, London. Inherited collection of books and manuscripts from his ancestors, the celebrated publishers of that name.
Nos. 260, 349, 522, 551, 602, 831.

MURTON, C. English bookbinder.
Nos. 126, 219, 244, 374, 413, 418, 419, 495, 517, 527, 560, 677, 728, 791, 860.

MYERS, THEODORE BAILEY, New York City. His heirs presented books to New York Public Library in 1899.
Nos. 112, 207.

INDEX

NEDHAM, EDWARD.
No. 536.

NEW YORK PUBLIC LIBRARY, Fifth Avenue, New York City. The Astor and Lenox Libraries and Tilden foundation, incorporated as the New York Public Library in 1895. Acquired the E. A. Duyckinck collection by gift in 1878; the T. B. Myers collection by gift in 1899.
Nos. 34, 57, 112, 153, 193, 207, 261, 291, 328, 350, 370, 398, 425, 443, 463, 464, 477, 505, 523, 552, 583, 603, 624, 643, 667, 702, 718, 747, 747*, 766, 783, 832, 856.

NIXON, JOHN, died 1818, Basinghall Street, London. Collector of English literature. Collection sold at Evans's: Part 1, 1817; Part 2, 1818.
Nos. 10, 723.

PALMER, EDWARD, Kirby Street, Hatton Garden, London. Books sold at auction, February 14, 1681.
No. 327.

PAYNE, JOHN, died, 1787. An English writer, bookseller, etc.
Nos. 248, 789.

PAYNE & FOSS, 1806-1825, Pall Mall, London. English booksellers; Thos. Payne (1752-1831) succeeded his father in book business in 1790; took in Henry Foss as partner, 1813.
Nos. 2, 123, 223, 234, 485, 531, 735.

PEARSON, MAJOR THOMAS. Collector of Early English. Books sold at auction, April, 1788. Several bought by King George III.
No. 589.

PENN, SIR WILLIAM, 1621-1670, Stoke Pogis, Buckinghamshire, England. Admiral under Cromwell and King Charles II. Father of William Penn of Pennsylvania.
Nos. 216, 740.

PERKINS, FREDERICK, 1780-1860, Chepstead, Kent, England. Collector of Early English books, manuscripts, prints, etc. Sold at auction, July, 1889.
Nos. 144, 197, 225, 348, 382, 513, 556, 570, 585, 691, 754, 800, 858, 875, 885.

PERRY, MARSDEN J., Providence, Rhode Island. American collector. Fine Shakespeare collection, sold "Halliwell Rarities" to H. C. Folger, March, 1907; has still a collection of folios, some quartos and Shakesperiana.
Nos. 28, 35, 58, 74, 77, 89, 100, 121, 143, 165, 184, 216, 262, 271, 297, 312, 316, 326, 341, 351, 366, 377, 392, 420, 444, 458, 474, 478, 506, 553, 570, 625, 636, 642, 655, 668, 690, 714, 740, 827, 849, 872.

PHIDSON, M. D.
No. 68.

PHINNEY, T. W., Newport, Rhode Island. Bequeathed one quarto to his daughter, Mrs. Wirt Robinson, West Point, New York.
No. 59.

PICKERING, WILLIAM, 1796-1854, Chancery Lane, London. Now Pickering & Chatto, 66 Haymarket, London. English booksellers.
Nos. 34, 91, 110, 113, 115, 209, 272, 281, 286, 294, 298, 317, 320, 352, 395, 399, 657, 833.

PIERCE. Books sold at auction, September, 1891.
No. 504.

PLUMMER OF MIDDLESTEAD, Selkirk, Scotland.
No. 3.

INDEX

POOR, HENRY W., died 1915, New York City. Books sold at auction: Part 1, November, 1908; Part 2, April, 1909; Part 3, February, 1909.
Nos. 88, 118.

POPE, ALEXANDER, 1688-1744. Poet and Shakespeare editor. Pope's quartos were left to Warburton, who put them into Mallet's sale in 1766. Their subsequent history is not known.
No. 650*.

POPE, MRS. N. Q., Brooklyn, New York. American collector; after her death, her husband sold her collection to Robert Hoe, December, 1895.
Nos. 19, 53, 61, 149, 263, 354, 492, 609, 695, 749, 782, 854, 883*.

PRATT. English bookbinder.
Nos. 206, 292, 600, 777, 827.

PRIVATE OWNER, NO. 1, England.
No. 400.

PUTTICK AND SIMPSON, 47 Leicester Square, London. English auctioneers.
No. 338.

QUARITCH, BERNARD, 11 Grafton Street, New Bond Street, London. Father, 1819-1899, and son, 1871-1913, English booksellers.
Nos. 22, 37, 56, 262, 265, 348, 351, 353, 372, 392, 397, 444, 445, 450, 501, 506, 507, 508, 509, 553, 554, 590, 683, 719, 785, 816, 873.

RAMAGE, J. & Co., 45 Creed Lane, Ludgate Hill, London. English bookbinders.
No. 664.

REED, ISAAC, 1742-1807, Staple Inn, London. Shakespeare editor. Books sold at King and Lochée's, November, 1807.
No. 138.

RHODES, WILLIAM BARNES, 1772-1826. English collector of the drama. Books sold at Sotheby's, April, 1825.
Nos. 390, 691.

RICHARDSON, GEORGE F., 1829-1912, Lowell, Massachusetts. Collected Early English books, now in possession of his widow.
Nos. 67, 604.

RICHMOND, GEORGE H. & CO., New York City. American booksellers.
No. 448.

RILEY. Bookbinder.
No. 801.

RIVIERE, ROBERT AND SON, 29 Heddon Street, Regent Street, London. English bookbinders.
Nos. 12, 55, 68, 90, 92, 118, 149, 165, 210, 245, 253, 265, 272, 274, 280, 281, 282, 295, 297, 353, 394, 399, 445, 492, 501, 508, 541, 545, 546, 622, 670, 671, 695, 711, 715, 719, 759, 817, 830*, 837, 873.

ROBINSON, MRS. WIRT, West Point, New York. Inherited one quarto from her father, T. W. Phinney of Newport, Rhode Island.
No. 59.

ROBSON, CHARLES, 1735-1794, Stockholm, Sweden. Early owner of unique Titus Andronicus, 1594.
No. 859.

INDEX

RODD, THOMAS, 1763-1822, London. English bookseller.
Nos. 24, 226, 238, 429, 489, 574, 680, 693, 863.

ROWFANT LIBRARY. See Locker-Lampson.

ROONEY, Trinity College, Dublin.
No. 1.

ROSENBACH, DR. A. S. W., 1320 Walnut Street, Philadelphia, Pennsylvania. American bookseller.
No. 245.

ROXBURGHE, JOHN KER, DUKE OF, 1740-1804. English collector. Books sold at auction, May-July, 1812.
Nos. 18, 31, 33, 79, 131, 138, 146, 263, 414, 513, 520, 550, 603, 681, 700, 747, 794, 805, 876.

SABIN, F. T., London. English bookseller.
Nos. 345, 546.

SANDARS, SAMUEL, 1837-1894, Trinity College, Cambridge. Bequeathed collection to Cambridge University, 1894.
Nos. 41, 821, 844.

SCHIFF, MORTIMER L., care Kuhn, Loeb & Co., 52 William Street, New York City. Collector of French and English books.
No. 283.

SEWELL, HENRY F. American collector. Gave prints to Boston Museum; books sold at auction: Part 1, November, 1896; Part 2, December, 1896; Part 3, January, 1897.
Nos. 97, 116, 195, 402, 622, 717.

SHAKESPEARE BIRTHPLACE LIBRARY, Stratford-on-Avon, England.
Nos. 353, 445, 446, 465, 509, 554.

SHAKESPEARE MEMORIAL LIBRARY, Stratford-on-Avon, England.
Nos. 479, 510.

SHAKSPERE SOCIETY OF PHILADELPHIA, Philadelphia, Pennsylvania. Founded by Asa I. Fish in 1851.
Nos. 605, 834.

SHAW, E.
No. 115.

SIMES, N. P. English collector of Bibles, Manuscripts, Early English and French. Books sold at auction, July, 1886.

No. 369.

SKYNNER, THOMAS, fl. 1621.
No. 487.

SMITH, A. R., London. English bookseller. Books sold, February, 1874.
Nos. 187, 465.

SMITH, GEORGE, London. Deputy Lieutenant of the Tower. Collected a general library. Books sold at auction, July 10, 1867.
Nos. 236, 828.

SMITH, GEORGE D., 547 Fifth Avenue, New York City. American bookseller.
Nos. 263, 354, 492, 650*, 695.

INDEX

SMITH, RUSSELL. English bookseller.
Nos. 639, 769.

SOTHEBY, WILKINSON & HODGE, London. English auctioneers. Began as S. Baker, c. 1744, and have carried on business continuously until the present day.
Nos. 27, 37, 90, 93, 172, 208, 226, 230, 280, 282, 317, 337, 345, 356, 377, 393, 399, 408, 420, 442, 460, 499, 539, 557, 570, 581, 592, 596, 620, 625, 667, 704, 709, 740, 747*, 759, 763, 768, 814, 817, 828, 829, 837, 851, 871.

SOTHERAN, HENRY, 43 Piccadilly, London. English booksellers, firm founded by Thomas Sotheran in 1812.
Nos. 644, 656.

STACE, MACHELL. Books sold: Part 1, December, 1808; Part 2, November, 1814; Part 3, April, 1835; Part 4, January, 1843.
No. 788.

STAFFORD, GEORGE GRANVILLE, MARQUIS OF. Son of Marquis of Stafford and Lady Louisa Egerton. In 1833 he became first Duke of Sutherland; see Bridgewater House.

STAPFER, MARC.
No. 14.

STAUNTON, WILLIAM, Longbridge, Warwickshire.
No. 629.

STEEVENS, GEORGE, 1736-1800. Shakespeare editor and English collector. Books sold at auction, May, 1800.
Nos. 18, 59, 127, 138, 146, 153, 176, 220, 227, 231, 327, 336, 417, 513, 519, 520, 525, 537, 550, 559, 582, 681, 687, 696, 700, 743, 747, 794, 805, 822, 876.

STEVENS, HENRY, now Henry Stevens, Son, & Stiles, Great Russell Street, London. American bookseller in London. Author of several bibliographical works.
Nos. 34, 57, 153, 193, 261, 328, 350, 362, 370, 398, 425, 443, 464, 477, 505, 523, 552, 583, 603, 624, 702, 718, 747, 747*, 766, 783, 832, 856.

STIKEMAN & CO., 114 West 32d Street, New York City. American bookbinders.
No. 74.

STORER, ANTHONY MORRIS, 1746-1799, Purley Park, Berkshire, England. Bequeathed library to Eton College, 1799.
Nos. 47, 183, 248, 339, 365, 391, 434, 457, 472, 542, 618, 713, 778, 825, 848, 882.

SUTHERLAND, DUKE OF. See Bridgewater House.

TERRY, DR. RODERICK, Newport, Rhode Island.
Nos. 263, 354.

THEOBALD, LEWIS, 1688-1744, London. Shakespeare editor and literary critic. Books sold at auction, October 30, 1744.
Nos. 43, 417, 532, 627, 743.

THOMAS, GEORGE H., died 1911, Philadelphia, Pennsylvania. American collector. Books sold privately after his death, at various times.
Nos. 245, 442.

THORLO, LORD. Books sold at Christie's, April, 1804.
No. 801.

THORPE, THOMAS. English bookseller.
Nos. 153, 338, 550.

INDEX

TITE, SIR WILLIAM, 1798-1873. English architect. Collector of Early English, Manuscripts, books in foreign languages. Books sold at auction, May, 1874.
Nos. 17, 31, 86, 134, 152, 163, 192, 215, 232, 368, 392, 424, 462, 537, 572, 597, 623, 681, 686, 699, 709, 732, 739, 799, 804, 809, 855.

TOWNSEND, WALTER, fl. 1894.
No. 22.

TRINITY COLLEGE, Cambridge, England. Acquired the Capell collection of plays, June, 1779.
Nos. 7, 21, 36, 60, 124, 135, 137, 154, 166, 175, 194, 217, 233, 235, 264, 329, 355, 371, 381, 401, 426, 447, 466, 480, 486, 511, 524, 532, 555, 571, 584, 606, 626, 674, 682, 703, 720, 733, 736, 748, 755, 767, 784, 789, 806, 815, 835, 857, 874, 884.

TROWBRIDGE, FREDERICK K., 115 East 37th Street, New York City. American collector.
Nos. 448, 512, 607.

TRYE, H. N., London. Probably a relative of Canon Trye, who lived near Cheltenham in the latter part of the 19th century. Mr. Trye sold a copy of Richard II, 1598, to Quaritch, January 21, 1890.
No. 683.

TUCKETT. English bookbinder; worked for British Museum.
Nos. 134, 326, 386, 416, 456, 528, 562, 807, 809, 820, 865.

UNIVERSITY OF MICHIGAN, Ann Arbor, Michigan.
Nos. 75, 114, 208, 318, 637, 644, 656, 669.

UTTERSON, ERNEST VERNON, 1776-1856. English collector of Early English books which he edited and reprinted at the Beldornie Press, Isle of Wight. Also collected Incunabula, books in foreign languages, Manuscripts. Books sold at auction: Part 1, April, 1852; Part 2, March, 1857.
Nos. 163, 356, 572, 604, 719, 814.

VALENTINE, P. A., 55 Wall Street, New York City. Collector of English literature.
Nos. 319, 449, 608.

VAN ANTWERP, WILLIAM C., 15 Broad Street, New York City. American collector. Books sold at auction in London, July, 1907.
Nos. 348, 509, 554, 837.

VERNON, fl. 1837.
No. 22.

VICKERY, JUDGE WILLIS, Cleveland, Ohio. American lawyer and collector. President of Rowfant Club.
Nos. 68, 280.

VOYNICH, W. M., 68 Shaftesbury Avenue, London. English bookseller.
Nos. 304, 315.

WALKER, FOUNTAINE. English collector. Books sold at Sotheby's, May, 1893.
No. 241.

WALLACE, WALTER S., South Orange, New Jersey. Collector of English literature.
No. 292.

WALTERS, CURTIS, 31 East 27th Street, New York City. American bookbinder.
Nos. 294, 657.

INDEX

WARNER, RICHARD, fl. 1749-1752.
Nos. 469, 757, 807.

WARWICK, FRANCIS R. C. G. GREVILLE, FIFTH EARL OF, Warwick Castle, Warwickshire, England. Sold Shakespeare quartos *en bloc* to H. C. Folger.
Nos. 29, 49, 78, 85, 103, 120, 141, 162, 173, 185, 204, 251, 270, 301, 313, 342, 421, 436, 461, 500, 595, 619, 632, 665, 797, 830, 851.

WAVELL, WILLIAM.
No. 881.

WAY, MRS. JOHN, fl. 1869.
No. 111.

WEBBER, JOHANNIS.
No. 610.

WHEATLEY, HENRY B., 96 King Henry's Road, London. Author of bibliographical and literary works. Collector of Early English books, fine bindings, etc.
Nos. 90, 209, 272, 281, 293, 670.

WHITE, ALFRED T., 14 Wall Street, New York City. Collector of Americana; some English books.
Nos. 356, 450.

WHITE, W. A., 14 Wall Street, New York City. American collector of Shakespeare, Blake and general Early English. Handlist issued, March, 1914.
Nos. 22, 37, 61, 69, 91, 97, 101, 115, 116, 144, 176, 195, 225, 226, 265, 273, 284, 294, 298, 320, 330, 357, 372, 382, 402, 403, 410, 427, 467, 481, 513, 556, 572, 585, 590, 609, 627, 638, 645, 657, 658, 683, 691, 704, 721, 749, 768, 785, 800, 816, 836, 858, 875, 885.

WHITE KNIGHTS (library of Fifth Duke of Marlborough, while Marquis of Blandford). Early English, romances and poems in various languages; books sold at Evans', June, 1819.
No. 794.

WIGHALOGER, MATTHEW.
No. 48.

WILLIAMS BOOK SHOP, Cheltenham, England. Early 19th century shop; the contents were sold *en bloc* on the death of Mr. Williams in the latter part of the 19th century.
No. 683.

WINANS, ROSS, died 1912, Baltimore, Maryland.
No. 507.

WINDSOR CASTLE, Windsor, England. Private royal library founded by William IV, largely augmented by Queen Victoria.
No. 514.

WINDUS, BENJAMIN GODFREY, Tottenham Green, England. Books sold at Sotheby's, March 23, 1868.
Nos. 148, 390, 548, 697.

WOLFRESTON, FRANCIS.
Nos. 362, 621, 709.

WOOD, ANTHONY à, 1632-1695, Oxford, England, author of Athenæ Oxonienses. Bequeathed some of his books to the Ashmolean Museum, Oxford, in 1695.
No. 611.

INDEX

WRENN, JOHN HENRY, died 1912, Chicago, Illinois. American collector. Books now in possession of his estate.
Nos. 92, 210, 274, 295, 671, 837.

YALE UNIVERSITY, New Haven, Connecticut. (See also Elizabethan Club.)
Nos. 119, 285.

YOUNG, CHARLES, fl. 1837.
No. 22.

ZAEHNSDORF, JOSEPH WILLIAM, 144 Shaftesbury Avenue, London. English bookbinder.
Nos. 56, 397, 590.